FLY-FISHING THE SALTWATER SHORELINE

FLY-FISHING THE SALTWATER SHORELINE

Ed Mitchell

STACKPOLE
BOOKS

Published by
STACKPOLE BOOKS
5067 Ritter Road
Mechanicsburg, PA 17055
www.stackpolebooks.com

Printed in the United States

10 9 8 7 6 5 4 3 2 1

First edition

Front jacket photo of author with striper by Phil Farnsworth

All photos and illustrations by the author, unless otherwise credited

Color plates of flies by Farnsworth/Blalock Photography

Library of Congress Cataloging-in-Publication Data

Mitchell, Ed, 1946-
Fly-fishing the saltwater shoreline/Ed Mitchell.—1st ed.
p. cm.
Includes bibliographical references.
ISBN 0-8117-0653-2
1. Saltwater fly fishing—Atlantic Coast (U.S.) I. Title.

SH464.A85 M58 2001
799.1'6614—dc21

2001018363

*To my lovely wife Sandy, my son Eddie—the wise guy—
and our loving yellow lab Snickers, the wonder dog.*

Contents

Acknowledgments   viii

Introduction   ix

Chapter One: How to Fish for Bonito and False Albacore   1

Chapter Two: How to Fish for Striped Bass   26

Chapter Three: How to Fish for Bluefish   55

Chapter Four: How to Fish for Weakfish and Hickory Shad   70

Chapter Five: Fly-Fishing the Edges   82

Chapter Six: Forage and Flies   131

Chapter Seven: Fishing the Migrations   163

Chapter Eight: Solving Common Problems   203

Chapter Nine: A Guide to Lobsterville Beach and Dogfish Bar   214

Bibliography   219

Index   221

Acknowledgments

The more I write about saltwater fly fishing, the more aware I am of my debt to others. I can't possibly thank all of them here, but some attempt must be made.

First off, thank you Capt. Joe Keegan for your assistance over the years; you have been a good friend. A tip of the hat to all the fine fly tiers whose work appears in this book. They are Capt. Joe Blados, Bill Catherwood, Phil Farnsworth, Jack Gartside, D. L.Goddard, Mark Lewchik, Brian Owens, Eric Petersen, Bob Popovics, John Timmermann, Bob Ververka, and Chris Windram. Special thanks goes out to Phil Farnsworth and Lisa Blalock for use of their studio in shooting the color fly plates. Couldn't have done it without your professional expertise. Thank you Capt. Brian Horsley for your help with North Carolina fishing. Thank you Bob Popovics and John DeFilippis for your help with New Jersey fishing. And a northbound thank you to John MacMillan of the Nova Scotia Department of Fisheries for his help with the Maritimes.

In closing let me extend gratitude to a number of editors. Thank you Art Scheck and Joe Healy at *Saltwater Fly Fishing*. Thank you David Ritchie at *Fly Fishing in Salt Waters*. Thank you Angus Cameron for helping me get started in this book-writing business. And last but not least, thank you Judith Schnell and Jon Rounds at Stackpole for helping to make this book a reality.

Introduction

This book is a practical text on the subject of saltwater fly fishing along the Atlantic coast. It does not cover offshore angling, but focuses entirely on casting from the beach or close to shore in a small boat. The places mentioned are my home waters and all lie in southern New England. Nevertheless, the information is relevant to fly rodders in many places along the Atlantic.

This work follows closely in the footsteps of my first book, *Fly Rodding the Coast*. In the six-year interim between these titles, the fish and the fishing haven't changed much, and thus both books cover similar ground. I learned some new things during that period, however, and wrote twenty magazine articles on the subject of the salt. All of that new thinking is included here.

In this book is a greatly expanded section on that wonderful brand of angling madness called fishing for bonito and false albacore, more properly know as little tunny. Given the increasing popularity of these two speedsters, this chapter should prove valuable to many people, be they tyros or seasoned anglers with tuna notches already in their belts. In addition, there's a chapter on fishing for weakfish and hickory shad, neither of which was covered in *Fly Rodding the Coast*. Six years ago, there wasn't much doing for either one; the two have now increasingly made themselves known.

You'll also find new information on how to search for a super striper from shore. The aim here is to guide the fly rodder to the bass of a lifetime. And that should interest a great many folks. Also new is a chapter on the seasonal migration of game fish. There is a more extensive coastal planner and a new section on solving common problems that should prove useful.

One of the most valuable parts of *Fly Rodding the Coast*, I believe, is the chapter on reading beaches. This book tackles that topic too, but this time around, I not only explain to readers how to find the good water, but show them how to fish it as well.

One more new item is a brief fishing guide to Lobsterville Beach and Dogfish Bar on Martha's Vineyard, which together are, arguably, the most famous strands in all of coastal fly rodding.

CHAPTER ONE

How to Fish for Bonito and False Albacore

My fly swung across Menemsha Inlet as the blue-green waters ebbed on a cloudy October morn. About me on the jetty wall, a small army of anglers flayed at the water, while to my back on the beach, others did the same. And we weren't alone. Off in the distance, boatloads of anglers bobbed in Menemsha Bight. Wadded together, their dark forms sat motionless under a canopy of gulls. On the jetty, on the beach, out in a boat—it really didn't matter. All of us were under the same spell. We were bonito bound.

The boaters were banging bonito at a fairly good clip. Or so I had heard. From the number of birds aloft, it had the look of a mighty good bite. On the jetty and on the beach, however, things were going nowhere fast. In three hours, only two people had landed bonito. Both of those lucky anglers were in the same spot, right at the jetty's tip. Unfortunately, there was no more additional room out there; it was already eyeball-to-eyeball when I arrived just after dawn. So I had taken up a spot about midway along the jetty wall, a place apparently no one else had wanted.

Like the tide, my confidence was running out. Not only had I never caught a bonito before, I was convinced of one thing—that not being at the end of the jetty was the kiss of death. Moreover, I was certain you needed an ebbing flow in order to catch these fish from the wall. The tide was still dropping, but it was about to go slack. Little did I know I was about to be proven dead wrong on both counts.

1

The current stalled briefly, then flipped and began to flood in. As it did so, I prepared to pack my bags and hit the road. Suddenly, without warning, the bonito were right in front of me, ripping up the inlet. Running hard, they raced up inside toward the harbor. Before I could get the fly back into the water, they were gone. I made a cast anyway, sure that I had just missed my only opportunity. It was a cast made more out of frustration than anything else.

Disappointed, I watched my fly glide across midchannel just under the surface. Then it happened. A bonito slowly ascended from the green depths of the channel. It remained suspended for a split second directly below my fly, then quickly rose up and grabbed it. At that instant, the current had caused a large bow to form in my fly line, so I felt no pull, no sensation whatsoever; only my eyes recorded the strike. I reacted as best I could, rearing the rod high. That desperate tactic hooked the fish, but barely. The fight was on for a minute, and then my long-awaited bonito was gone.

Those events took place well over a dozen years ago. I didn't get a bonito that day, but a fire had been lit inside of me. I ached to catch one of those elusive and mysterious fish. It was not until the following fall that I actually landed a bonito, and that same autumn I had the good fortune to beach a couple of false albacore as well. Now, many seasons later, I still pursue them both with the same burning desire. And no, I don't regret that first day on the jetty in Menemsha. Yeah, I made mistakes, but those mistakes and the ones that followed taught me a great deal. As the old saying goes, sometimes you have to fail before you can succeed.

Atlantic bonito and false albacore (little tunny) are the glamour game fish of recent years, and it's easy to understand why. Both are powerful opponents, capable of long, lightning-fast runs and sustained fights. At times they are difficult to find and at times difficult to hook. So to be successful, you need to get your ducks in a row. What's more, the season for them is relatively short, often measured in weeks rather than months. All told, they provide plenty of excitement and plenty of challenge. Who could ask for more?

FINDING THE FISH

Finding fish is always a two-part equation: You have to know when and where to look. The first half involves understanding how fish react to tide, light, and weather, as well as knowing something about the seasons—when the fish typically arrive and leave. Chapter 7 includes a coastal calendar that outlines the seasons for false albacore and Atlantic bonito, as well as striped bass, blue-fish, and other species.

Both Atlantic bonito and false albacore are blue-water creatures, citizens of the open sea, so the majority of them live well away from shore. Fortunately for us, however, in some areas they do come very close to land. And it's these areas that are of the most interest to fly rodders. But bonito and false albacore are not widespread in the waters near shore. Far from it. Unlike striped bass and bluefish, which prowl all over the place, the action for these two tunas is isolated in pockets.

Places that attract them near shore generally have three criteria: They hold large numbers of schooling forage fish, they have strong tidal currents, and they are places where deep water is not far away. Typically, in southern New England, these requirements are met by the following kinds of structure: reefs or underwater ledges; inlets to estuaries, especially salt ponds and their adjacent beaches; rips off points of land; warm-water power-plant outflows; and harbors and bays, particularly their entrance areas.

In all of these locations, both species gravitate to what anglers call edges. Edges are an integral part of fishing for striped bass, bluefish, and weakfish as well, and thus they are of critical importance to coastal anglers, especially to those on foot. In brief, edges are places where the bottom or the water itself undergoes some type of marked change. That change might be in depth—for instance, where a shallow bottom drops away to deeper water—or in water speed, such as where fast and slow currents meet.

Seasonal Changes

In southern New England, when the fish first arrive, they feed away from shore, but as the season continues, some gradually move closer to land. The trend usually reverses by mid-October, before the fish leave for the season. The fish that were feeding in close move back out to feed in deeper locations. The best locations to look for the fish change accordingly. Reefs, ledges, and the tidal rips off points of land are the first places the tuna show during the season and the last places they hang out before leaving in the fall. They are also most likely to host the biggest bites. A few of the more famous locations in the Northeast include the waters off Montauk Point, the Race and Plum Gut in the Long Island Sound, and the Watch Hill reefs in Rhode Island.

Inlet fishing starts a little later and ends a little earlier. Still, inlets can be red hot, and it's in the inlets and their adjacent beaches that shoreline anglers most often get their best shots. Famous locations include Menemsha Inlet and the Gut at Cape Pogue on Martha's Vineyard; the salt pond openings along the south arm of Cape Cod in Falmouth; the inlets, locally known as breachways, along the southwest coast of Rhode Island; the inlets on the north shore of Long Island, such as Mattituck Inlet and Goldsmith's Inlet in Southold; and the inlet to Shinnecock Bay on the south shore of Long Island.

While inlets are without a doubt hot spots, bonito and false albacore do, at times, run up inside salt ponds and even some coastal rivers. But they generally do not go far, preferring areas with deep water relatively nearby and very little freshwater intrusion. Hence, in salt ponds, expect these two small tunas to stay mostly in the channels and rarely reach the back areas of the ponds where salinity is apt to be lowest. And only those coastal rivers with deep water and high salinity in their lower reaches will host these fish.

Harbors and bays have the same seasons as the inlets. Known ones include Edgartown Harbor, Woods Hole, Point Judith Harbor, Narragansett Bay, Little Narragansett Bay, and Stonington Harbor, to name a few. Much of the fishing may be at the harbor entrances, but if bait stacks up back inside, these tunas are capable of running all the way to the back of the bay or harbor, even at times busting bait under the boat docks.

The number of bonito and false albacore in southern New England vacillates considerably from year to year. While the size of the stock may have something to do with it, and the natural cycle of boom and bust certainly plays a role, the major factors are likely weather changes and physical events such as the presence of warm-water rings breaking off the Gulf Stream. As a result, some seasons there are tons of tuna up against the beach, and other years you can't buy a bite. You just have to get used to it.

The timing of the fish's arrival at a given location is subject to change. If the fish do not show up when you think they should, don't give up. Check back around the next moon. Like striped bass and bluefish, bonito and false albacore seem to move inshore and offshore on the stronger tides. Hence, a place that has had no action can suddenly blow wide open.

GETTING OFF ON THE RIGHT FOOT

If you have a fair degree of experience fishing for striped bass and bluefish, you may feel you're adequately prepared for Atlantic bonito and false albacore.

Yes, you can use the same type of tackle and in some cases the same flies, but these tunas are different. For one thing, you can't simply start blind-casting every shoreline within range. The tuna are not spread out, but rather highly concentrated into a few select spots. Even when you do locate them, the tuna are very often moving much faster than other species, and therefore, you really have to be on your toes, ever ready to move. When they come to the top, they rarely spend as much time there as bass or blues. One moment the tuna are busting everywhere, a second later they are gone. It can be wild. All told, even an experienced angler may get only one shot into them during the course of a day.

Preparations

These tunas are going to test not only your fish-fighting skills, but your tackle too, so it's imperative that your hooks are sharp and your knots strong. All your gear must be in tip-top condition, ready to roll. So check and set your reel's drag, and check your knots in the leader, to the fly line, and to the backing as well. Stretch and clean your fly lines before heading out, so your casting will be at its best. (Chapter 8 explains how to properly stretch your fly line and how to avoid tangles in general.) Then look at the condition of the backing. It should be wound neatly on the spool. When in doubt, peel off the first hundred yards of backing to make sure the wraps aren't crossed over each other in a way that may lead to a jam, and reload it neatly under firm pressure.

Spotting Bonito and False Albacore

To successfully hunt for these two rocketships, you must be able to recognize signs of their presence. On some days, the tuna can be seen jumping clear of the water. Their football shape is easy to identify, especially if the fish are back-lit. If none jump, however, the untrained eye may confuse a school of feeding bonito or false albacore with a school of feeding bass or bluefish. All of these species can make a considerable commotion on the surface, but an experienced angler knows that these tunas feed with their own signature style.

Bonito and false albacore rarely stay up on top feeding for more than a few seconds, whereas bass and bluefish tend to stay up much longer. Furthermore, schools of bonito and false albacore travel at a much faster speed—they're in front of you one moment and a hundred yards off the next. Bass and blues often leave swirl marks as they eat; tuna do not. Bonito and false albacore frequently either tear across the surface, slicing a line through the water, or slam

When false albacore feed near the surface, birds often mark the action.

into the bait so hard that water sprays upward. If you are very close to the fish, you might also look for their tails. In bright light, as these two tunas streak by, their unique, black, sickle-shaped tails are sometimes plainly visible.

When a large number of bonito or false albacore come to the top and feed, they are likely to attract a flock of gulls. Bass and blues do the same, but once again, there are differences. Tuna feeding near the shoreline don't do so in large numbers as bass and blues often do, so they don't attract gulls. Thus, if you see gulls working in close, say within 200 feet of the shore, the fish are unlikely to be tuna. Out from shore, gulls may be an indication of the presence of tuna.

Atlantic bonito, overall, are a tad more erratic in their behavior, not quite as likely to feed in a discernible pattern the way their cousin the Atlantic false albacore does. Thus bonito can be harder to figure out. Compounding the difficulty, bonito are more difficult to hook. And even when you hook one, a fairly high percentage of them get off. This is because they do not take the fly very deeply, as a false albacore or a striper normally does. Rather, a bonito seems to prefer to grasp the fly well forward in its mouth, using its teeth to lock on to it. Hence, the fly is in a very narrow and bony portion of the jaw, which makes driving home the hook more difficult.

For this reason, bonito flies should not be tied so that the tail or wing extends well beyond the hook bend. This would only encourage short strikes.

Instead, keep the wing or tail fairly short so the bonito has to take the hook into its mouth in order to hold the fly.

Even this, however, will not solve all your hooking troubles. Bonito do not always approach the fly from the rear. At times, they slam the fly from the side. This also makes your job more difficult, because as the fish closes its mouth down on the hook, it may well roll flat so that the point of the hook is facing toward the teeth instead of into the jaw. There's nothing you can do about that.

TACTICS FROM SHORE

Years ago, I was walking back to the car after a morning of searching the beach for bonito. The fish had never shown up, and several anglers including myself had spent a couple hours casting over empty water. It happens in this game. I was just about in the car when one angler stopped and said, "Face it Ed, this tuna game is strictly for boaters."

It's understandable why he made that remark. No question, boaters take the lion's share of bonito and false albacore each year. Nevertheless, you can catch them from the beach, and doing so is one mighty big thrill. So if you're the kind of person that is willing to face tall odds, and to be patient and perseverant, I highly recommend you try taking tuna from terra firma. There are big risks but big rewards.

The first step in fishing for these speedsters—from shore or from a boat—is to determine which are the prime weeks of the season. The season for these tunas, especially from shore, is a limited one, far less generous than the season for striped bass or bluefish. Expect it to be anything from a few days to six weeks total. Supplement the information provided in this book's coastal planner by talking with local fly shops. If there's a tuna bite from shore in your state, they'll know about it and can tell you exactly when to be on the water.

With a limited season, you must pick the beaches to fish with the utmost care. Location is everything. Therefore, you should focus on places with an established history of being productive for these two species. Ask around, particularly in the off-season, when anglers tend to be more talkative about their exploits. Atlantic bonito and false albacore can conceivably show up on any type of shoreline, but inlets and their immediate adjoining beaches are by far the best bets. Inlets are narrow gateways through which tremendous quantities of bait migrate with the changing seasons. That bait may hang near the mouth and along the nearest shoreline for weeks before leaving for open water.

Once you know when and where to fish, you're zeroing in on success, but there's still plenty more to learn. Above all else, you cannot hope to hit the bull's-eye unless you have some idea how to properly fly-fish a variety of different types of shorelines. In fact, this skill most clearly defines the coastal fly rodder's game.

After you've picked a beach or inlet to fish, it may seem that the business of selecting a location to fish is over. It's not. Expect every shoreline, even the ones with the finest reputations, to contain microcosms, smaller pieces of real estate that are in reality the prime fishing grounds. These are the edges—those changes in the bottom and the current that game fish love to prowl. And because these edges are so important, you'll see local experts constantly jockeying to fish in specific spots.

With bonito and false albacore fishing, this phenomenon is often very pronounced. The reason for it is simple: These two tunas prefer their food on the run, often eating in a high-speed drive-through style, and they frequently run along the same bottom contour lines time and again. Consequently, they generally come within fly-rod range only in a few specific places. Thus one 50-foot section of shoreline can consistently give up over 50 percent of the fish caught on that beach during the season.

When tuna run a beach, they are not going to attract a flock of gulls, so watching the birds won't help you determine exactly where to fish. The most effective way to uncover the right spots is to fish the same beach several days in a row. Ideally, you would try the morning bite, take a siesta, and then return for the matinee. In that way, you can learn exactly when and where the fish show up most often in that location. Experience pays off. If you simply can't spend the necessary time learning a spot well, befriend someone who has. Much of this tuna terrain has a fanatic following, a handful of hard-core anglers who rarely miss a good tide. Knowing one is a giant step in your angling success. You can not only get the inside track on how the fish react in a given location, but by staying in touch, you can learn when the action picks up.

Regardless of what type of shoreline you select, the same basic rules apply. Don't wait for the fish to show up before you start casting. Keep the fly wet; work the water. Periodically stop and double-check your tackle. Does the tippet have a wind knot in it? Is the hook point still sharp? Is the drag still properly set?

Often a fish strikes suddenly after a long lull in the action. When this happens, it can catch you off guard. To avoid missing any precious strikes, here are a few things to do. Make it a habit to keep the rod tip down—even touching the water—so you're always in contact with the fly. To avoid having the line yanked from your grip, dry your hands occasionally. And whether you use a one-handed or two-handed strip, make a conscious attempt to grasp the line firmly between your fingers during the retrieve.

Typically, the fish suddenly erupt on the surface with little warning. If you're lucky, you'll get a cast into them before they disappear, but whether you get a shot or not, don't leave. The tuna are likely to return to the same spot in a short time—perhaps twenty minutes or so. Once the tuna disrupt the schools of bait, they zoom off to look elsewhere. Meanwhile, the schools of bait re-form. Once the bait is balled up again, the tuna return for another attack.

Jetty Fishing

Since a lot of bonito and false albacore fishing centers on inlets, a great many of the tuna caught from shore are caught by anglers casting into an inlet while standing on a jetty wall. In this situation, I usually opt for a fast-sinking line, especially when the current is strong. I cast straight out or slightly upcurrent in order to give the fly a chance to sink. I then place the rod up under my casting arm in preparation for the retrieve. While the fly is swinging with the current, I retrieve at a moderate pace. Once the fly hangs below me in the flow, I wait a moment before bringing it back for the next cast. If you're using a sinking line that has a floating running line, try to mend during the swing to remove the bow in the line caused by the current. And always keep the rod tip pointed down at the water.

The jetty's tip is often a good place to hit pay dirt, particularly on an ebbing tide. Unfortunately, it's often crowded for that reason, but there are other places to fish. Pay special attention to any offset in the wall. Bends cause current changes and provide places for bait to hide. And as a rule, where the bait is packed in, so go the tuna. Also occasionally turn and fish the opposite side of the jetty wall, the one facing away from the inlet. Fish may show up on this side of the wall as well. Regardless of where you fish along the wall, try to avoid areas densely packed with lobster pots. Tuna have a real talent for tangling you up on these things.

Always scope out a safe route down to the water before you start fishing. You'll need it to land your prize. And always be very careful on rocks covered with seaweed or algae. It's very easy to take a fall. Steel cleats and a wading staff can be mighty handy for that reason. Use care; go slow.

As good as the inlets are, there are times when the tuna prefer to race back and forth along the beach to either side of the inlet. Chasing them on foot is nearly impossible, but careful observation will help you discover specific portions of the beach that get more of the tuna's time. One of the most consistent gems is the bowl formed where the beach meets the jetty. Schools of bait often ball up in this pocket, and the tuna know it. In fact, one of the best things you can do when fishing a beach is to stay near the bait. In other words, fish only the portion of the beach where the bait appears to be the most concentrated. The tuna target these areas.

When working on the beach, I'm more apt to swap the fast-sinking fly line for an intermediate one. I cast out, give things a moment to settle, and then start my retrieve. A moderate speed is fine, something on the order of a foot of line a second. And once again, I like to place the rod under my arm during the retrieve. The strike could come at any time and frequently does so with little or no warning. Remember that story I told you about my first bonito? Always be ready for the fact that these speed demons like to show just when you least expect it. So even when the fishing is slow, don't drop your guard. Remain alert, and keep in touch with the fly at all times.

Typically, things go like this: The tuna suddenly appear out of nowhere and slam into the school of bait, dispersing it. If your fly is in the water at that moment, you have an excellent shot at a hookup. Within seconds, however, expect the tuna to tear off toward a different location. As I mentioned before, don't leave at this point. Gradually, the bait in front of you will re-form its school, and the tuna will likely pay a return visit. Note, however, that the interval between attacks could be upward of twenty minutes. Be patient.

Any place you fish has its own idiosyncrasies, little quirks that can improve your odds of catching fish. And the only way you learn them is by being observant of your surroundings. On one jetty I fish, during slack tide the local lobsterman shows up to pull his pots. As he lifts his pots, the bait in the trap falls into the water. After filling them with fresh baiting, the pots are returned back down. In effect, the lobsterman is creating a chum line. Soon schools of baitfish concentrate in the area and you have a chance of bonito making a pass through. So I follow the lobsterman down the wall, fishing where the pots have just been reset. There is only one downside—there's a risk that a tuna will wrap me on a pot, but it's a chance worth taking.

When Things Are Slow

If fish do not show up in a location where they've been seen regularly day after day, keep your eyes peeled. Look in the water. Has the bait moved? Schools of bait may relocate up or down the beach a ways from day to day, especially if there has been a day of high wind. Expect the fish to follow. Therefore, when a normally hot spot goes cold, start searching around for the bait; it might be a short walk from where you're standing.

Still can't find the bait or the fish? If you're fishing an inlet with a deep channel, try going down with a fast-sinking line. Cast and then count the line down, allowing it to sink a long, long way. These tuna do not always feed on the surface. In fact, they may do a lot of their chewing well down out of sight. So it's possible that the tuna are right in front of you, but running deep along the bottom. It's always worth a shot.

When Fishing Is Hot

When the fish erupt all over the place, don't get buck fever. Stay cool. Use the same smooth casting rhythm you've used right along. Any attempt to boom out a cast often results in a tragic tangle. When you feel the fish take, concentrate on getting the line on the reel while maintaining some tension. Once the fish is running hard, swing your stripping basket out of the way. Now, if necessary, you're ready to move. As the run slows, lower the rod tip a bit under tension. Then, when the fish turns toward you, lift the rod tip gradually as needed to keep tight while you reel.

TACTICS FROM A BOAT

Even though bonito and false albacore can run right along the water's edge at times, most of these fish are caught from boats. These include a variety of crafts: seaworthy center consoles, tin boats, rowing dories, inflatables, kayaks, and canoes. I use a McKenzie drift boat, the same fly-fishing craft so popular on the rivers of the West.

Gear and Flies

Never get onboard a boat with your rod still in a tube. Always have it assembled and strung up with a fly ahead of time. This is for two reasons: It's easy to rig a rod on land and much harder in a rocking boat, and you may well hit fish a short ride from the dock. And those fish may be the only ones you encounter all day.

It's a common custom to store all gear under a hatch, under a seat, or in the console. That's fine, and it makes sense, but a small amount of critical gear should be on your person ready to go. In your jacket pockets, carry a box of flies, a spool of tippet material, and a hook hone. And on your belt should be a pair of pliers in a holster. In that way you are ready to operate as soon as fish are found.

Reading the Birds
It's important for a boating angler to learn to read the behavior of the seabirds. Birds know where the fish are long before you do, and thus by watching the birds you can greatly increase your success ratio. That goes for bass and blues as well as for bonito and false albacore, although the birds behave a bit differently around tuna.

The bird that most aids anglers is the ever-present herring gull. Herring gulls do follow these tunas, but often you'll see more laughing gulls taking on this type of chase. Laughing gulls, unlike herring gulls, have black heads, and for that reason they are also called hooded gulls. Laughing gulls outcompete the herring gulls on tuna chases likely because they are more agile and therefore better equipped to chase these high-speed, erratic fish.

Whichever gull happens to be present, by watching their behavior you can get a sense of what the tuna are up to at the moment. When the fish dive deep, the gulls circle around, flying in all directions. As the fish come nearer to the top, the gulls tighten their formation and slowly descend toward the water. If you see the gulls dipping to the water or sitting right down on the waves, the fish are feeding immediately below them. And if the gulls actually sit on the water, you can be sure there are no bluefish around. No gull would stick its feet into a bluefish blitz.

Not only can gulls alert you that the fish are about to surface, but they can also tell you where they went. As a blitz goes on, a school of bait may split up into two or more groups that move in different directions. When that happens, the feeding pattern suddenly changes as the tuna charge off in pursuit of the various schools. In such cases, the birds will split up and follow too. By watching them, you can determine where the action is headed. And by noting where the birds are most numerous, you can pinpoint the hottest action.

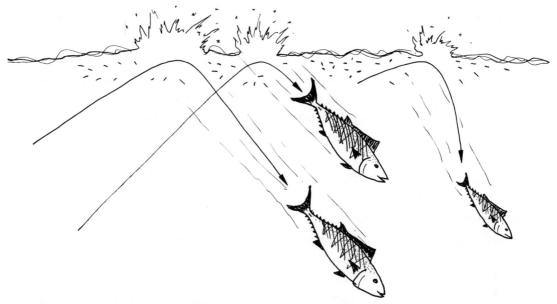

In a heavy current, bonito and false albacore may rocket to the top and then go straight back down. If you cast to the explosion, you're too late; the fish is already gone.

Presentation Is Important

Even when you're casting right into the fish, you may fail to get a hookup. When this happens, anglers quickly blame the fly or the size of the tippet. In truth, the problem is more apt to be presentation. Because bonito and false albacore accelerate to the surface, smash bait, and then dive deep, all without shifting gears, fishing blitzes can be difficult. If you cast directly at a busting fish, by the time your fly arrives, that fish is back down. Casting directly at the spot where you saw the tuna break is like shooting at the tail of a duck; you miss a lot. A better tactic is to gauge which direction the fish are headed, and drop the fly in front of them. Learn to lead them a little.

The shape of a tuna's tail gives it great speed but does not offer enough surface area for it to make high-speed turns. Tuna can make tight maneuvers when cruising at lower throttle, however. Frequently anglers find themselves casting at right angles to the direction in which the tuna are headed. If the tuna are in turbo mode, your hookup rate may not be as good as you'd like. A better presentation is one that drops the fly into the school's path and then moves it parallel to the herd. It not only looks natural, but it also makes an in-line target. A fly hanging in the current or slowly sinking can be deadly too. In all cases, you want to present an easy meal, one the fish lock on to and then nail on the run.

Running and Gunning

Once you've located the fish, you need to get a fly in front of their faces. To do it, power boaters like to employ a tactic called running and gunning. The motor is popped into neutral and left idling. Then all aboard start scanning the water for signs of life. As soon as the fish erupt on the surface, the motor is immediately engaged, and the race is on. The idea is to get to the quarry as quickly as possible, before it has a chance to go back down. As the boat nears the spot, the motor goes back into neutral, and all aboard cast like demons.

This tactic is as old as the hills and probably got its start with boaters fishing blitzes of striped bass and bluefish. But whereas stripers and blues tend to stay on the surface for minutes at a time, unfortunately these tunas are frequently up for only a matter of seconds. Hence, if this method is to work well on tuna, the casters aboard must be able to deliver the fly the instant the boat stops. Any delay, and your hookup ratio takes a nosedive.

This running and gunning has other problems as well. For one thing, the commotion often puts the fish down. Worse yet, if several boats are working the same school of fish, these boaters can find themselves in direct competition. Soon tempers flare, for inevitably one boat cuts another off en route to the fish. Things then get ugly. Last summer in Vineyard Sound, during one of these bouts of "reef rage," a boat deliberately rammed another at full speed, putting a hole in the other boat's hull. Crazy.

When two or more anglers start casting wildly, trouble is a-brewing, with tangled lines and hooks where they shouldn't be. Because this method is as chaotic as a Chinese fire drill, it's an invitation to broken rods and even gear lost overboard. When the captain signals it's time to move, rather than reel up the fly line and store the rods in a rack, anglers place their equipment on the floor of the boat. Not only is it quicker, but when they reach the fish, the rod and line are ready to go. The downside is in what can occur as the boat is traveling. A pounding boat can do a job on both rod and reel, and if the rod is left near the back of the boat, it can bounce right off the stern. If the wind sucks your fly line overboard behind the boat, it may wrap on the prop and instantly be severed, and if enough line gets into the water, it can create sufficient force to take the rod with it.

Positioning the Boat

There are alternatives to running and gunning. Both bonito and false albacore tend to be pattern feeders. Once you find them, expect them to repeatedly attack the area in a predictable manner as the school of bait is scattered and regroups. If you sit back and watch, you can see it happen. Typically, false alba-core explode first at the head of a rip, along the edge where the glassy water meets the turbulent waters of the rip. Seconds later, they reappear farther down the rip, explode on top again, only to disappear again. Then they reap-pear even farther downcurrent. After a lull, the false albacore return to the edge at the head of the rip and repeat the process. They usually work in the same direction as the current, so expect them to come at you from uptide.

Once you understand the pattern, you can set up the boat to take advan-tage of it. One way to do it is to position the boat at the head of the rip, imme-diately upcurrent from the edge where the fish regularly appear. Holding the boat in this spot can be accomplished by either stemming the current with the motor or dropping anchor. In both cases, the bow should be pointed into the flow. Of the two methods, dropping anchor requires more care, since anchoring in a current can be very dangerous. Never anchor in a navigation channel or any other water where there is heavy traffic.

When done correctly, anglers can cast off the transom so their flies swing through the exact area where the fish were seen previously. Don't wait for the fish to return before casting. The idea is to keep the fly in the water as much as possible so that the instant the fish return, it's directly in their path. It's even possible to leave the fly hanging straight back in the current. I've seen it work.

At times, schools of baitfish may seek refuge by hiding directly under the hull of your boat. This is a problem, since there is no way to present a fly to any tuna feeding on this bait short of just hanging it over the side. If the bait stacks up heavily under the boat, try quickly moving the boat to one side and then having everyone immediately cast back to the spot where the boat was a moment ago.

Setting Up a Drift

Another approach is to drift down through the rip, traveling over the water where the fish are seen most often. This is perhaps the best method of all. Once again, don't wait for the fish to surface. As the boat drifts with the current, con-stantly cover the water to either side, hoping to be in the right spot at the right time. If conditions are fairly calm, you may want to position the boat so it drifts broadside to the current. This allows for plenty of room between a caster in the bow and a caster in the stern. Once you reach the tail end of the rip, circle the boat back to the head for another drift. Do not drive directly over the water you want to fish. Travel out to the side, giving other boats plenty of casting room.

Occasionally you find schools of false albacore feeding in open water where there is no discernible current. Even here they may well feed in a pattern, repeatedly hitting the same areas. Since there is no current with which to set up a drift, position the boat upwind of the fish, and then allow the breeze to push you through the prime water while you blind-cast.

Bonito versus False Albacore

False albacore not only seem to be more numerous than bonito, but they seem to be able to outcompete them, too. When the false albacore move into town, the bonito often become hard to find. So if you want to find bonito, it's best to focus your efforts when false albacore are not around. This is true regardless of whether you're fishing from a boat or from shore. Here in southern New England, generally in August false albacore have yet to appear, but bonito are available. After the false albacore depart in the fall, there is another short window of opportunity for late-season bonito. This is tough fishing, as the bonito tend to stay deep after the water dips below 60 degrees. But these fish are usually the biggest bonito of the entire season.

The author with an early November bonito caught off Watch Hill, Rhode Island. Capt. Mike Roback

If you want to target bonito while the false albacore are in town, there are some things to keep in mind. Since false albacore are more powerful and more aggressive than bonito, when both feed in the same area, the bonito may be pushed deep or to the side of the main action. If you're determined to catch a bonito, the best bet is to fish deeper, under and often to the side of the false albacore blitz. It seems that the bonito follow the false albacore, feeding on what the false albacore leave behind much in the way stripers may follow marauding bluefish. This tactic has worked for me several times. Fishing through an area vacated moments earlier by blitzing false albacore can also result in bonito. So as the false albacore action tapers off, stay around and work your fly deep to see if bonito are passing by.

When Things Are Slow

As wonderful as it is to have the tuna on the top, you are bound to run into days when the fish simply are not cooperating. The popular solution to this problem is to put the boat in gear and do some exploring. Try to visit all the known feeding spots within a given locale, attempting to hit each of them at a good stage of the tide. You may get lucky immediately, but that's not always the case. It's best to have the gas tank topped off, because this may take some real searching. I know of guides who have covered over 60 miles of water in a single day trying to get their clients into the action.

Besides slow days, there are slow periods—several days, weeks, even an entire season when the tuna are hard to find. When this happens, you have to rethink things. While there is no easy answer to this situation, there's one tactic that has worked for me. Typically, boaters blow into an area, and if they don't see tuna on top within three minutes, they hightail it to another location. But even when the fishing has been good in a general region, the tuna may show only every fifteen minutes or so. The key may be to bite the bullet and wait—possibly for an hour or more. Like beach fishing, this is definitely not a game for the impatient. I start by picking a place that is well known as a false albacore hangout in most years. Upon arrival, I start scanning the water for signs of tuna. If nothing is doing, I set up a drift and begin blind-casting the water, all the time looking for the least sign of my quarry.

Using this tactic, on several occasions I have caught a brief glimpse of the tuna. In one location, after a considerable wait, I saw a band of false albacore pass through immediately as the current began to flood. Their numbers were few—about a dozen fish—and they attacked a particular spot where silver-sides schooled up in the water flowing around the corner of a small island. Within ten minutes, the false albacore were gone.

That initial visit resulted in no hookups. But the next day, I arrived just before the current started and set up the boat within casting distance of that corner. On cue, the fish showed, just like the day before. And I got one fish before the action shut down. On subsequent days, things went about the same—one hookup per trip. No, that's not fantastic fishing. Still, the fish I got came at a time when other boaters, even some of the most knowledgeable ones around, went fishless.

The Mystery Days

There are times when the fish are visible but you just can't get them to take any fly in your box no matter how you present it. So what is going on? Everything we throw at these fish is designed to imitate baitfish, but these fish also eat other things. And I think that is why we encounter these mystery days.

On occasion, you'll come across false albacore gently rolling on the surface. You see their backs, the dorsal fins appearing and then disappearing, followed by their tails. This rolling maneuver is done in an out-of-character, slow, easy manner. And when you see it, the fish can rarely be provoked into striking the typical streamers and epoxy flies that so commonly work. Clearly, their prey in these situations must be slow moving. That would appear to rule out baitfish. And so it is not surprising that the usual flies are of little value here. So what are they eating? In southern New England waters, we have crab hatches in September, which release thousands of these tiny creatures to drift with the tide. My guess is that these crab hatches are the main reason for this mysterious feeding behavior. But there could be additional things on the menu as well, including other small crustaceans, such as shrimp, or possibly jellyfish.

THE RIGHT TIDE AND TIME OF DAY

The Right Tide from Shore

When fishing from shore for either bonito or false albacore, I prefer a rising tide. It frequently brings the fish closer to shore. This is especially true when fishing an inlet. On the ebb, the bonito and false albacore tend to feed outside the inlet and are therefore outside casting range, except perhaps for a few anglers at the jetty tip. When the tide turns incoming, those same fish may rush inside, practically at your feet. Don't forget that when fishing an inlet, the time of current and the time of tide can be considerably different.

The Right Tide from a Boat

When fishing from a boat, tide selection is slightly less important than when fishing from the beach, but you do want moving water, not a slack tide. If you plan to fish the waters immediately outside an inlet, then an ebbing current is probably best. Again, keep in mind that there is a difference between the time of current and the time of tide. If you are going to fish rips over reefs or off points of land, then generally speaking, either tide may work well. Be prepared to learn, however. Some rips are much more productive when the water rolls in one direction versus the other. Local knowledge can be very important. It's always a good idea to talk with other anglers who have recently fished a location you have in mind. Often feeding patterns develop where only a certain stage of the tide hosts the action. Knowing that ahead of time is in your best interests.

The character of the fishing may change as the tide progresses. As the current builds, expect the fish to become increasingly aggressive. That's the good news. But there is a downside. The more the current increases, the more the fish tend to feed in increasingly tighter lanes. Because they are so concentrated, you're either right in them or out of luck.

During stages of the tide when the current is not strong, the fish and the bait are likely to be more dispersed throughout the rip. Oddly enough, this may actually improve your chances of hooking up. With scattered bait and no strong current to fight, the tuna may be more spread out and more willing to travel farther to inhale your fly.

The Right Light Level

Both species are capable of feeding right through the daylight hours, but generally speaking, the fishing you will experience has peaks and valleys during any given day. While tide plays a significant role in that, so does light level. Surface activity usually peaks during those hours when the sun's light is striking the water on a slant, from early to midmorning and from mid- to late afternoon. Likely the angled light produces more contrast near the surface and allows predators to better see their prey. Undoubtedly a considerable amount

John Wadsworth holds a false albacore he caught from the author's drift boat in Long Island Sound in early October. The fish hit in the early morning—often the best time for false albacore and bonito—on a running tide.

of feeding also takes place deep, but it's difficult to take advantage of it since you can't be sure where the fish are.

Since both light and tide are elements in the game, it makes sense, whether you fish from a boat or from the shore, to fish when the right tide coincides with the right time of day. For example, when fishing an inlet, shore-based anglers should pick a day with flooding current during either the early morning or early afternoon. Anglers on a boat working the inlet would want an ebbing current instead. Whether you are onshore or afloat, I think morning tides hold the better bite. Expect the fish to begin feeding actively immediately after the sun breaks the horizon, spilling light over the waters.

As the light fades each day, the tuna seem to disappear. Likely they go out a ways from shore and sit near the bottom in a school, waiting for dawn in order to resume their feeding. Though I've never heard of anyone hooking up in total darkness, tuna have been caught under the lights at night in the outflow to Millstone Nuclear Plant in Waterford, Connecticut. I've also witnessed them being caught in the false light just prior to dawn, in a location where the false albacore had been busy regularly during the daylight hours. It was late October, forty-five minutes before the scheduled sunrise. These fish gave no sign of their presence—no jumps, no splashes, nothing. It appears that they were slowly cruising around. Anglers would pick them up by simply covering the water. In such cases, blind-casting pays off.

Another year, in this same spot, this false light action lasted into the second week of November. The best bite came under clear skies and a bright full moon. I got six, but the anglers standing in the prime spots on a rock wall got as many as twice that. You could actually look down in the water and see the false albacore cruising by eating peanut bunker in the moonlight. Once again the tuna made no real ruckus. And they would take any fly you threw at them. Things got going around 5:00 A.M., an hour and a half before sunrise. By 7:30 A.M. it was over. In the dark, a slow retrieve worked best, but as things brightened, you had to pick up the speed. It was just like a predawn bite of striped bass. Amazing.

FIGHTING AND LANDING BONITO AND FALSE ALBACORE

False albacore commonly hit the fly so hard that they are hooked and running before you have a chance to do much of anything. Most of the time, false albacore hook themselves, and barring a bad knot or a tackle malfunction, you're likely to eventually bring the fish in. Bonito, on the other hand, are hard to hook and hold, likely because they tend to grasp the fly in the forward portion of the mouth rather than inhale it. Since you won't know which tuna has taken the fly, try to set the hook with the rod as the fish turns and runs.

Get in a Safe Position
If the boat is pitching in a choppy sea, it's best to bend slightly at the knees and brace yourself. Flats-style boats, particularly those with neither a bow rail nor a casting brace, are tricky in this regard, since there are few places to grab hold of. Often the only solution is to step down from the casting deck. This places you lower in the boat, where you're less likely to take a fall.

When fighting fish in the sea, high-sided boats are excellent, as they permit you to lean against the gunwale. Ideally, this gunwale should extend above the kneecaps and have a padded combing. Then you can lock your knees as you lean on the side of the boat.

The Long Run

Both of these tunas are as fast as greased lightning. As a rule, the false albacore can run farther and is more consistent in making a long run. I've only ever hooked two false albacore that did not burn straight away into the backing. Both of those fish turned out to be chock full of immature menhaden. A small percentage of bonito you hook won't tear off on a lightning-fast run, but will fight relatively close. This is especially true of those under 5 pounds. And overall, the bonito are a smidgen less powerful and more apt to run in an erratic fashion. Nevertheless, both of these fish will test your skill.

Once you've cleared the line through the guides and the line is on the reel, let the fish run under steady pressure. A false albacore of 9 pounds or larger has the strength to sprint between 100 and 150 fifty yards in a single burst. If it looks like the fish will go farther than that, have the captain immediately put the boat in gear and go after it. But boat speed must be only as fast as you can retrieve line.

If you're using a direct-drive reel, as most anglers do, it's imperative to keep your hands clear of the reel handle during the run. With an antireverse reel, this is not a problem. Whichever type of reel you use, avoid touching the backing as it races off the reel; it can burn or cut you. This is especially true with the new ultrathin backing materials.

Eventually the fish will stop and turn around, coming toward you slowly. Reel quickly to keep the line taut. Some of these speedsters will make a second or even a third run, but rarely is it anywhere near as long.

Running under the Boat

Once you get the fish in close, it may attempt to run under the boat. If your drag is set a bit tight, things can get hairy. The rod bends sharply, but worse yet, the pressure on the leader increases greatly. When this happens, some anglers get the jitters and attempt to loosen the drag. Don't! If you think you're at risk of popping the tippet, back-reel instead. Back-reeling is a simple trick that works beautifully, although only with direct-drive reels. With the rod tip pointed down at the water, turn the reel handle slowly in the opposite direction, releasing line to the fish under tension. Two turns is normally all it takes. The forces on the rod and leader will instantly subside. What's more, you've lost very little line and can quickly regain it as things settle down.

Another thing to remember when a fish dives under the boat is to keep the rod from touching the gunwale; the rod could snap instantly. Try to move as quickly as possible to either the bow or the stern of the boat, whichever is closer. In order for you to move, some line has to come off the reel. Here again, back-reeling is a great help. When you reach the end of the boat, guide the rod tip around the hull so you can continue the fight on the opposite side of the boat.

A fly rod's long length is a real help in making this maneuver, although it has its drawbacks too. This rod length is especially welcome when you're forced to go around a transom with an outboard motor, making it easy to pass the line safely around to the other side. In recent years, this is even more of an advantage, because many boat manufacturers now build their outboard mod-els with transom brackets that set the motor even farther back. These brackets may help performance, but they are a real nuisance for serious anglers.

At the Gunwale

Perhaps the hardest part of the fight happens just when you think the war is won. As these members of the tuna tribe sense the end is nearing, they invari-ably sound, diving deep and refusing to come up. This leaves you standing at the gunwale with the rod doubled over. Now a fly rod is a great angling device, and it has its advantages, but a great lifting tool it is not. If you doubt me, these fish are going to prove it to you. So if you hope to win these boatside tug-of-wars, you need to maximize the lifting ability of the fly rod by pumping the rod. It's the same basic tactic you'll use with bass and blues as well, although with tuna there is one added twist.

With the fish directly below the boat, lower the rod tip gradually to the water while reeling in line. The rod must remain bent and the line tight at all times. Once the tip reaches the water, stop reeling and then slowly lift the rod to a roughly horizontal position. As you lift, keep the line from exiting off the reel by pinching the fly line tight to the rod blank with the index finger of your rod hand. If your reel has rim control, you can palm the reel instead.

You don't want to lift with so much force as to pop the tippet, but at this stage the fish is weak, and smoothly applying pressure rarely results in prob-lems. Once the rod has been lifted, reel back down to the water, releasing your grip on the line if necessary. Then lift again. Repeat this process until the fish is at the surface.

Now here's the twist with tuna. During the final stage of the fight, these fish will not only bore deep, but they will swim in circles. It's helpful to time the lifting of the rod to correspond with the moment when the tuna's circle brings it closest to the boat. Holding the bent rod approximately horizontal to the water, wait until the tuna starts to swing toward the gunwale. As the fish nears, quickly reel while lowering the rod tip. During this procedure, the rod must remain bowed, and the line should have no slack. As the fish passes by, lift the rod smoothly back to the horizontal. In so doing, you will have lifted the fish's head nearer to the surface and thereby forced it to circle higher in the water column. In a sense, you are trying to unscrew the fish out of the water column.

Landing and Releasing
Some boaters use nets to land their fish, but I rarely do. For one thing, most of the large nets made for salt water are rough and scrape the fish's sides. If you plan to release the fish, this reduces its chance of survival. It's best to use nets only if you plan to keep a fish for the table or if the seas are so rough as to make reaching over the gunwale difficult or dangerous.

Once they become tired, both of these tiny tunas are relatively easy to land by hand. Simply wait until the fish is at the surface on its side. Lean over the gunwale carefully, and reach down and grasp it at the tail wrist. If you're alone in the boat, do whatever you can to unhook the fish rapidly. If you have help, hold the fish horizontal to the deck, with its belly skyward. It should remain fairly quiet. Then have your partner remove the hook.

If you want to release the fish alive, get it back in the water pronto. Don't cradle the fish in the water the way you see anglers release trout. That technique can be used with bass and blues, but it's not effective with these fish. Reach over the side of the boat, holding the fish by the tail wrist, with its head pointed down at the water. The fish should be a distance of 2, even 3, feet from the surface. The idea is to accelerate the fish into the water so it receives a blast of water through the gills. In fact, I recommend that rather than simply letting go, you propel the fish downward toward the water with a little force. These fish are not very buoyant and sink readily. When done properly, you'll see bubbles pour out the fish's gills during the descent. Expect the fish to level off and zoom away.

If you're helping a friend land a tuna, don't leave your fly hanging in the water, particularly where there is current. A fly hanging in the current is an attractive target for a false albacore, and if one of these tunas yanks on it, you could lose your rod and reel.

Gauging the Weight of Your Fish

It is common practice these days to discuss fish in terms of length rather than pounds. For one thing, most anglers have a tape measure on hand, but far fewer have an accurate scale. And if you try to guess the weight by looking at the fish, you are often wrong.

These tunas are much heavier per inch than a bass or bluefish. When a striper reaches 30 inches in length, it usually tips the scales at around 10 pounds. A blue is about the same. A false albacore might, on the other hand, weigh upward of 12 or 13 pounds at that same length, and a bonito about 11 pounds.

Big Flies, Big Tuna

Big bass and big blues like big flies. Turns out these tunas do too. Sure, bonito and false albacore are size selective at times, and carrying flies to match the prevalent bait is de rigueur. But the biggest bonito and the biggest false albacore I've ever caught were both taken on large white flies of about 7 inches in length riding 3/0 hooks. Both events took place late in the season. In the case of the false albacore, I had been fishing a large school for hours and taking some with a small fly. Just for fun, I put on the big fly and cast it into the melee. A big false albacore greyhounded across the top, coming from 30 feet away to nail it. It proved to me that these fish, like striped bass and blues, sometimes like a lot of feathers. So don't leave the full-figured flies at home.

CHAPTER TWO

How to Fish for Striped Bass

Evening had settled slowly over Vineyard Sound as the tide kicked to the west, ebbing toward Devil's Bridge. During the first two hours of current, the fishing was fairly good. We had stripers in several spots along the winding shores of Dogfish Bar. A fish here, a fish there. Big white Deceivers had done the trick, but as the last light faded, we cut them off and switched to black versions of the same. A dark fly would be the fare in the night ahead.

By the third hour of the ebb, the water level had receded and the tidal currents had increased in speed, pulling hard in their journey westward, as overhead swept the beam of Gay Head Light. Where there were once broad areas of moving water, there were now sharply defined rip lines. And in these narrowing lanes, the bass and the bait congregated to feed. Things were shaping up.

Gradually, the muted sound of slurping striped bass intensified. It was steady and unmistakable; hundreds of stripers were on the chew. They were out a ways, beyond our reach from shore. So we waded forward into the retreating water, ever closer, until finally we were within casting range.

The fish were fussy. Without a doubt, our flies were going right through their midst. And equally without question, we had few hookups to show for it. Clearly the big flies that had been so productive earlier in the evening were simply not working. Rummaging through our fly boxes, we searched for the cure. Gradually it became apparent that smaller flies worked, and the smaller

26

we went, the better the results. Best of all were small, 2-inch-long sand eel flies, tiny creations by saltwater standards. But even after we found what they would eat, too many casts were going unanswered. Something else was still wrong.

By trial and error, we discovered that the retrieve had to be painfully slow, barely creeping along. Once we had that part of the puzzle in place, the doors swung open; we began to hook up big time.

The strikes were hardly strikes at all. The fly simply stopped cold in its tracks, as if it had run up against some invisible wall. Then for a split instant nothing at all would happen, until you pulled the line taut to drive the hook home. Suddenly the rod would throb as the big bass went haywire, shook its head, and then thundered downcurrent. The war was on.

Coastal striped bass are predatory nomads, wanderers along the Atlantic shore. It is an existence they carved out of time and honed over sand, surf, and stone. Stripers belong here. And in their quest for survival, like all wild creatures, they abide by the necessities of each moment. Through the waves and under the stars they go, moving with a change in the light, a shift in the tide— fleeting shapes on the edges of an emerald world.

More than any other fish, striped bass have been my North Star. Why it is that some wildlife becomes symbols of the topography they inhabit? I can't be sure, but it happens. They captivate us. Perhaps we see them as the embodiment of a particular place—as if their size, shape, and physical being were somehow distilled from the very terrain. Perhaps it's because the spirit with which they conduct their lives echoes some attribute of our own. Perhaps it is all or none of these things.

FINDING STRIPED BASS

As with bonito and false albacore, finding striped bass is a two-part process: You need to know when and where to look. To be successful in your search for stripers, you must understand the effects of season, light, wind, weather, and tide, and know what types of locations the fish gravitate to.

Striped bass are likely the most adaptable game fish along the Atlantic coast. They are capable of surviving a wide range of water temperatures and consequently are found from the Canadian Maritimes all the way to Florida, although they are most numerous between Maine and North Carolina. Additionally, stripers can live in both fresh and salt water, an ability held by only a small percent of game fish species. As a result, these fish can be caught not only along a large portion of the Atlantic coast, but in coastal rivers and salt ponds as well.

Striped bass are voracious feeders capable of eating a wide variety of forage and of hunting both in daylight and at night. Over time, striped bass grow quite large, well in excess of 50 pounds. Typically, the fly-caught striper is between 3 and 8 pounds, or roughly upward of 28 inches in length. Bass of 30 to 33 inches—approximately 10 to 13 pounds—are reasonably common catches, and they are excellent fighters. A yard-long bass is certainly harder to find, but it's quite possible, especially if you're willing to do your homework. Stripers of 40 inches or better are memorable fish and all too rare on a fly.

The length-to-weight ratio for stripers can vary considerably. Most bass are fat and sassy, but a few are long and lean. Likely the difference is due to the availability of adequate forage. But there may be something else going on here too. It has long seemed to me that there are two races of striped bass on the coast. Granted, this distinction is often blurred, and the visual differences are subtle. Nevertheless, I believe two races exist. One has a longer lower jaw, a more pointed snout, and a very robust body, thick, well conditioned, and streamlined, with a slight hump on the shoulder. The other has a blunter head and the more typical striper shape, and frequently tends to be much leaner. The former I see mainly on the Vineyard during the spring run. They are very strong adversaries. The majority of the stripers in Rhode Island and Long Island Sound fall into the latter category. These fish have less spunk.

Although striped bass are adaptable creatures, there are limits to what they can do. Stripers chase schools of bait across open water, but they are at their best where there is plenty of cover from which to spring an ambush, and that cover is most abundant near shore. So unlike bluefish, bonito, or false albacore, striped bass feed, for the most part, within a half mile of land. And clearly that is good news for beach-based anglers and small boat owners alike.

Habitat

Striped bass are found on all types of shorelines—sandy strands, rocky coastlines, protected beaches, exposed beaches. There is, however, a general distinction between locations that attract small bass versus their larger kin. School bass, those 10 pounds and less, are more tolerant of warm water than their elders. The larger stripers typically inhabit cooler, deeper haunts, whereas smaller bass are frequently found in shallower, warmer waters. Where bass of both sizes mingle, you can expect the big boys to be the deepest members of the crew.

TACTICS FROM SHORE

Over the years, I've caught thousands of striped bass on a fly rod from shore—from 4 inches to over 40 pounds—and in all types of situations: on sunny afternoons, in total downpours, on calm days, in the middle of northeasters, at dusk, at dawn, at night, and everything in between. You name it; it has happened.

Nevertheless, at times striped bass can be elusive, even in years when their numbers are fairly abundant. How can an aggressive predator that lives in a wide variety of coastal habitats be elusive? Striped bass don't feed continuously around the clock. They eat and rest, eat and rest. And when the bass are resting—or perhaps I should say digesting—there are periods when the finest fly and the longest cast go unanswered. This on again, off again feeding behavior is not completely random, however. Stripers prefer to feed when environmental conditions stack the deck in their favor. And when you understand those conditions, you can plan your fishing around them. Of the factors influencing those conditions, light and tide are the most consistent and predictable, but wind and weather play a role as well.

Light
Both on land and underwater, most ambush-style predators prefer to hunt in low light. There's no better place to launch an attack than from the shadows. Consequently, bass often do their heaviest feeding in twilight conditions—which is to say after sunset and before dawn. Time after time, my experience on the water has borne this out. When the light is low, the fishing is best. In fact, I'll even go a step further and say that light as a factor is more important than tide. Whether the water is up or down, when the light is low, you should go for it.

Exceptions to this occur at the extremes of the season. In early spring, when water temperatures are marginal, sufficient warmth is more essential than low light. Therefore, fishing in the early afternoon, the warmest part of the day, is more likely to bear fruit than fishing in darkness. In the fall, bass are filling their bellies with winter in mind. As a result, daytime blitzes are common and are a very exciting part of the fishing. As the autumn run winds down, light may again be the main factor. In my waters, by late October, it's not uncommon to find brief flurries at dusk or dawn, and the daylight hours are largely dead.

Light penetrates water, yet only to a certain depth. That depth is determined by the strength of the sun and water clarity. Leaving the clarity issue aside for the moment, one thing is sure: In shallow water, light is able to influence a greater percentage of the total water column and may even illuminate things from bottom to top. In deeper water, the light influences a smaller percentage of the total water column. Therefore, the impact that the light level has on your striper fishing is usually inversely correlated with the depth of the water you're fishing.

Since the water is shallowest close to shore, light level is far more of an issue when fishing from the beach than when fishing farther out in a boat. And when fishing from shore in broad daylight, a deep shoreline is more apt to be consistently productive than a shallow one. However, during times of the year when the water is still relatively cool, shallow water can be productive for bass even in the brightest light.

Tide

A moving tide—one that is either flooding in or ebbing out—is almost always better than a slack tide, with two limited exceptions. Striped bass in a swift, deep rip are frequently feeding well below the surface, out of the flow, and can be difficult to reach with a fly. As the tide slows or goes slack, those same bass may come up toward the surface and be vulnerable to a fly. Also, the biggest bass are lazy feeders; they don't want to waste energy bucking a current. Hence, there may be spots where the largest bass nose in to feed right at slack tide.

Perhaps the most critical thing to understand is that the influence of tides is highly local. One spot may fish better on a rising tide and another may fish best on the ebb. For beginners, this is often an issue of great consternation. They want one tide to be the answer for all locations, and who can blame them? But the marine environment is a varied terrain, and one can't reasonably expect the influence of tide to be identical in all areas, even two places 300 yards apart.

Still, here's a starting point for those new to the striper game. When fishing the mouth of an inlet, an ebbing tide is a pretty safe bet. The baitfish flow out of the inlet with the current and the bass are there to meet them. If you arrive during a rising tide, fish farther up inside the inlet. The bait and bass are likely there. When fishing a beach, you can safely assume that the bass come closest to shore during the hours when the water level is fairly high. That translates into the last three hours of the rising tide and the first three hours of the ebb. An hour of slack high tide lies right in the middle, providing a nice break for coffee and a sandwich.

One way to get a better handle on this tide thing is to understand the effect tides have on the feeding behavior of bass. As tides move in and out, they produce current and turbulence, and bass like to feed in both. That's why a moving tide, be it ebb or flood, typically produces better fishing than a slack tide, and the stage of the tide that creates the strongest current or greatest turbulence on a particular shoreline is likely to hold the most consistent action. Also, the days of the month on which the tides are strongest are apt to hold better bites than the days when the tides are average or below average in strength.

Besides current and turbulence, tides alter the water levels near shore. A flooding tide raises them, permitting striped bass to enter shallow areas where forage may be hiding. An ebbing tide eliminates that access. Thus you can expect stripers to move into shallow beaches and flats on rising tides and exit these locations during the ebb. Likewise, expect bass to move up inside bays, coves, harbors, and salt ponds on the flooding tide and drop back toward the mouth when the tide reverses.

As you gain experience with a particular shoreline, try to discover which combinations of light and tide most often result in good striper fishing. At one spot I know, an ebbing tide that starts before dawn and carries through first light regularly produces fine action. So I study my tide charts ahead of time, circling those days when the tide crests immediately before first light. Since the time of tide advances roughly an hour a day, this opportunity lasts for only about three consecutive days at best. That three-day window occurs twice a month.

Wind and Weather

Because wind and weather can't be predicted far enough ahead with any certainty, anglers must react to changes in wind and weather as they occur. It's just something you have to get used to.

Much of the time, the effects of wind and weather are subtle, but during the spring and fall, wind and weather can play a significant role in your fishing success. In the spring, prevailing southwest winds are what you want. They keep the fish moving and the fishing on track. Northerly winds, during that same period, shut the fishing down rapidly. In the fall, a northerly blow may well stir the stripers up to feed, but the stronger and more often north winds are around, the quicker the season ends.

As a good general rule, regardless of the time of year, the fishing is better when there is at least some wind. And you will undoubtedly see some occasions when a strong wind ignites a furious bite. A gusty wind preceding a front or a thunderstorm may cause stripers to feed ravenously. At that moment, any fly will work, but as soon as the wind passes, the fishing returns to normal.

Calm conditions are less likely to create a feeding bonanza, particularly where big bass are concerned. Nevertheless, some fly rodders enjoy working glassy water, because any striper chewing near the surface can be spotted for a country mile. I prefer the combination of calm conditions and fog. For whatever reason, it seems to help me catch fish.

When wind moves water, it concentrates the largest single food source in the sea: plankton. Consequently, plankton stacks up along shorelines that face into the wind. That plankton attracts foraging fish, which in turn draw striped bass. So an onshore wind is often to the benefit of beach anglers, even though it makes casting more work.

Prevailing winds promote stable weather, and stable weather typically produces stable fishing. So if the action has been fairly good, it's likely to remain that way as long as the wind and weather hold. If the action has been poor, however, it may remain poor.

A change in the weather—the passage of a front—is announced by a shift in the wind. When the wind shifts from its prevailing direction, expect a change in the fishing. This phenomenon is most evident during the spring and fall migration periods and least visible during the middle of the season. Regardless of the time of year, the best fishing often is immediately prior to a front's passage. Rainy low-pressure days are usually productive, whereas high-pressure days, with their beautiful blue skies, generally hold poor striper fishing.

Edges

Once you understand what conditions tend to bring striper bass to the dinner table, the next step is to figure out where they are going to dine. There's an old saying that 90 percent of the fish are located in 10 percent of the water. There's a lot of truth in that statement. And implicit in that saying is this: Instead of trying to cover all the water in front of you, you should focus on that 10 percent that holds the majority of fish. Doing that will cause your success ratio to skyrocket.

So how do you determine where that 10 percent is? If there's one rule that defines how you fish for striped bass, it's this: You work the edges. An edge is an area of transition where the water or the bottom undergoes a rapid change. This change may be in water depth, in water speed or turbulence, or in the composition of the bottom, say from sand to rock. With an edge, the change takes place somewhat abruptly. A gently sloping bottom that increases a foot in depth over a hundred-yard span does not qualify as an edge, but a bottom that drops away 2 feet or more in a span of 10 feet is very definitely an edge.

Typical edges include points, sandbars, cuts, sloughs, rock piles, undercut banks, flats, channels, and the rips associated with all of them. Edges are areas of rich habitat, attracting a wide variety of forage for stripers to feed upon. Equally important, edges allow striped bass to play their strong suit. With their broad, shovel-shaped tails, striped bass are at home in strong current and turbulence; they can even blast bait in a breaking wave. Edges are places where water takes on these types of motion. Finally, edges supply another key component of the hunt: the necessary cover from which bass can bushwhack their prey.

Thus, if you want to be able to consistently catch striped bass—or bluefish or weakfish—from shore, you must be able to find and properly fish edges. Sure, we've all heard the stories about novice anglers stumbling upon huge bass on their first outings. But luck is fickle, and it never carries an angler over the long haul. Only knowledge and skill do. Since edges are so important to fishing for many species, chapter 5 is devoted entirely to this subject.

Daytime Fishing

Fishing for striped bass in the daylight is a fun experience, and it doesn't require you to lose any sleep. When striped bass feed during the day, occasionally they are in plain view. Much of the time, however, they are not visible either on the surface or below it. As a result, most striper fishing is done blind—by searching the water in hopes of intercepting the fish.

To search the water effectively, you should do two things. First, pick a fly that is highly visible under the present conditions. In clear water, white is my favorite color. It stands out nicely, particularly over a rocky bottom. In

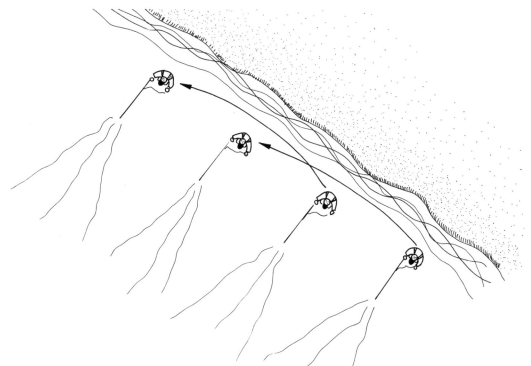

You and a partner can quickly search a large area by fan-casting and then moving past each other as you work down the beach.

discolored water, such as in many coastal rivers or on days when a steady wind has churned up the bottom, a yellow or chartreuse streamer is better. Second, don't just cast straight ahead. Instead, cover each fishy-looking area in shotgun fashion. Make an array of casts, fanning out in several directions.

When fishing during early spring, carry some weighted flies and a sinking line. At this time of year, bass are usually near the bottom. In fact, along the beach, stripers sit deepest in spring. For that same reason, poppers are not terribly effective during the opening weeks of the season. Save them for when the water is at least 55 degrees.

Under daylight conditions, I assume that if I use a fair-size fly and fan-cast the water, any striper nearby will quickly see the fly. Hence, if after targeting a few hundred feet of water for fifteen minutes, I don't get a hit, I move down the beach to the next spot. That assumption is not always correct, but over the years, it appears to have been right more often than not.

When the sun is up, there's also the possibility of seeing cruising bass and then casting to them. This brand of action is known as sight fishing, and increasingly anglers are becoming interested in it. And why shouldn't they be? Sight fishing adds an exciting dimension to the sport. You hunt for the quarry, see it, and cast to it, just as in the revered art of bonefishing. In order for sight fishing to work, however, you need several conditions to come together, and some special angling skills. This is discussed in depth in the chapter on edges.

Blitz on the Beach
One day you may walk down to the beach and see hundreds of gulls screaming overhead and hundreds of striped bass ripping up the water underneath those birds. Typically in these situations, as long as the fish are within range, it's hard to go wrong. Any fly, any retrieve works. Still, there are strategy and tackle considerations that will enhance your success.

The specific type of baitfish involved may require some adjustments in terms of what you tie on the end of the line and the speed at which you bring it back. In June on the Vineyard, it might be juvenile Atlantic herring. On Cape Cod, it might be sand eels. In the fall on the Rhode Island coast, it might be bay anchovy. In Long Island Sound, it might be juvenile menhaden—peanut bunker. Each event has its own set of tactics, detailed at length in chapter 6.

If the fishing is fast and furious, your leader is going to take a serious beating. And if you're not careful, eventually you'll get broken off. For that reason, in a blitz it's good to either cut back the leader or go to a heavier tippet. That way you can catch as many fish as possible with little worry about getting broken off. The fly will get mangled in this brawl. But surprisingly, it can get practically destroyed and still work.

Regardless of what bait is involved, predator and prey are likely to move along the shoreline, so you need to stay in touch with the fish as best you can. The obvious approach is to follow the blitz as it progresses down the beach, although running in waders is never a picnic.

But sometimes the blitz has moved too far or too fast, or obstacles are in your way. When that happens, don't automatically give up on the bite. Many times, the bass circle back to the same area. Be patient. Also, there are likely stragglers around, stripers feeding behind the main school. Some of them are likely near you, so cast and move until you find one. A second bite often occurs later, after the sun has gone down. After all, there's probably a good deal of injured bait lying around for the picking.

Dusk and Dawn Fishing

Though I love to fish for striped bass during the day, dusk and dawn fishing are two of my favorite times to be on the water. The dawn bite is typically a short window of action, anywhere from twenty minutes to an hour in length. It generally starts about an hour to an hour and a half before the scheduled sunrise, builds with the sun's first faint glows, and shuts off as the light spreads over the water. If you arrive after the sun has broken the horizon, you may miss the action.

There are exceptions, particularly in the fall, when the bite may last well into the morning. A cloudy morning, what sailors call a high dawn, is a bonus, since the clouds delay the light reaching the water. Fog is a help for the same reason. On a foggy morning, the action can extend considerably longer, at least until the fog begins to burn off with the heat of the rising sun.

Dusk fishing typically runs for a longer duration than the dawn bite. As soon as shadows start in late afternoon, expect some bass to move into the shallows to feed. In June, for instance, that might translate into 5:00 P.M. The fishing usually builds slowly as the light fades and often reaches a peak right as the sun disappears. This burst of action may last for another half hour or so, but usually it tapers off quickly as full darkness moves in. Don't let the lull fool you; the bass may be back big-time during the night.

Fishing from Shore at Night

In many locations, night fishing offers the single best shot at stripers from shore, in terms of both numbers of fish and size. But for many people, making the transition from sunlight to starlight is not always easy. Usually, the first time they head into the night, everything goes awry. Not only do they feel out of sync with their surroundings, worse yet, they rapidly lose confidence. And as a result, for some of them, their venture into the dark becomes a one-night stand. But knowing some basic tactics can make night fishing a whole lot easier.

The best time for night fishing depends on the season. In southern New England, night fishing comes into its own in late May and extends right through the fall. During the warmer months, the deeper parts of the night are most productive. Hence, I pick a day when the right stage of the tide for a given beach occurs late—near midnight or beyond. I also prefer dark nights around the new moon over ones with a bright full moon, particularly in places with clear, shallow water. In the cooler parts of the year, May and again in October and November, the hours around dusk and dawn are good bets. If I had to pick, I'd take dusk in the spring and dawn in the fall.

Fishing an unfamiliar beach in broad daylight can be a pleasant experience. Navigating a strange place at night, however, is rarely so simple and often a ticket to trouble. Therefore, it's imperative that you develop a good mental map of the beach first. A mental map is an internal sense of how the local terrain is laid out. In the middle of the night, most of us can roll out of bed and find our way to the bathroom without ever flipping a light switch. We simply know our homes that well. You need to develop the same type of familiarity when fishing a beach at night.

To develop a mental map, you and your fishing partner should scout out the beach during the day, preferably at the same stage of tide you intend to fish under the stars. I suggest that you start your night adventures on relatively shallow, protected shorelines. Focus your efforts on finding three aspects of the shoreline: the best travel routes to and from the water and along the beach; the best-looking edges to fish; and the locations of any potential hazards, such as steep drop-offs, holes, undercut banks, swift currents, or slippery footing. Under cover of darkness, fish frequently cruise into shallower water than they do during the day. Therefore, portions of the beach that you might write off during the day as too shallow may be productive in darkness.

Also, watch for landmarks—objects large or distinctive enough to help you navigate at night. Look inland along the horizon for things that will make bold outlines against the night sky, such as cottages, telephone poles, streetlights, or trees. Look on the beach, too, especially for immovable objects with memorable shapes, such as a grouping of large rocks, a particular point in the shoreline, or a jetty.

Perhaps more than any other form of fishing, night fishing requires forethought. So make sure your equipment is ready before you head out to fish. That means stretching fly lines, sharpening hooks, fixing leaders, inspecting knots, and so on. Comfort is important as well, so choose appropriate clothing. Pack a candy bar or two, and take along a water bottle. And don't forget bug repellent.

Also check your flashlight, which should be waterproof. Some lights are way too powerful—more suited to landing a corporate jet than a striped bass.

They will kill your night vision, and the flood of light they emit will make you persona non grata with the rest of the anglers on the beach. I like small, penlight-size lights with a focused beam. The Mini Maglite is one that is tough and user-friendly. If you are going to carry only one light, have spare batteries and even a spare bulb along. I carry two lights, one of which has a reddish amber filter. I use it for changing flies, tying knots, and releasing fish. The colored beam is soft on the eyes, and when you shut it off, your night vision returns quickly. The other light has a clear lens, and I use it as a backup or for maximum illumination while walking back to car.

When you arrive on the beach at night, you and your partner should move slowly, especially at first. It takes up to forty-five minutes for your eyes to fully adjust to the dark. As the two of you progress along the shore, look for the landmarks you identified during the day to get your bearings. Establish a place to meet in case the two of you accidentally get separated.

One of the most important aspects of night fishing is getting into a consistent rhythm. Don't try to boom out all the fly line. Instead, work for a smooth casting stroke that delivers a comfortable amount of line without tangles. Keep repeating it until you are into a steady groove.

At night, the steady sea breeze of a summer afternoon often swings around and comes off the land. To take advantage of it, try shortening your backcast a bit and aiming your forward cast slightly higher.

As you fish, listen to the night. On calm, protected shorelines, you can often hear the fish feed. You may even see swirls in the starlight. While moving along the beach, train a tightly focused beam at the water's edge. This will often reveal the presence of bait. Obviously, where the bait is most abundant, the other fish will be too. Small streamers work at night, yet larger ones that push water are frequently a better bet. Fish feeding in shallow water seem especially attuned to anything moving overhead, so carry some sliders, too.

Regardless of the pattern you pick, the leader can be short—7 feet max. Keep your retrieve slow; the fly should barely creep back to you. A slow retrieve makes it harder to stay in touch with the fly, so it's critical that you pay attention. Get sensitive to the subtle weight (resistance) of the fly at the end of the line. If you can't feel it, you will miss strikes. Keeping the rod tip very low to the water helps—in fact, it is imperative—but keeping the rod tip pointed at the fly, even as the fly swings across a current, is also important. As a wave passes under the fly line, you tend to momentarily lose contact with the fly.

When you feel this happen, increase the retrieve speed a hair until you again feel the fly. Then, as the wave passes by, decrease the retrieve to its original pace.

Make it a habit to periodically stop and check the fly to be sure it's not fouled. If it fouls repeatedly, replace it with a different fly. In fact, patterns that tend to foul should not have a place in your fly box. Remove any weed from the fly or leader, and inspect the hook point. A low backcast, particularly on a rock beach, can dull the hook and in some cases bend or snap the point right off. Be sure your fly is in top fish-catching form.

In a rip, the hottest fishing may be associated with the lanes of fastest current, especially later in the ebb. Since your vision is limited at night, let the line locate these lanes for you. Cast across different portions of the rip, paying attention to the speed at which the fly line swings downcurrent. When you find the fastest flow, cover the water well. Follow the fly's path with the rod tip, or you'll miss fish.

Catching Big Bass

One of the most memorable moments for a coastal fly rodder has to be catching a striped bass of 20 pounds or more from the beach. The power, the sheer weight, the sight of that shovel-shaped tail slapping the surf—it's unforgettable.

Given the pressures of the workaday world, most anglers fish a limited number of times per year. As a result, the single biggest obstacle they face is planning their time on the water wisely. Now if you're satisfied with schoolie bass, that's not hard to do. But if you yearn for a bass longer than a yardstick, the place to begin is by identifying which months hold the best fishing for big bass in your part of the coast.

A big bass could latch onto your fly at just about any time of year, but far and away the most productive moments for a jumbo striper from shore occur during the annual spring and fall migration. Each of these periods is roughly six weeks long, yet in both cases it's toward the end of the migratory surge that your big-bass chances are best. Big bass are the last to leave the spawning grounds and therefore the last members of their tribe to hit the coastal highway. As a result, these fish are not mixed in with the first surge of stripers shooting up the coast in the spring. And because of their tolerance of cold water, they're also the last ones to head home in the fall.

So in reality, what we have is roughly a month-long window of opportunity in the spring and another month-long window in the fall. In southern New England, that translates into late May to late June, and late October to late November. If you fish farther north or south, you'll have to adjust these dates. On the fall end of things, in New Jersey, it's early November into early December, and up in Maine, it's early September into early October.

At this point, the hunt for big bass has been narrowed down to a sixty-day season. Manageable. Now let's try to take it a step further. Inside those two month-long windows, there are peak periods, times when the odds tip more in your favor. Striped bass seem most active around the stronger tides of the new and full moons. Therefore, fishing during these moon tides increases your odds of meeting up with a big, hungry bass.

Open your tide book to the months in question, and mark the day of each of these migration moons. (In the *Eldridge Tide and Pilot Book,* you'll find the days of the moon listed in the back.) You have to adjust this according to the region. For example, in southern New England, you would check off the last moon of May and the two moons of June, followed by the last moon of October and the two moons of November. If you're fishing in the fall in Maine, I'd suggest the two moons of September and maybe the first moon of October. On the outer beaches of Cape Cod, I'd pick the last moon of September and both moons of October. On the south shore of Long Island, I'd opt for the moons of November. Farther south, at Sandy Hook, New Jersey, the migration is later, and I'd choose the moons of November and the first moon of December.

The next step is to note that each moon hosts upward of six days during which the tides are above normal in height. Circle these days in your tide book. You now have defined approximately thirty-six prime days to find a trophy bass.

If any moon does not host above-normal tides, that moon is in apogee. Apogee moons are those that occur when the moon is at its maximum distance from the earth. An apogee moon tide is really no stronger than a quarter-moon tide, and therefore I suggest you cross that moon off the list. You likely will lose at least one of the six moons you checked off, thereby reducing your prime-day total to thirty.

Besides adjusting by region, you need to adjust your fishing around the weather. As a rule, warmer-than-normal weather makes for a longer season by kick-starting fishing earlier in the year and delaying the return to the south. A slightly cooler-than-normal spring delays good beach fishing by a week. An even colder spring may set beach action back two weeks or more. On the other end, a cold fall means that the fishing starts and ends earlier than usual. A warm fall is the reverse.

In both spring and fall, the approach of a strong storm can trigger a brief but memorable blitz. In the spring, these are likely thunderstorms; in the fall, they're apt to be northeasters. Your personal safety is number one, so use common sense.

Beach-bound anglers do better on big bass during low-light conditions. Therefore, during those thirty prime days, any outing you attempt should concentrate on dawn, dusk, or night fishing. Base your decision on the time of the tide. All things being equal, in my experience, dusk is a bit better than dawn in the spring, but in the fall, the reverse is true. If you're night fishing, late-night tides—those that occur between 11 P.M. and 1 A.M.—are superior during the spring migration. In the late fall, that has never seemed to be the case. At that time of year, tides in early evening or just prior to first light seem to have the edge.

Whether a new or a full moon is more productive at night depends on the depth of the water you intend to fish. Shore-based anglers typically work relatively shallow locations. Here a new moon is best. In these locations, the light from a full moon penetrates a fair percentage of the water column and seems to discourage big bass from aggressively feeding. Over deeper water, however, the light from the moon does not necessarily reach the fish and hence is often not a problem.

Where to Look

The places where you regularly bail schoolies are not usually the places to catch bruiser bass. So focusing on big bass usually means forgoing the steady action supplied by smaller bass. Overall, this means avoiding extremely shallow shorelines or very warm water. Instead, lean toward windy, exposed locations with some depth or at least deep water nearby. Often the migration of big striped bass is closely coordinated with the migration of key forage fish. Therefore, large bass are frequently found where schools of migratory forage fish tend to congregate. These tend to be two types of shoreline areas: inlets and river mouths, along with their adjoining beaches, and points of land.

Purchase some marine charts of your area, and circle the inlets and points within driving range. Now go back to your tide book and look up the times of tides for these spots during the prime days you determined, noting particularly how these tides relate to dawn, dusk, or night. With the inlets and river mouths, an ebbing flow is usually best. The current may not actually start until one, two, or even three hours after the time of high tide. The right tide for a point of land is hard to generalize. Some fish better on the flood, others on the ebb.

During the spring, inlets and river mouths usually outproduce the points, so focus your energies there. In the fall, however, things are different. Typically, the forage schools first show in the inlets and river mouths. After a time, they move to the adjacent beaches, and then they stage off the points, before finally migrating away from shore. Try to follow along.

Sad but true, big bass are not equally dispersed along the Atlantic coast. So like it or not, the state in which you plan to fish may determine to a degree your chances of hooking up a truly big bass.

Several years ago, the Atlantic States Marine Fisheries Commission (ASMFC) began estimating the size of the striper stock using a mathematical model called a virtual population analysis (VPA). The VPA calculates the number of fish in different age groups and estimates the number of fish of various ages that were landed state by state. These numbers show that anglers in some states did far better on older bass than anglers in other states. The VPA counts bass according to age, not length. Let's assume that big bass are ten years or older. In years when forage is highly abundant, such a fish might weigh 30 pounds, but in other years, it might be only a little over half that. According to the VPA, in 1998, Massachusetts recreational anglers landed 93,532 bass age ten and older. (This number also includes fish released.) By comparison, in Maryland, recreational anglers landed 21,999; in Connecticut, 18,408; in Rhode Island, 11,823; in New Hampshire, 2,545; and in Maine, 1,504.

Beach Etiquette and Safety

In recent years, the number of fly anglers on the beach, day and night, has risen dramatically. And because of it, you need to be increasingly careful about people walking behind you while you're casting. Casters should try to be cognizant of people approaching from either side. When you are the one approaching, try warning the caster by calling out, "Coming behind you!" This often does the trick. And I think you're best off passing as close behind the caster as possible. Walking high on the beach may put you out of range, but you can be sure casters can't hear or see you, and on a long backcast you may still get hit.

Increasingly, fly casters are wearing protective eyewear, the type used in many other sports. You may want to consider using such eye protection, especially at night or on windy days.

TACTICS FROM A BOAT

Fishing for striped bass from a boat is similar in a number of ways to fishing from shore. Nevertheless, working from a boat does have its special character. As with beach fishing, 90 percent of the fish are likely found in 10 percent of the water. Therefore, fishing edges remains an important part of your angling strategy. The edges boaters cover, however, are typically deeper than ones anglers cover from shore. Because of that greater depth, light level is not as big a factor in boat fishing. This is because in deeper waters, light does not penetrate as much of the water column. Thus boat anglers have a much better chance than onshore fishers of finding feeding striped bass during the daylight hours. Be that as it may, boaters can still expect to see more surface activity and overall do a bit better in low-light periods than in the middle of the day.

Tides also are important to boaters but a little less critical than they are to the beach-bound angler. Boaters are far more mobile, so when the tide goes slack in one location, they can relocate to another spot where the tide is still

Boaters should watch for packs of busy gulls, which often accompany surface-feeding stripers.

running. That is a major advantage. In addition, since the water is deeper away from shore, typically there is enough depth to give striped bass access to any location, even at low tide. Nevertheless, even away from the beach, tides still are the principal cause of current and turbulence, so boaters also benefit by matching the right stage of the tide to the right location, and the right light level as well.

Boaters must factor in wind and weather too, although these conditions also are a bit less of an angling concern here. Wind and weather are very much a safety issue for boaters, however. Never go to sea when conditions are dangerous or remain out when conditions put you at risk.

In general, as with shore fishing, windy days are better than calm days. Stable weather produces predictable fishing. Overcast, low-pressure days are frequently more productive than high-pressure, bluebird days, although high pressure is more of a problem for anglers on the beach, since it tends to drive bass away from shore into deep water. At that point, at least boaters still have a shot at them.

As boaters often work edges that are deeper than the ones worked from shore, it is imperative that they own and know how to cast fast-sinking fly lines. By fast, I mean lines that sink at 5 inches or more a second. These lines are often the difference between catching fish and getting skunked. However, they can be a bear to cast, especially for novice anglers. It is far better to practice with them on your own than to attempt to learn how to use one in a rocking boat, where you will put yourself and others aboard at risk of getting hit with the fly.

Full-length sinking lines are fine, but the most popular lines are essentially designed like a shooting head, although the head and the running line are, in this case, one piece. My personal preference in this type of line is the Air Flow Depth Finder. I use a 400-grain model on my 10-weight rod and find that it casts quite nicely and sinks like a stone. Some anglers, however, go to 11- and 12-weight rods and throw even heavier lines. Be warned that these big guns are a lot of work and require considerable strength to operate for any length of time.

How deep do these lines allow you to deliver a fly? I've caught bass on lead-core sinking lines down to roughly 22 feet. But that seems about the limit to which fly rodding is practical. Far more often, you'll be looking for situations in which the fish are somewhere between 8 and 15 feet down.

As a good operating rule, always expect the bass to be below the level to which the light penetrates the water column. To get an idea how far down that is, tie on a light-colored fly and then lower it overboard. Allow it to sink on a slack line as you slowly count. As soon as the fly disappears from view, stop counting. Thereafter, each time you cast, allow the fly to sink while you count it down to the required depth before beginning your retrieve. If it takes more than a ten count to deliver the fly below the light, consider switching to either a faster-sinking line or a weighted fly.

While sinking lines are mandatory aboard a boat, I would not leave the dock without an intermediate fly line as well. Though fishing for striped bass from a boat frequently means going deep, over the course of a season boaters probably encounter more surface blitzes than one ever gets to see from shore. This is due in part to the boater's ability to cover ground and in part to the fact

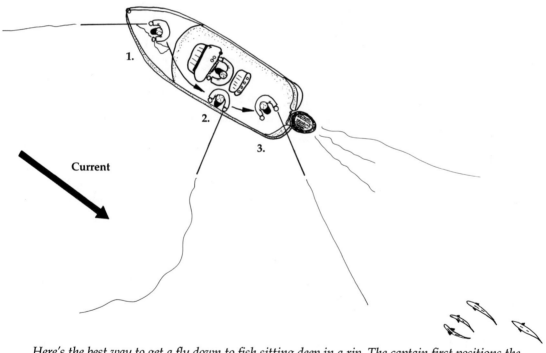

Here's the best way to get a fly down to fish sitting deep in a rip. The captain first positions the boat upcurrent and stems the tide with the motor, then:
1. The angler moves to the bow and casts a sinking line upcurrent.
2. The angler walks slowly toward the transom, allowing the line to sink freely.
3. At the transom, the angler waits for the line to tighten and then swing through the hot spot.

that when schools of bait are in open water, stripers frequently attack by driving them to the surface. Sometimes you'll simply come across the melee without warning. More often, when bass drive bait to the surface, you will likely see plenty of birds working overhead. Unlike the bonito and false albacore fishing, however, once the stripers come topside, they usually stay for a while. That makes it much easier to intercept the school and deliver a fly.

Once you're within casting range, most of the time you can do little wrong; you chuck the fly out, and bang, you're quickly hooked up. Nevertheless, when you see bass busting on top in broad daylight, many of them are actually rising up out from the depths to hit the bait. Therefore, while a fly near the surface is going to catch fish, a fly riding deeper is likely to be seen by more stripers and do even better.

If the bass go back down by the time you reach them, stay in the area and sit with the motor running. Very often the bass return to the top in a minute or two. During the wait, everyone aboard should be scanning the surface and watching the birds in an effort to gauge where the action will erupt next. Once the fish return to the surface, head directly at them. Shut down the motor before you reach them, so you can drift into the blitz rather than run right through it. This is much the same tactic I referred to as "running and gunning" back in the chapter on bonito and false albacore.

Some surface action is the result of only a handful of feeding fish, and there will be only a few swirls in the area. At such times, it may pay to hold your cast for a moment and study the water for signs of a striper. As soon as a swirl pops up, deliver the fly immediately to the area. If you see a few swirls clumped together, drop the fly in the center. In this way, several fish may see the fly and compete for it, ensuring an aggressive take.

Working a Shoreline with a Boat

While boaters certainly have the option of covering deeper water away from shore, there are times when they want to work a productive shoreline. To do it, you have several options. When there are calm conditions and no current, you may be able to move within casting range of the shore and simply shut down the motor and begin casting. You could also leave the motor at idle or anchor. The most popular and arguably the most productive method, however, is to set up a drift. To do it, you'll need a cooperative wind or current, one that will push the boat along the shoreline rather than straight in or out.

Even when you have the right conditions, a good, long drift requires that the boat be positioned with care. The basic idea is to get upwind or upcurrent of the area you want to fish and then allow the boat to drift. Whether you need to be upwind or upcurrent depends on which is strongest and is therefore the principal force moving the hull. By the way, the art of drifting is not reserved for covering shorelines. Any place you feel holds striped bass is likely conducive to this approach. Reefs and their associated rips are good examples. The same tactic described for bonito and false albacore applies for striped bass.

When drifting a shoreline, how close you need to get to land depends on where you think the fish are holding. On occasion, you may be drawn to a particular shoreline by the presence of birds and busting fish. In such a case, where to cast is obvious. More often, however, you'll be working blind, paying special attention to any edges, be they drop-offs, holes, current lines, or whatever. If you're not sure where the fish are, you can make several drifts, working tighter and tighter to shore each time. Where there is deep water next to the beach, the fish may be practically on the shore, and you may have to drop the fly almost on the beach in order to score.

If you elect to take your boat in close, you should always keep in mind fairness to others. Always give any anglers on shore plenty of room. I recommend that you do not drift directly in front of them unless you're at least 300 feet from their position. Given the mobility boaters enjoy and the limited amount of public access available to anglers on shore, that is only fair.

Another concern is safety. Wherever you work tight to a shoreline, the idea is to get the boat close enough that the best water is within range without getting the boat in harm's way. Submerged rocks are one hazard. On occasion, you may come across one that is too deep to see right off but shallow enough that you can bang the hull or the lower unit on it. Paying a visit at low tide is one way to learn the terrain. Still, even when you know where the submerged rocks are, they have a way of creeping up on you. A sturdy push pole of some sort is a great help for that reason. When a rock appears in your line of drift, the pole can be used to push the boat off. Unless you are drifting rapidly, the boat is very heavy, or conditions are rough, this should work. Another idea is to have one or more electric trolling motors rigged up. These nearly silent engines allow you to correct your line of drift with the flip of a switch.

Beyond submerged rocks and obstacles, there is another serious concern boaters face when working next to the beach: a surging sea. A surging sea is one where waves lift suddenly as they approach the shore, and then ride hard into the beach. Typically, you find this type of a surge on exposed shorelines bearing the full brunt of the Atlantic.

When you see one of these situations, you should always sit back a distance and watch the waves for several minutes in order to gauge the risk. If you opt to go in and cast, it is imperative to have someone at the helm ready to direct the boat out at a moment's notice. Even with an alert captain, if the motor fails, you could quickly find yourself in trouble. Also, the valley or trough between two large waves may hold surprisingly shallow water—so little, in fact, that you could conceivably go aground.

Sight-Fishing from a Boat

Boaters are increasingly interested in sight fishing for striped bass, wherever water depth allows. Boaters have two distinct advantages: Standing on the deck of a boat, you're perched up higher than someone wading and therefore can see fish significantly better. And boaters can sight fish in water that is either too deep for waders or inaccessible on foot.

One method for sight fishing from a boat involves slowly moving across a flat. The boat must be powered silently—by push pole, electric motor, or simply drifting under the influence of the wind and tide. A boat with its outboard running in shallow water is bound to push stripers away, so as you come into a productive area, shut the motor down plenty early and then move silently into location.

Another method is to anchor the boat and wait for the fish to come to you. Here is an example. The boat might be positioned on a flat just off the channel. Naturally, you'd like to position the boat with the sun and wind at your back, although this is not always possible. If you'll be standing in the bow, it's best to try to get the anchor tied off the stern so the anchor line is out of the way. If two anglers plan to cast, it becomes more difficult. With two anchor lines, you can get the boat set up broadside to the prime water. In this configuration, the length of the hull separates the bow and stern casters. Note that by anchoring in this way, you may get considerably more water slapping against the boat.

Boaters have to be very careful during an ebbing tide. If you stay too long in a shallow area on a dropping tide, you might get stranded. A lapse of judgment can leave you and your boat high and dry waiting for the next flooding tide.

Landing Stripers

Just as with bonito and false albacore, I prefer not to use a net when landing striped bass. However, if you are working from a high-sided boat in rough water, a net may be the only practical answer. Unlike the two tunas, bass can't be handled by grasping them just forward of the tail. For one thing, on a bass, the caudal peduncle is not rigid enough. Second, when the fishing gods smile down on you, you'll have a bass so big you simply can't get your hand around the tail wrist. Pleasant surprise. I also don't recommend trying to grasp a striper by placing your hand down over its back. The spines in the dorsal fin are very sharp and can easily pierce your skin, and because of the fish slime involved, any cut could get infected. Nor do I recommend that you lift fish by the gill plate. The potential of damaging the fish is too high, and the gill plates are also sharp.

When you need to grasp a bass, try one of two methods. Small striped bass, those under 10 pounds, can be successfully handled by lipping them in the way freshwater anglers handle largemouth bass. You do this by making a loosely formed fist. Lower the fist to the fish's mouth, and then insert your thumb inside the lower jaw. Now squeeze the thumb downward firmly, pinching the

Large striped bass can be held by the lower jaw, but you should also support them with a hand under the belly.

jaw against your index finger. Striped bass over 10 pounds can be lipped too, but you must also simultaneously support its weight by placing your other hand under its belly. To do otherwise is to risk damaging the fish's jaw.

If someone else aboard can help you land your fish, it makes things much easier. Once your friend has a grip on the fish, ease up on the rod, allowing most of the bend to come out of it. Don't let the fly suddenly pull free from the fish's mouth. Because of the tension on the line caused by the bent rod, it can fly back in the face of the person helping you land the fish.

After landing a couple fish, check the tippet for frays, particularly when fishing in an area known for sharp obstacles such as shell-covered rocks. If the action is fast and furious, I'll simply cut out the offending part of the tippet. Truth be known, in an all-out blitz, I've cut the leader right back into the 25-pound-test midsection and still caught all the bass I wanted. In slower situations, I will replace the tippet. Even if the tippet remains unfrayed, you should retie the knot from time to time.

Tide and Light

Experienced charter captains who have fished all their lives for striped bass will tell you that bass can be caught at any time of day and in any type of weather, provided you know where to find them and what to present them. True enough. But does that mean that fly-rodding for stripers is simply a matter of heading out whenever you feel like it? Yes and no. You can certainly fish whenever the urge or opportunity strikes, but don't expect to be consistently successful.

Here's the problem: What the average charter captain does to catch bass in the middle of the day doesn't involve using flies. More likely, it involves drifting live bait. And it may well entail delivering that bait well below the surface. During a cold front or during the brightest hours of the day, stripers might be 30 or more feet down, too deep to easily present a fly to. So overall, fly rodders will do best if they concentrate their efforts on situations and conditions that make bass vulnerable to fly gear. Common sense, really; nothing more.

When planning your trip, pick a day when the tide is changing while the light is changing. Moving water at either dusk or dawn is a fairly dependable choice. From late spring into summer, I prefer dusk fishing, and in the summer and fall, I prefer dawn.

HOOKING, FIGHTING, AND LANDING STRIPED BASS

Setting the Hook

Striped bass inhale a fly. Therefore, they take the fly well inside the mouth, and hooking up should not be a problem—as long as you follow some basic rules. The single largest problem anglers encounter driving the hook home is the presence of slack in the line. This slack commonly comes from holding the rod tip too high during the retrieve. How high is too high? If your rod is roughly parallel to the horizon, you'll miss some fish. But if you keep the rod tip down during the retrieve—close to, or even in, the water—you'll miss very few. This simple step eliminates most of the slack between you and the fish and greatly increases your hookup ratio.

Since boat anglers are standing well above the water, keeping the rod tip too high is often more of a problem than for anglers working from shore. It can be a problem for shore-based anglers as well, however, particularly when standing up on a jetty or even a rock. Keep the rod tip down.

For retrieving the fly, I like the underarm style. Using that method, the hookup is accomplished by continuing to retrieve line for a moment. When you feel the strike, simply continue to retrieve for another second. The line will stretch a bit, and you'll quickly feel the weight of the fish at the other end. Now, without lifting the rod tip, let the fish turn and run. As it does, allow some line to slip out through the guides, but keep some tension on that line with your fingers. The idea here is to get the fish up on the reel. You want to remove any fly line lying in the stripping basket or on the deck of the boat. Once the fly line is on the reel, lift the rod and begin fighting the fish.

Small schoolie bass, those under 4 pounds, are not strong enough to pull out a lot of line, and therefore you may want to handle them differently. Set the hook in the same fashion, but once it becomes apparent that the fish is not very big, pinch the fly line to the rod blank, and lift the rod. At this point, you have the option of either reeling up the excess line in your stripping basket or playing the fish by slowly stripping in the line. If you elect to play the fish in this way, you won't have to pull line off the reel in order to make a fresh cast.

The Fight

Striped bass can't make the kind of jet-propelled runs you get from a false albacore, but they put up a powerful fight. The fighting ability of a bass is noticeably affected by several factors. The best battles come when the water is between 50 and 65 degrees. Below or above that, the fish are more sluggish.

Condition also makes a huge difference. Most stripers you see are fairly healthy looking, but the weight-to-length ratio of bass varies. Occasionally you do see skinny stripers. They are all head, and as you would expect, these scrawny bass have less strength. At the other end of the spectrum are the super stripers, fish so thick and heavy for their size that you can hardly believe your eyes. When you lock horns with one of these guys, you're in for a tug-of-war.

If you catch enough stripers, you'll eventually run across two genetic deformities. One is a bass with a bent spine. These fight poorly and rarely are seen over 20 inches. Apparently they just don't live very long. The other is an odd-looking creature sometimes referred to as a pugnose. This bass has almost no upper jaw and a short, pushed-in forehead. The biggest pugnose I ever caught went about 32 inches. Angling lore has it that pugnose bass fight very hard, well out of proportion to their size. My experience bears that out.

Overall, striped bass generally seem to be in their fighting prime between 15 and 45 pounds. Typically, it's rare, even for these guys, to run over 100 yards, and most bass you hook are going to go less than that distance—if you apply sufficient pressure. Therein lies the key. Watch the bend in the rod; it's a good indicator of the actual force you are applying to the fish.

A heavy, well-conditioned bass in the 35- to 45-pound range, however, is an exception. Even against a seasoned fly rodder, they can go over 100 yards. I know; it has happened to me. An inexperienced fly rodder can quickly lose a lot of line or get spooled. Clearly, anyway you cut it, these fish are going to test you and your tackle to the limit.

Other considerations affect the fight as well. A fish in a current is always a tougher dude, no doubt. And a foul-hooked bass, one hooked outside the mouth, is tougher yet. You simply can't seem to wear that fish down. One of the longest fights I ever had on fly rod was a bass hooked in that fashion. It measured a little less than 45 inches and took me forever to bring to the sand.

More Fighting Tactics

Beyond using the rod effectively, there are other tactics you can employ. Whether you are in a boat or on the beach, once the fish stops running, try to immediately gain ground by reeling in line. Often the fish is tired at this point and will come toward you if pressured. If it does come, keep it coming.

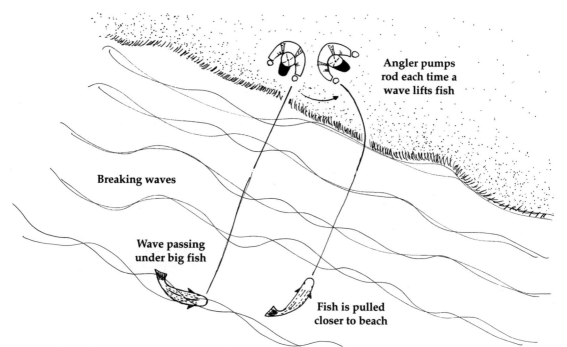

A big bass in breaking surf is hard to land. Try this trick when a wave lifts the fish: sweep the rod low and to the side. This will cause the fish to move toward you. When the next wave lifts the fish, do the same thing.

Continue to reel as long as possible, regaining as much line as you can, until the fish runs again.

If you are in a boat, another way to gain back line is to have the captain slowly motor after the fish. The boat should move only as fast as the angler can reel in line. In rough conditions, take a wide, secure stance or brace yourself in some way during the struggle, particularly when the boat is in gear. Ask others in the boat to be ready to grab you should you stumble.

On shore, it's a different story. When you hook one of these tanks from the beach, it often will swim out as far as the first steep drop-off, stop, and then move in low gear parallel to the shoreline. At this point, you can gain line by walking in the same direction while maintaining constant pressure on the fish. If there are other anglers in your path, yell to them that you have a fish on. I've never seen an angler refuse to step back and let a fellow angler through.

When they get tired, these jumbos like to hold their ground and refuse to budge. Pumping the rod is a great way to get them moving again. You need to know how to do it smoothly and without generating any slack. If the fish is near the surface or in relatively shallow water, you can coordinate pumping the rod with the passing of waves. I use this tactic regularly on open beaches. As a wave approaches the position of your quarry, reel down quickly, lowering the rod tip to horizontal. There should be no slack. As the waves pass under your bass, pull back smoothly on the rod. The lift generated by the wave, combined with the pressure of the rod, almost always slides the fish closer to shore. Granted, you may gain only a few feet, but if you gain with each wave, you'll win the war.

At the Gunwale

Stripers are not apt to circle alongside the boat as a tuna does, but you do have to pump a bass in order to get it to the surface. Short pumps are better than long sweeps of the rod.

Landing

One of the easiest methods of landing and unhooking your bass is to slide it up on the beach. In calm conditions, get the bass in close, and then simply back up a few feet to bring the fish ashore. In heavy waves or surf, you must take more care. Time it so that you're pulling the bass in as a wave comes up on the beach. As the wave retreats, your fish may be sucked back toward the water. Don't try to hold it tight. Take a couple steps forward while reeling so there is no slack line. Then use the next wave to drive the fish higher up the intertidal zone. Once the fish is on the beach, move quickly to it, bend over, grab the leader, and then take a couple steps up the beach, sliding the fish beyond the reach of the waves. Now you can kneel and unhook it.

If you're wading, you can bring the bass to hand without going ashore. Be careful not to bend the tip of the rod over sharply as you reach for the fish. Over the years, I've seen dozens of fly rods broken in this fashion. Instead, push the rod to the rear as far as your arm allows, steering the fish toward your free hand. Once you have your hand on the leader, take all pressure off the rod tip. Look back if you're not sure. Then place the rod under one arm to free up both hands for the remaining work.

CHAPTER THREE

How to Fish for Bluefish

The lunch plates disappeared into the sink, and moments later we were behind the wheel, roaring off down the road. Frankly, after a full night of fishing for striped bass, I was finding it a little hard to clear the cobwebs, but no complaints. We had a mission in mind.

Last night, when we were coming off the beach, we met an angler who told us that his buddy had caught a slew of bluefish in Menemsha Inlet that morning. Seems he got them off the jetty on the ebb, but when the current turned around noon, the fish stormed inside the inlet and up into the salt pond. The action was red hot, although the blues were not gigantic—4 to 6 pounds. Still, they would be riot on a 7- or 8-weight fly rod. And besides, it was a little special to have this many blues here on the opening days in June.

As we pulled into the parking lot, you could see birds working in the inlet, and from the tilt of the navigation marker in the channel, the current was already rushing in. After hopping into our waders, we jumped over the dunes and rushed down to the water. And lo and behold, the blues were right there.

Baitfish sprayed across the surface in sheets, as the blues did their best to TKO everything in sight. Man, were we psyched. When bluefish go hog-wild like that, fishing is going to be goof-proof. For the next three hours we caught them, sometimes on every cast, and it never seemed to matter much what was on the end of the line. Streamers, slides, poppers—they all got bit. No wonder, wherever you go, anglers love the blues.

In terms of size, bluefish run the gamut from less than a pound up to 20 pounds or more. The typical bluefish on a fly is between 2 and 7 or 8 pounds in weight. Blues between 9 and 12 pounds are nevertheless fairly common and provide quite a struggle on a fly rod. Bluefish in the low teens are less common on a fly but still possible, especially for knowledgeable anglers. Anything over 15 pounds is truly a memorable fish, and one that will sorely test you and your equipment.

Atlantic bonito have a mouth full of teeth, but it's uncommon for anglers to get cut off by them. And I don't know a single angler who was ever bitten by one. Blues are a different story. Bluefish have razor-sharp teeth and they regularly use them. And if blues can bite baitfish in two, they can cut through your monofilament leader like oleo. Never cast into a school of bluefish without a shock tippet, be it wire or heavy mono. It's imperative. And never put your hand in a bluefish's mouth. They can really cut you up. Use your pliers to get your fly back.

FINDING BLUEFISH

Bluefish typically range from Florida to Massachusetts, although in some years the largest blues travel up into the Gulf of Maine. So like striped bass, bluefish have a fairly wide geographic range. Unlike striped bass, however, bluefish are tolerant of fresh water only to a minimal degree. Hence they do not ascend coastal rivers very far, and where they do, they tend to ride upstream only as far as the salt wedge allows. Bluefish are also less tolerant of cold water. Generally speaking, it's rare to see them unless the water is well over 50 degrees.

Bluefish are regularly found near shore, frequently in the same haunts used by striped bass, and the two species are often mixed together. The bluefish is less of an ambush-style predator than the striped bass, and the evidence of that is clearly seen in the shape of the tail. Rather than being a broad paddle like that of bass, the bluefish has a forked tail. This translates into less acceleration from a dead stop but more high-end speed. As a result, blues are better equipped to chase schools of baitfish across open water, and they are frequently found feeding away from the beach and even far offshore.

Like striped bass, bonito, and false albacore, bluefish typically prowl in packs composed of similar-size adults. As a rule, the smaller blues tend to travel closest to shore, and the largest ones prefer deeper water. The only exception is when there are adult menhaden next to the beach. That brings the big blues in a hurry.

Given the bluefish's ability to operate away from shore, a good many of them are caught in open water by anglers in boats. When blues are abundant, anglers working from shore regularly catch them as well. In terms of shoreline preferences, bluefish frequent a wide variety of habitats, patrolling sandy shores, rocky shores, rips, bays, harbors, points, inlets, and flats.

Bluefish love to blitz baitfish on the surface, especially in the fall. It's their signature style. No surprise, then, that a good percent of bluefishing is done by anglers who sight the surface action and then move toward it. Once bluefish get going on the top, they like to stay up a while. The bite just goes on and on.

Many blues also are caught by blind-casting the water. When blind-casting, the same 90 percent, 10 percent rule as for striped bass holds true for bluefish too. In order to consistently locate bluefish by blind-casting, concentrate on the water most apt to hold them. Edges are key.

FORAGE

Blues love adult menhaden, but they'll eat just about anything. Research has documented over seventy different types of forage in their guts. Small bluefish in bays and harbors seem to feed primarily on silversides. Larger blues like silversides too, but often they chow down on squid, butterfish, juvenile and adult herring of all kinds, and small weakfish. And on several occasions, I've watched big blues making a meal out of little blues. It happens. And it wouldn't surprise me if blues plucked the occasional small bird off the surface.

Is there anything they don't like? I've never seen blues in a worm hatch, although it may well take place. And while bluefish eat plenty of sand eels, they don't seem to fully share the stripers' fervor for them.

TACTICS FROM SHORE

Fly rodders working from shore will find that fishing for blues and stripers is quite similar. Blues often hold along the same types of edges that stripers frequent, and the same stages of the tide can prove effective for both. Blues and stripers pretty much eat from the same menu and can be taken with the same flies.

A big bluefish on a light fly rod is a battle to remember.

There are, however, some notable differences between these two fine game fish. Bluefish spend less time stalking shorelines and more time hanging off the beach in rips. In addition, bluefish seem to be more strictly a schooling predator, less apt to fan out and spread throughout a bay or cove in the way stripers do. This makes it harder to catch bluefish consistently by blind casting, although you certainly can catch them that way.

As with striped bass, the two most predictable factors affecting the feeding behavior of bluefish are light and tide. Low-light situations do encourage bluefish to move closer to shore and feed, but overall low light is noticeably less critical to bluefish than to striped bass. Likely this is simply because bass are more ambush oriented than blues.

Still, bluefish love to rev up their engines right at sunup, and their feeding frenzies are often connected with dawn. Striped bass like early morning too, but the bluefish's schedule is not quite the same. Stripers start before the sun arrives and close up shop as the sun fully strikes the water; blues wait for the sun to arrive and just keep rolling along into midmorning, much like bonito and false albacore.

Bluefish action generally slows as the sun reaches its zenith and then builds again into late afternoon. Dusk is also a productive time to fish for blues, but as darkness descends, it's uncertain what bluefish will do. Many times I've seen blues and bass feeding together at dusk, only to have the blues leave as night takes over. Nevertheless, I've had some fine fishing for blues after dark, so they are definitely able to feed nocturnally.

Bluefish typically feed most heavily when the tide is pulling hardest. In an inlet, ebbing currents frequently host the hottest action, but elsewhere it is difficult to generalize. Moving water, regardless of direction, is often all you need. As with striped bass, bluefish tend to ride into shorelines on rising water and fall back on the ebb. This is especially the case with the bigger bluefish but less so with the small guys.

Light and Tide

When fishing from shore, you should always look for days when the right stage of the tide occurs at the right light level. That remains true regardless of what species of game fish you seek. Moving water at first light is a great bluefish combo. If the tide is rising, look for the blues to stage an attack at the head of a bay, cove, or harbor. If the tide is ebbing at dawn, look for the blues to be farther back toward open water, concentrating their efforts where strong rip lines form. A moving tide in midmorning or late afternoon also holds promise, although the action is more apt to be out from shore.

Wind and weather can be figured into your bluefish plans as well. Warm, stable weather is usually a ticket to good bluefishing. Even dead calm days are no real hindrance; blues are just as likely to come to the top and chew, perhaps even more so than in windier conditions. Also note than on those hot days, the approach of a thunderstorm often spurs a bluefish blitz, just as it does for striped bass, although lightning is a safety hazard.

Overcast or foggy days often encourage bluefish to work in shallow areas and stay closer to shore. Such conditions are excellent for working poppers. Cold fronts are likely to drive bluefish deep, particularly in the spring, and it may be a day or two before they return near shore. Periods of heavy rain may lower the salinity near shore, driving blues away from land, especially in the vicinity of coastal river mouths. Given a choice, fish the shoreline that faces into the wind, as that's where the forage fish are apt to be most numerous. If the wind is very strong for a prolonged period, so that the water becomes discolored, expect bluefishing to taper off until such time as the water clears.

During the fall run, bluefish get really cranked up and cream schools of bait endlessly. During these autumn blitzes, tide, light level, and weather may not mean much. The blues just eat and eat, day after day, regardless.

Bluefish aren't always in the mood to gobble up the world, however; at times they can be wary. I've had monster blues nip at the tail of a fly rather than take it entirely into their mouths. When I set the hook, I could feel them holding on to the fly for a second before they let go. In situations like that, changing retrieve speeds and fly size may well spur a sudden strong take. Try going faster first, and then try a larger fly.

I believe that bluefish have excellent overhead vision and can see above the water fairly well. I base that on the fact that I've occasionally cast a fly out and had a blue nail it the instant it landed on the water. The fish must have seen it coming. Hence, if the fish are right at the top and within 20 feet, they likely can see you, especially if you're standing up high on a jetty or the deck of a boat. So if the fish refuse to nail your fly, try casting out and then crouching down during the retrieve. I've seen it work.

Day vs. Night

Anglers catch bluefish both during the day and under the stars. Compared with striped bass, however, bluefish are less apt to feed at night. If you find bass and blues together during the day, bluefish seem the more aggressive of the two and are typically easier to catch. Their preference for hunting in the light is evident in the way they feed. At night, blues eat fairly quietly, but as soon as the sun arrives, they go into high gear. Then they pretty much eat continuously, chewing like demons, rarely taking a break the way bass do. As a result, when you find bluefish in the light, they're usually in a striking mood. Little surprise, then, that anglers know bluefish best for their daylight antics. That is when the action is best.

But while bluefish are justly famous for the daytime blitzes, they are also capable of feeding at night. And in my experience, the bigger bluefish are just as ready to roll under the stars as their little brothers. I've caught a lot of bluefish from shore, and some of the biggest monsters—3-foot-long blues—latched on in the middle of the night.

In the dark, don't expect bluefish to sip at the surface or make a gentle popping sound the way striped bass often do. And while schools of bass at night may dine together on top, it is rare for schools of blues to do so. The only indication of bluefish I've ever seen at night is an occasional large boil. Rather than pick off small pieces of bait at the top, blues are more inclined to whack things hard below the surface. So hard, in fact, that you may hear it if you're standing close enough. The first time you experience this, it can be a bit unsettling.

After dark, striped bass are not inclined to clobber a popper, but bluefish will. So a noisy surface offering can raise a blue, no matter what the light conditions. But unlike during the day, at night you're best off using a slow retrieve. Setting the hook with a popper must be done quickly after a blue latches on, the opposite of the correct technique with bass. This is because a bluefish quickly sinks its teeth into your popper. Once it has firmly locked its jaw, setting the hook becomes difficult. You can yank all you want, but you may just be moving the fish's head, not the hook.

When you finally land your bluefish and go to get that popper back, you might be surprised at what you find. There may be little left. A really big blue can mess up even a 2/0 hook. After you extract it, if the hook is bent, consider retiring it. The same holds true for streamers and sliders; blues are capable of shredding them, too. And if the first blue doesn't, the next one might.

Cold-Water Blues

Water temperature is another factor in fishing for blues. In cold water down around 50 degrees, blues may be very sluggish and actually sit on the bottom, waiting for an easy meal. In clear water, they may be visible to the discerning eye, a hanging shadow not unlike a barracuda.

In cold water, they're not able to fight with the same fury as during the warmer months. One November, I latched on to a 15-pounder on a trout rod with a reel that had no drag. I landed that chopper after quite a struggle, but had it been the middle of the summer, that fish might have left me in the dust.

In cool water, bluefish also are less prone to chase an artificial, be it a fly or a plug, and more likely to gobble up a baited hook. This is the reverse of their feeding behavior during most of the season. Something moving along draws more strikes than something sitting still, especially when the light is up. Still, there may be days on the beach in late season when the blues that come to the hook are all taken with menhaden chunks on the bottom. If that seems to be the case, try using as large a fly as you can cast, and drop the retrieve speed down, too. A large, slow-moving meal may seem too good to turn down.

Retrieve Speed
Many anglers believe that a fast retrieve is the only style to which bluefish will respond. It's true that a fast retrieve works well at times and a very slow retrieve can result in refusals or in blues simply nipping at the fly. Nevertheless, a moderate pace is usually all you need in most daytime situations. The one exception is with poppers. Here, it does seem that a fairly fast retrieve out-produces other speeds. And the stop-and-go method, so effective with striped bass, holds less allure for blues. Crank the popper across the top and keep it coming. At night, however, regardless of the fly you're using, fish for blues with the same slow retrieve you use for striped bass.

Blues at Their Finest
If you want to experience blues at their very finest, target them in shallow water, less than 8 feet deep. With no room to dive, blues streak off on blistering runs, and if there's no deep water for some distance, the runs are long indeed.

Moreover, shallow water has two other things to offer. In the shallows, blues go airborne more often, tailwalking across the waves. It's great stuff. And because you don't have to lift the fish up from the depths, you can hunt with a lighter fly. That sweetens the whole deal.

Fishing a Blitz on the Beach
Some of the most exciting bluefish action occurs when blues—or bass, for that matter—pin a big school of bait right against the beach. If the water is clear, you can witness the whole feeding frenzy as if it were taking place in an aquarium. So intense is the attack that the bait actually leaps onto the sand in an effort to escape. An attack like this can be over in a matter of minutes, but often enough it lasts for an hour or more. And it may even repeat the following day at the same time.

Many years ago, scientific research done on bluefish revealed some interesting facts about how they feed, facts that every bluefish angler should know. As a blitz starts, the bluefish may single out the smallest members of a school of bait. This makes sense when you consider the little guys are likely the weakest and slowest of the bunch. But later, after the blues get gorged, they tend to target the biggest bait they see. Why, I have no idea, but it means the angler should switch to larger flies as the frenzy goes on.

In my experience, typically during a blitz the color and type of fly you use make little difference. All things seem to work. But if the bait is big, such as adult menhaden, the garden-variety 3- or 4-inch streamer is not going to be very effective. You'll need a fairly large fly, something on the order of 7 or 8 inches long, in order to get the interest of a blue.

If the action suddenly drops off, the bait and the blues have moved down the beach. If you don't have a four-wheel drive at your disposal, or the energy to chase the fish on foot, don't despair. Many times I've seen the action erupt a second time in the same spot, after a short respite. Even if a full-blown blitz does not recur in that exact spot, there is often some residual action, even though the main body of fish has gone. Slower, to be sure, but fun nevertheless.

To hunt for these residual fish, don't rely on short casts; begin reaching out with your best throw, covering as much water as possible. At the same time, watch for signs of nervous water or a slick. If you see a patch, cast there quickly. If you've been using a streamer, switch to a popper. Poppers call bluefish from some distance and are a good choice as the action tapers off.

If you chase the fish, try to gauge how fast they are traveling. By the time you reach the next bit of activity, the fish might be getting ready to move again. It can drive you crazy. Therefore, it may be best to get ahead of them slightly rather than stop at the first sign of action. If you're on foot, try not to run with loose line in your stripping basket. It'll tangle, causing you to lose precious time. Reel up and swing your stripping basket behind you; that way, you can see your feet and are far less likely to trip or stumble.

TACTICS FROM A BOAT

Most blues, like most bonito and false albacore, are caught from boats. This is not an indication that shore fishing for bluefish is unproductive, but rather that more bluefish are found away from the beach. The simple reason is that bluefish are more likely to feed far out from the beach than striped bass are. Truth is, bluefish are even caught offshore in the big, blue waters tuna prefer.

Bluefish love to stack up in a rip, and when they do, they are typically very willing biters. The same boat tactics as for bonito and false albacore work fine with blues. Hold the boat at the head of the rip and swing flies back in the current, or drift down the rip, casting to the sides.

Fishing a Blitz from a Boat

The classic scenario is the bluefish blitz. These legendary feeding orgies often take place out in a rip under flocks of wheeling gulls. With a little luck, you can see one of these frenzies for several miles. Once you get within casting range, the action is usually instantaneous. At such times, everyone in the boat may be hooked up simultaneously. It's great fun: bucking rods, screaming anglers.

Here are some guidelines to fish by during the battle. If, during the fight, your fish comes free, don't sweat it. Immediately drop the rod tip and start to retrieve again, even if there's very little line out. You'll be surprised how often a second strike can be enticed, or even a third in some cases. Quickly check your leader for frays by running your hand down the monofilament after releasing each blue. Replace any worn sections. When helping a friend land his or her fish, don't leave your fly hanging overboard in the water. An unexpected strike could pull your rod and reel overboard.

In deep water, a blue is far more apt to dive than to run straight out. This doesn't mean that they are going to come in easily, only that the fight is more commonly a slugfest at the gunwale. Here again, as with striped bass, your skill at pumping the rod wins the war. As your bluefish comes into sight, you may see other blues following along. This is an opportunity for any anglers aboard who are not hooked up. A quick cast in the vicinity should do it.

Is there ever a time when blitzing blues are fussy? Yes, especially when they are chewing on adult menhaden. In that type of bite, a small fly isn't likely to produce well; these blues want a big meal. A large fly, one at least 6 or 7 inches long, should work. A popper may do fine, too. And a long slider dragged over their heads is a killer as well.

When a big blitz goes on for some time, you may get your fill of angling for the moment, but if you'd like to catch some bass too, here is a tip. When bluefish spend time chopping up a school of bait, a good deal of the meal falls to the bottom. These leftovers in effect are chum, calling other fish to the area. Striped bass are famous for following behind or under bluefish, dining on the free lunch. A sinking fly line may get you a bass right in the middle of the bluefish blitz. Another idea is to come back later when the blitz is over and search the area with a large fly. It may produce some fine bass.

Slicks

Gulls often give away the position of feeding bluefish, but anglers should be on the lookout for other signs as well. One of the best is a slick—a becalmed patch of water that, from a distance, looks lighter in color than the surrounding water and a bit shiny. If you are downwind, you may even smell the oil. It's a sweet odor difficult to describe.

When you find a slick, it does not necessarily mean the blues are directly below. The blues and the bait may have moved on since the slick was formed, although it's likely that the fish are still somewhere in the immediate area. Or the slick itself may have moved. On a windy day or in a current, a slick quickly drifts away from its original site.

Therefore, when you reach the slick, begin casting into it while at the same time scanning the water in all directions for additional signs of bluefish. If the water you're casting over is relatively deep and there are no signs of blues on top, cover it with sinking lines. Go down. Once you've made certain there are no fish below you, search the area for other slicks.

Silver Flakes

While searching the water for bluefish, you may come to a spot where the water looks sparkly. As you peer down over the side of the boat, the water looks as though it holds suspended particles of mica or metal. These are actually scales from chopped-up baitfish, a sure sign of rampaging blues. This occurs most often when blues are feeding on baby menhaden. Other baits, such as silversides and sand eels, have little in the way of scales. Once again, however, it does not mean the blues are directly below your boat; it means they are likely nearby.

Daisy Chaining

If you fish southern New England waters long enough, you may eventually see a school of bluefish slowly milling around on the surface with their tails and dorsal fins showing. It is quite a sight. It remains unknown just what this business is about, but it appears to be connected to spawning. Most likely these blues are bonding as a group before traveling off into deeper water to reproduce.

These somewhat rare events usually take place on calm, warm days in early summer. At least, that's when I've seen them occur in Long Island Sound.

I've never had the good fortune to see blues acting in this mysterious manner while I was wading; it's always been while I was aboard a boat, although once or twice we were fairly close to shore. The few times I have seen this, the fish were fairly large, and it occurred during years when the bluefish in Long Island Sound were very numerous.

When you see this take place, you might assume that these blues would be easy to catch. Not so. If approached, they frequently prove to be skittish and may quickly descend when a fly is thrown into their midst. But patience can pay off. Shut off the motor and stay absolutely quiet. Start casting over the water with a variety of flies, poppers, and streamers, and by all means try a sinking line. After a short while, the fish may slowly return into view and begin following your fly. With luck, one will bite.

Chumming

Most fly rodders prefer to find bluefish without the aid of chum. In fact, it's fair to say that in general, fly anglers are not crazy about the practice. Nevertheless, bluefish respond readily to a chum line. Ground menhaden is very effective. Anchor the boat from the bow, and feed the chum over the transom. A current running away from the transom will spread your offering.

Half a Striped Bass

Occasionally in the fall, especially late in October or even early November, you may hook a small striper and wind up landing only half a bass. You land the head and a portion of the body, but the rest has been bitten off. When this happens, some anglers immediately assume that it was the work of a shark. It's possible, but unlikely. Odds are that the tail end of your would-be catch is in the mouth of large blue. Probably a mid-teen-size fish, at least. Yes, a big blue can bite right through a small bass. But nature plays no favorites—striped bass are known for swallowing small blues as well.

The first time this happens to you, it leaves you for a second wondering what to do next. If you're standing in the water, you'll be tempted to get out. It may be the prudent thing to do, although the odds of your getting bitten are extremely low. Truth is, in all the years I've fished, I've never heard of an angler in waders being attacked by a bluefish—or a shark, for that matter.

Whether you stay in the water or get on the beach, the challenge becomes seeing if you can hook that big blue or one of its comrades. Don't be surprised, however, if this turns out to be difficult. Sure, the blue that hacked off the back half of your bass seemed mighty aggressive, but that big guy has probably slipped away from the dinner table at least for the moment. And in the cool water of late fall, jumbo bluefish are not apt to blast a fly unless it looks like a big, easy meal. Switching to something large, whether it's a streamer, slider, or popper, is the first step. A popper may be the single best bet. Work it patiently. It may well take repeated casts before one of these huge blues strikes.

HOOKING, FIGHTING, AND LANDING A BLUEFISH

Hooking

You hook a bluefish in much the same manner as a striper. With the rod up under your arm, once you feel the take, you retrieve rapidly until you are solid to the fish. Then, as the fish turns and runs, you ease line out through the guides under tension until the fish is up on the reel. Poppers are an exception to this rule, however. When a striper takes a popper, it's best to delay your strike for an instant to give the fish a chance to pull the popper under and turn. When a blue whacks a popper, on the other hand, don't delay—strike immediately.

You need to use a wire or heavy mono shock tippet, or you stand a fair chance of getting bitten off. This goes for both large and small blues. Number 6 solid tobacco-colored wire works reasonably well, although it tends to kink after a few fish and will require straightening. A short piece of 40-pound mono makes a fair alternative, but the biggest blues can slice this up fairly quickly.

If you're caught by surprise and have no heavy monofilament or wire on hand, here are some tips that will help you land a few fish. Instead of using a single tippet, use two or more on your leader. Each is an additional insurance policy. Connect them by loop to the midsection, and then tie each of them to the fly. Don't be concerned if they are not all exactly the same length. Yes, this rig looks ratty, but it works in a jam.

Another way to prevent getting bitten off is to strike immediately. Any delay and the fish has a greater chance to engulf the fly and thereby slice the tippet. This is true even when using a shock tippet. Be vigilant. Once a blue is hooked up, play the fish a little more lightly than you normally would. This reduces the stress on the tippet and helps it endure, especially when badly frayed. A long, drawn-out fight should be avoided as well. Also try dropping your retrieve speed. In daylight, bluefish respond most aggressively to a moderate or fast retrieve speed, but they are most apt to take the fly deeply if they charge it hard. If you retrieve slowly during daylight hours, you're apt to get refusals or have the fish nip at the back end of the fly. Still, the fish you do catch are likely to have the fly well forward in the mouth, if you set the hook in time.

On numerous occasions, I've hooked bluefish on 2-inch-long sand eel patterns connected to 12-pound-test mono. In all cases, the fly was barely creeping. When I beached those blues, they had the fly at the front edge of the mouth, and the tippet was untouched. If I picked up the speed, however, the blues hit the sand eel fly much harder and almost invariably cut me off. Apparently, bluefish are capable of gently mouthing slow-swimming bait. This goes counter to their image as cautionless eaters. Yet it makes sense that blues, like any predator, would not waste energy unnecessarily, using only as much force as required to secure their prey.

Fighting

Blues can crank, believe me. Pound for pound, they have an edge over bass in both power and stamina. How far can they run? On a long, shallow flat, I hooked a 17-pound bluefish that roared off well over 100 yards. That was under ideal conditions, however. In reality, most blues, like striped bass, run for less than a 100 yards if adequately pressured.

Expect a bluefish to jump after its first run. Usually there's a brief pause as the run slows, and a moment later your fish comes up and dances across the top. Bowing to the fish as done with tarpon is not wise here. If the leader drapes across the blue's mouth, the fish may well cut through it. A bluefish is also apt to jump at the end of the fight, just when you think you have it licked. And if you have enough bend in the rod, the fish is going to come right at you. This surprises the daylights out of some folks.

Little guys—those in the 4- to 6-pound range—are fine on a 7-weight rod. In the 8- to 12-pound class, however, I suggest at least an 8-weight, and a 9 is better. Any blue larger than 12 pounds requires more rod. A 9-weight will do, but if the blues are running 16 pounds or bigger, a 10-weight is better yet.

Landing

To land a bluefish tail it, grasping it right at the tail wrist, something not possible with a bass. Then lift the fish free of the water. If you have help, hold the

Bluefish have powerful jaws and razor-sharp teeth. Never put your fingers in a bluefish's mouth. Always use a pair of pliers to remove your fly.

fish parallel to the ground but belly up skyward. Have your partner remove the hook with a pair of pliers. Pliers are really mandatory in this operation, so be sure you have them with you when you set out to fish. Bluefish follow you with their eyes, and bringing your hand close to their mouth is likely to make them snap at you. Take care.

Small bluefish are often caught on big flies, and when that happens, they may bleed. Bluefish seem to bleed far more than striped bass do. Nevertheless, I've rarely seen a bluefish that did not recover immediately and swim off like a shot. Still, you should use barbless hooks so that the removal is quick and as easy as possible on the fish. Besides, a barbless hook makes unhooking the fish so much easier.

If you plan to take a bluefish home for dinner, do yourself a favor: Bleed it completely, and then place the fish on ice. You'll get a much better-tasting meal for your effort.

CHAPTER FOUR

How to Fish for Weakfish and Hickory Shad

Two species have recently made a comeback in the waters of southern New England, and it's hoped that both of them will be around for some time to come. One is the hickory shad, a silvery fish that acts and looks like a tiny tarpon. This little leaper has quickly won a fly-rod following in many places, and with good reason. It takes flies well and puts up a mighty fine account of itself, especially on a trout-size fly rod. The other is the weakfish. Here in southern New England it's been a quarter century since they were numerous, so anglers are extremely pleased to see them make a comeback. Weakfish are considerably larger than the hickory shad, bold to a fly, and good looking to boot. As a food fish, weakfish have a tasty but soft flesh that does not keep well. All told, I believe their rebuilding population is going to have a far-reaching impact on saltwater fly fishing along the Atlantic.

WEAKFISH

The weakfish, *Cynoscion regalis,* is regal looking, all right. Brilliantly decked out, it's thought by some anglers to be the most attractive near-shore Atlantic game fish. Along the back are shades of blue-green, and the flanks are iridescent silver, with numerous small black spots and touches of gold, lavender, and pale blue. Fins along the lower belly are accented in yellow in smaller weakfish, but in larger fish they take on an orange glow, particularly during the spawn.

Cynoscion is from the Greek for dog. Weakfish are members of the drum or croaker family, and it's something the male weakfish quickly testifies to. In your hand, they make an odd barking sound by internally rubbing the swim bladder. It's quite a surprise to most anglers the first time they land one.

Weakfish are most abundant in the mid-Atlantic, from Virginia to New Jersey. They are found in fair numbers down to Florida, too, and in years when the population is on the upswing, they swim as far north as Martha's Vineyard and Cape Cod.

Along the mid-Atlantic seaboard, they're called weakfish, sea trout, gray trout, or simply trout, although they should not be confused with their smaller cousin the spotted seatrout, or with freshwater trout, for that matter. From New Jersey northward, weakfish is a more common handle. And from Connecticut to Cape Cod, the venerable old term squeteague is in widespread use.

Weakfish grow at greatly varying rates. There are two somewhat related theories why this is so. One speculates that during the last fifty years, young weaks have grown to sexual maturity much faster because of commercial overfishing. That is, to survive, they've had to reach reproductive size before getting harvested. The other theory speculates that low population densities promote fast growth, and high ones inhibit it.

Regardless, weaks do not usually reach the weights attained by striped bass and bluefish. Still the average fly-rod weakfish is of respectable size, between 3 and 7 pounds. Eight-pound weaks are not unusual, although they may be close to ten years of age. Anything over 8 pounds is a big old weak and often referred to by anglers as a tiderunner. When the population is healthy, tiderunners of 10 to 12 pounds are occasionally caught, especially from Long Island to Cape Cod, where weaks tend to be larger and can reach 15 to 17 pounds. These giant tiderunners are rare beasts. Twenty-five years ago, they were more often caught on live bait or jigs than on flies. But there were few saltwater fly rodders back then, and perhaps more big tiderunners will fall to flies this time around.

With catch and release being such a large part of our sport, it is common practice for fly rodders to use a fish's length as a gauge of its weight. When judging weakfish by their length, however, you should not use the same length-to-weight ratio you would with striped bass or bluefish. In general, weaks are of a somewhat lighter build and do not have the thick, muscular bodies of the striped bass. Therefore, they weigh less for their length than you might expect. For instance a 10-pound bass is often about 30 inches long, whereas a weakfish of that length may be only 8 pounds or so.

Front and center in a weakfish's upper jaw is a pair of large, pointed teeth. Those daggers and the fact that a weakfish's eyes glow like opals in the beam of a flashlight give them a kind of vampirelike look when caught at night. Day or night, these canines are sharp, so keep your hands clear. Don't be surprised, however, if one or both fangs are missing. Apparently these teeth are easily broken off and quickly grow back. In spite of this toothy look, shock tippets are not really needed, except when you're looking for the largest members of the tribe.

Finding and Fishing for Weakfish

There is one trait of weakfish that anglers should never forget: They are extremely clannish. True, other game fish form schools, but weakfish take it to extremes. Weakfish don't fan out on flats in search of food as do striped bass. They always stick together. Only the monster tiderunners are less apt to swim in a herd. This stick-togetherness means weakfishing is usually feast or famine. They are hard to find, especially if you don't know where to look, but once you find them, you're in them good and should catch a bunch.

Small to middle-size weakfish prefer protected environs. Coastal river mouths, bays, harbors, and salt ponds are excellent places to look for them—much the same locations as for school-size bass. This brings them in range of both shore-based anglers and those casting from small boats. As spring gives way to summer, these locations warm considerably, and weakfish tend to drop back to deeper water, although they may make a return visit to the shallows in early fall. Big weaks are more apt to be found where you find big bass, in cooler locations back from shore.

Like striped bass, weakfish follow schools of feeding blues, picking up the scraps. Weaks do it, however, in their own way. Stripers are close behind or immediately below the bluefish school. Tiderunners do the same, but smaller weakfish keep their distance. Seems big blues often make chowder out of them. So when a school of blues passes by, you may want to hang around for a while. Twenty minutes later the weaks may show.

The weakfish is an ambush-style predator, and you can see it in the design of the tail. It's squared off much like a striper's, rather than forked like a blue's. Like striped bass, weakfish are built to feed near shore where there is ample cover from which to spring an attack. So here again it's the edges that hold the action. Fact is, weakfishing is all about edges, whether they're sandbars, sloughs, rips, holes, or edges of channels. And since weakfish hang together, you either fish the edges or miss out on the bite. It's that simple.

Weakfish are ideally suited to the fly rod. They take a fly well and are often found in protected waters where fly rods are most at home. The relatively forgiving nature of the fly rod compared with stiffer tackle, such as spin or plug gear, reduces the chances of the angler pulling the hook free from their soft mouths. And because the majority of weakfish are under 10 pounds, you can use even a freshwater-size fly rod if you wish. For most weakfishing, a 6- or 7-weight rod is strong enough.

Light and Tide

Given that weakfish are bushwhackers like striped bass, weakfish have the same preferences as bass in regard to light and tide, and the two species are often caught together. Expect weakfish to move closer to shore on a flooding tide and then drop back to deeper water on the ebb. And like bass, weakfish

Weakfish often bite best in low light. This nice pair was caught on a May evening on the Connecticut coast.

feed most in low-light conditions. Dawn fishing is always a good bet; as the sun rises, the weaks fall back to deeper haunts. The action should return at dusk and often continues right through the night.

Regardless of these similarities, fishing for weakfish has its distinctions from fishing for bass. Big bass love a roaring surf, but weaks, even big tiderunners, prefer calmer conditions. Given this desire for flatter water, on open beaches weaks don't favor situations that foster waves, such as onshore winds, winds opposed to the tide, or breaking waves crossing a sandbar, all of which stripers really like. This affinity for glassy water also carries over to the tides. Along exposed beaches, expect weaks to avoid rising water and instead feed from slack high down to low tide.

Another difference between bass and weaks is that bass can handle fresh water, but weaks can't. In fact, weakfish are not even particularly fond of brackish water. Consider too that weaks are less likely than bass or bluefish to blitz schools of bait in open water. (However, I recently saw a Bob Popovics video made in New Jersey that shows them blitzing baitfish on the surface, and, interestingly, making a distinctive sound—a soft slapping noise unlike the sharper ruckus made by bass or blues.) Of all the species discussed thus far, weakfish are the most restricted in terms of places they can feed. They have to hunt in fairly protected waters, where there is at least moderate salinity, and they have to be near edges.

Weaks will feed near the surface but usually after dark. On the other hand, they will grub right on the bottom any time of day. Therefore, getting the fly down can be an essential part of your tactic, particularly in daylight. Where the water is fairly deep, that means sinking fly lines are mandatory. But even where water depths are under 6 feet, you may want to use a weighted fly. After the near-shore bite in May, weakfish in southern New England waters drop back to depths of 20 feet or more, so a fast-sinking line is a must.

In general, weaks are drawn to places where the bottom has some vegetation, such as eelgrass or *Spartina*. This kind of habitat seems to hold their preferred foods. Vegetated bottoms are typically found in protected areas where there is little in the way of wind and wave. Hence your basic strategy for finding weaks should be to search for schools in confined areas such as bays, coves, harbors, and the lower ends of tidal creeks.

In these locations, look for places where there are shallows in close proximity to water with much greater depth. For example, in the spring, harbors with relatively deep channels adjacent to flats make for ideal fishing grounds. Weakfish are extremely sensitive to sudden cold snaps and need to have escape routes so that when a cold front approaches, they can quickly drop back to deeper water.

When fishing in harbors at night, try where lights from marinas and docks spill over the water. Weaks are attracted by these things much in the way stripers are. Likely the artificial illumination draws baitfish and shrimp to the surface, presenting weaks with an easy meal. An ideal combination would be lights over a spot that also hosts current.

Big weakfish—tiderunners—are somewhat of an exception and do feed along open beaches, and in the mild surf as well as in heavy currents. They are particularly fond of inlets and jetties. In addition, the adjoining beaches to either side of an inlet are prime tiderunner habitat. Along the beach, they like sloughs and the cuts between sandbars. Overall, they often sit back farther from the water's edge than bass or blues. When fishing in all of these locations, it's imperative to concentrate on the edges.

Forage

Weakfish munch on schooling forage fish such as sand eels, silversides, and especially juvenile menhaden and mummichogs. But they also eat other items, including crabs, marine worms, and a special favorite—grass shrimp. Tiderunners eat these same items yet also tackle much larger prey, like scup, alewives, blueback herring, or adult menhaden.

Chumming is a highly effective way to draw a school of weakfish, and the traditional chum of choice is live shrimp. Once weakfish start to feed in the chum line, you can serve them a streamer fly, which they will quickly nail.

Flies

Since weakfish feed on the same forage base as other predators, special flies are not needed for them. Typical saltwater streamer patterns on hooks up to 2/0 are just fine. Capt. Jim White of Rhode Island tells me that yellow is the best color of all. I don't doubt it, but records indicate that fly rodders have successfully used many color combinations, including red over white and yellow over red. Years ago, even the freshwater Mickey Finn was used with good results.

Shrimp flies, while not in extensive use by fly rodders in New England, certainly catch weakfish, as well as striped bass. The late Paul Kukonen of

Worcester, Massachusetts, raconteur extraordinaire, was one of the first to develop such flies for weaks, and he did so over sixty years ago. Fly-rod poppers work too, but scale them down a bit from the ones you would select for bass or blues. You may want to try sweetening the mix by trailing a shrimp fly off the bend of the popper on a short piece of mono.

Shock Tippets

Generally speaking, toothy fish require the use of a shock tippet, but how important a shock tippet is depends to a fair degree on how a given species consumes its food. Toothy species that tend to overrun or inhale their food present the greatest danger of cutting you off.

Weakfish tend to whack a fly at the head, in striped bass style, but they do not often cut you off. The fly is typically held in the corner of the mouth. This is especially true with the smaller weakfish, those less than 8 pounds. So things usually go well, although you may want to check your leader for frays. If larger tiderunners are your primary target, a mono shock tippet makes sense.

Fighting and Landing

Fighting a weakfish on a fly rod is a good deal of fun. A weakfish can hit hard or take the fly softly, but either way, once the battle commences, a weakfish often fights in its own distinctive way. Frequently, it surges ahead in short runs, each one punctuated with a brief pause. This style of struggle causes the rod tip to dip down for a moment and then slowly rise back up. It's a trademark of this fine game fish. Once you've seen this behavior, you won't forget it.

After a surge, the weakfish may turn and fall back toward you, creating slack in the line. Be ready to take it up so as to remain tight to the fish. In terms of power and endurance, though they're a fun fish to catch, weakfish don't seem to be in the same league as bass and blues. Weaks seem less hardy than bass or bluefish and therefore take a bit longer to revive, so care is needed if catch and release is your game plan.

As many anglers learn the hard way, a weakfish's jaw is not made of the same tough stuff you find on a bass or a blue. (Speculation has it that this weak jaw is in fact the source of the name weakfish. No one is certain of that, however, and other theories exist.) Never try to horse these babies in; the hook can yank free without warning. When using barbless hooks, the fly frequently falls out on its own accord as you land the fish.

Because of the soft mouth, let weaks run; don't try to hold them. During the fight, do as little lifting with the rod as possible; instead, allow the weakfish to fight subsurface until very tired. This further reduces the odds of the hook ripping free.

If you wish to keep or photograph your catch, care is required during the landing process, as this is when many weaks are lost. From a boat, a landing net is a great aid. From shore, try to gently beach the fish rather than unhook it in the water. If the beach is sloped and there are waves against it, you need to be especially careful. Use the incoming waves to help you drive the fish up the slope of the beach, but if a receding wave grabs hold of your prize, don't hold the fish tight. Let it slide back into the foam and then try again with the next incoming wave.

Once the fish is on the sand, reach down and pick it up carefully rather than drag it up the beach with the line. Often as the fish hits the sand, the hook pops free, so be ready. When removing the fly, because weaks have teeth, don't stick your fingers in the mouth. Overall, if you plan to release the fish, it is important to handle it gently and get it back in the water as quickly as possible.

HICKORY SHAD

If the idea of using trout-size fly rods in the salt appeals to you, the hickory shad fits the bill even better than the weakfish. It's a compact little warrior that rarely weighs more than 2 pounds, but it's a pocket rocket on the end of a line and a fine fly-rod game fish.

Like its larger cousin the American shad, the hickory shad is a member of the herring family, so it's related to alewives, bluebacks, menhaden, and Atlantic sea herring. Hickory shad have an extensive range much like the striped bass and are found along the entire Atlantic coast from the Canadian Maritimes. They also are anadromous, capable of traveling extensively in fresh water.

Hickory shad have collected their share of aliases. At the turn of the last century, they were widely known as tailor herring, tailor shad, or Mattowacca, which is rooted in the Native American word for Long Island—Mattowaka. Presently, along the Rhode Island and Connecticut coast, anglers call them hicks or simply shad.

Hickories have paddle-shaped bodies, tall from back to belly but quite thin in cross section. In southern New England, they typically run between 14 and

Hickory shad are great fun on a light fly rod. They hit hard and jump like miniature tarpon.

18 inches in length. Bigger ones do exist, reaching upward of 2 feet and 3 pounds. In spite of their diminutive size, hickories are a blast to catch. They eagerly whack a fly; they jump and give you quite a scrap. Truth is, if hickories grew to 10 pounds, they would be one tough customer on a fly rod.

Like weakfish, the hickory shad population seems to be very cyclic. Prior to 1990, I had never seen a hickory shad along the Connecticut coast, even though I had fished it heavily for years. By the mid-1990s, however, hickory shad had become regular fixtures in Long Island Sound, especially in the late fall. By the end of the decade, they were around from spring right through to winter and had increased in both number and average size. It's my guess that hickories are presently filling a near-shore niche left vacant by the downswing in bluefish. If

I'm right, when bluefish are again plentiful along our shorelines, hickory shad will rapidly fade into the background.

Finding Hickory Shad

Similarly to weakfish, hickory shad are commonly found close to shore in sheltered areas such as bays and harbors. Unlike weakfish, however, hickory shad are quite tolerant of fresh water, fully able to run up coastal rivers a considerable distance. I've caught them 50 miles up the Connecticut River from Long Island Sound. Hicks have a decidedly forked tail and are not strictly ambush predators, so though they do hug edges, they do not do so with the same all-consuming passion as a weakfish. Instead, you'll see hicks chasing schools of bait across open expanses of bays and coves. And when in this mode, hicks herd schools of bait to the surface much in the same way small bluefish frequently do. When feeding on top, the two are easily confused.

As with other saltwater game fish, when fishing for hickory shad, you have to figure in the tide. Very often hicks do not actively feed unless the water is moving. So generally speaking, slack tide is a poor time to fish for them. Hicks also tend to travel a considerable distance with the stage of tide, moving up inside tidal rivers and bays on the flood and dropping down on the ebb. This is particularly true when they are feeding on baby menhaden, since they also travel back and forth on the tide. Because hickory shad are sensitive to the stage of the tide, you may find the fish, only to have them quickly disappear, high-tailing it to another location where the tidal current is now more to their liking. The wise angler learns to follow.

Given the hickory shad's preference for moving water, you should look for them in places where the current sweeps around, under, or alongside a man-made structure. Bridge abutments, piers, and docks are typical examples. Likewise, the shad tend to hug the edges of a current much like American shad do during their spring run upriver. For instance, in a tidal creek they often herd bait near the bank. Another similarity is that they both seem to prefer to stay out of bright sunlight. They accomplish this in several ways, staying deep in the current for the most part or being active only early and late in the day.

Hickories bite well in the dark. During the summer months, it's now common to catch them from dusk right through to dawn, feeding in locations often associated with small striped bass.

Forage

Hickory shad feast on the same menu of small forage fish as the other game fish discussed here—sand eels, silversides, juvenile menhaden, and mummichogs. In these situations, the shad push the bait along the surface, causing it to spray from the water. Often the commotion is large enough that you may think it's a school of small stripers or blues making the ruckus.

Hickory shad can also feed along a protected beach, mixing in with other game fish, especially striped bass. For example, about three years ago, hickory shad begin showing up along the north shore of Martha's Vineyard. There they would feed on sand eels at dusk with the striped bass, and the bite lasted well into the night. Big bass love to eat hickory shad, so wherever hickory shad are mixed with bass, especially adjacent to deep water, there's a chance that jumbo bass are lurking nearby. It's best to carry a few truly big flies with you.

Flies

Shad are not terrible fussy about flies, but some do seem to outproduce others. They like a subsurface fly, particularly one that jigs up and down a bit on the retrieve. Hence a weighted fly, such as a Clouser Deep Minnow or a Popovics Jiggy, is my first choice. Bead-eyed bonefish flies, such as a Crazy Charlie, also work well for the same reason. While the subsurface flies account for most hicks, I've also caught them on small foam sliders designed to imitate juvenile sand eels. This is a good deal of fun, since when hooked on the surface, hickories immediately cartwheel across the top. My guess is that very small freshwater-size poppers, a couple notches up from what one would use for bluegills, would also be a blast.

Regardless of the pattern, these shads have small mouths, and hook sizes should reflect that fact. Size 2 hooks seem about right, size 1 works, but anything larger is getting risky. Overall, hicks like bright colors such as chartreuse or yellow, and your fly should have some flash material as well.

The common shad dart sold to spin fishermen pursuing American shad also works well on hickories. It's a might heavy for the smallest fly rod, but it can be cast far enough on a 5-weight or larger rod. These darts come in several colors. I find that chartreuse is the best. Setting the hook with either a weighted fly or a shad dart is not usually a big problem, since these hickories slam the fly with a vengeance out of proportion to their size. Nevertheless, short strikes can be expected, particularly from the smaller shad.

A jigging motion is often most effective, particularly so during the cold-water months of spring and fall, and less so during the warmth of summer. When working in a current, you can use the conventional down-and-across presentation, but at the end of the swing, permit the fly to hang for several seconds. Like striped bass, hickory shad will whack a fly holding in the current.

Fighting and Landing
Once you hook a hick, the real challenge is hanging on to it. These pocket rockets are excellent jumpers and can vault out of the water, frequently throwing the hook in the process. Once you see it happen, you'll know why I called them tiny tarpon. It's an appropriate handle, since the highly sought-after silver king of the tropics is closely related to the herring family as well. Every time I see a hickory shad leap, I am reminded of that fact.

Though hickory shad leap like tarpon, they lack the tarpon's concrete jaw. Hicks have very tender mouths, even softer than the jaw of a weakfish. Hicks can shake the hook free during a jump, and frequently the hook simply pulls out during the struggle. But if they get off before you can land them, so much the better. They're not good eating, so you'll be releasing them anyway. It's really the strike and first jump or two you're after. Hicks are fragile; even the least bit of handling causes them to shed scales. So if they're able to release themselves without any handling, so much the better.

CHAPTER FIVE

Fly-Fishing the Edges

When you pick up your fly rod and walk out onto the coast, one thought burns in your mind: "Will I find fish?" It's a fair question. Finding fish can be a real challenge. The territory is immense. The fish come and go with the seasons. And when they are in town, they move in response to wind, light, and tide.

In spite of it all, fear not. The fish you seek are driven by fixed needs, and moreover, they are, to a degree, creatures of habit, often returning again and again—year in and year out—to the same locations. Food is perhaps the strongest of these needs. Hence, where prey exists, so do predators. Thus it follows that finding game fish involves, to a degree, finding forage. To do that, you must understand forage fish—know how they live and where they go.

Even when predator and prey exist along a shoreline, they are rarely uniformly spread out. Always assume that a small percentage of the water before you holds the vast majority of the available fish. It is a fundamental truth. Invariably, your fishing success is highly dependent upon your ability to identify those spots, move to them, and then properly present a fly.

Experienced saltwater anglers are extremely proficient at this game; they quickly fillet any shoreline into its productive and unproductive waters. It's a matter of knowing where to look and what to look for. And what are they looking for? Prey, for one thing, but edges are equally important. Game fish travel along, feed along, and hold along edges.

Edges Defined
An edge is an area of transition where the water or the bottom undergoes an abrupt change. This change can be in water depth; in the motion of the water, from slow to fast or calm to turbulent; or in the composition of the bottom, say from sand to rock.

The less change you find in the bottom or in the shape of the shoreline, the less fish you are apt to come across. Therefore, a saltwater angler should always have an eye out for fishing locations that offer variety and variation.

The majority of edges you'll encounter fit into two broad categories: They are either concave or convex areas of the bottom. A depression or hole would be a concave area, and a sandbar or reef a convex one. The shape of either type of structure causes a change in water depth and thus qualifies as an edge.

Prime Edges
Edges are rich environs, places where the habitat aids fish in their struggle to survive. Nevertheless, all edges are not equal; some provide better habitat than others. And for that reason, these prime edges attract more bait and more game fish. In some cases, their ability to attract is simply a question of size. The predators and prey along any shoreline frequently are drawn to the largest edges—the ones with the greatest amount of change. The deepest hole and the most extensive sandbar on the beach would meet that criteria. Thus they are prime edges.

Size is not the only element that makes an edge prime. Complexity—how many different kinds of changes an edge possesses—is also a factor. Concave and convex areas in the bottom both create changes in water depth. When the tide pushes water over them or waves move water by them, additional changes can take place. For a time, these edges may also be areas of turbulence and possibly strong current. When that happens, the habitat is significantly improved, and the ability of these edges to attract game fish soars. And for however long those conditions last, those edges are prime.

Coastal anglers run into this scenario time and again. They discover an edge; it fishes reasonably well, but under certain conditions of tide, wind, and wave, it fishes far better. With time, wise anglers piece it all together, remembering which

Steep drop-offs are prime edges and are often easy to spot. Here, a channel meets a sandbar.

stage of the tide and which wind directions produced the better fishing. In short, they learn from experience when a particular edge is likely to be prime.

Developing an Eye for Edges

On occasion, beaches give up fish without a fuss. You walk out onto the sand, and the sky is filled with gulls diving over feeding fish, or the water's surface is broken with swirls or dotted with slicks. But most of the time, it's not that easy. And as a consequence, your fishing success hinges directly on your ability to hunt the fish down—to find and fish the most promising edges.

Finding edges is, at times, a piece of cake. A sandbar that rides high and dry at low tide is quite obvious. More often, however, edges are hidden to some degree. Still, nearly all edges give some sign of their existence.

Shape and Slope

The shape of the shoreline and its slope as it enters the water are two important clues to the character of the adjoining bottom. These two aspects of a beach can help you quickly locate a good many edges on any beach. Here is how to read

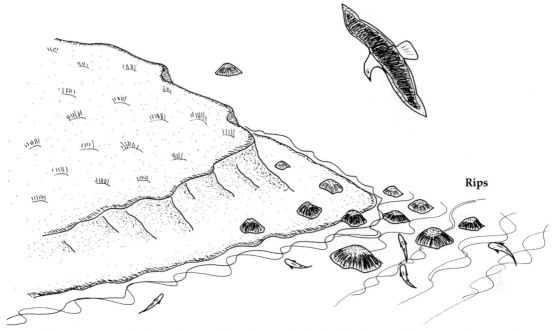

Rips

Points are one of the best places to fish. They are loaded with edges and often home to current and waves.

them: Walk down to the water and sight along the water's edge, taking in 200 or more yards of shoreline. The straighter the shoreline, the more uniform the adjacent bottom is likely to be, and the less likely that there is much in the way of edges. Consequently, fish are not apt to regularly hold here, especially ambush feeders like striped bass, which need cover to operate. Conversely, the more irregular the shoreline, the more likely that the bottom near shore is uneven—concave and convex—and the more likely you are to find edges and fish. Or think of it this way: When the bottom next to the shore is concave and convex, the shoreline echoes those shapes. Where the bottom is concave, the shoreline tends to be concave too, cupping inward. And where the bottom is convex, the shoreline tends to be convex, jutting out to meet the structure.

Though it's often practical to do this with fairly short sections of shore, you don't have to confine yourself to studying a few hundred yards of beach at a time. If you have miles of shoreline in front of you, to be expedient you'll want to scan larger chunks. Generally speaking, pay particular attention to the largest points you see. Often they contain the best edges, and they frequently have current as well.

As you're observing the shape of the shoreline, you should occasionally turn your attention to the slope of the beach as well. Where the beach slopes very gradually on entering the water, the bottom is likely shallow and fairly flat for a considerable distance out from shore. Which is to say, it will have few sharp edges and therefore few places for fish to ambush bait. On the other hand, where the slope of the beach is steeper, the bottom drops away more rapidly, tending to be convex. There you will find more edges and more places for fish to feed.

Signs on the Surface

Beyond the information provided by the shape and slope of the beach, the water itself has a story to tell. Because edges alter water depth or speed, the water over an edge reflects the changes and therefore looks different than in surrounding areas. There are three main types of differences: change in the color of the water, disturbances that suggest the presence of turbulence or current, or waves that behave oddly as they pass over a section of bottom. Sometimes you may see an edge that has all three. When an edge is large and well defined, these changes in appearance are apt to be dramatic and hard to miss. Smaller edges, however, may produce only very subtle changes in the surface, and if you are to find them you must be alert. And that highlights one of my central beliefs: Good anglers are keen observers.

Three Keys to Finding Fish

With these thoughts in mind, there are three basic keys to finding fish. These are just starting points, but on any beach, they will get you on track. First, look for signs of feeding fish, and immediately get within casting range if possible. Second, if feeding fish are not visible, look for bait, and try to fish where it's most concentrated. Finally, if there are no signs of fish and the bait is spread out, study the shape and slope of the shoreline, as well as the surface of the water, to find the edges, for where the edges are, there the bait and the game fish are most likely to be.

Whether you find fish or not, recognize that every venture onto the coast is a learning experience. Win or lose, you take something home with you.

HOW TO FISH TROUGHS

As waves break against a sandy beach, they roll over with considerable energy, producing a band of turbulence just below the waterline. This turbulence is called the backwash, and it constantly digs away at the bottom. As a result, there is a concave depression running the entire length of the beach just seaward of the water's edge. This edge is commonly known as a trough.

Where clarity allows, you can see this edge as darkening of the water immediately beyond the water's edge. Polarized sunglasses are a big help, reducing glare off the water and increasing contrast. No fly rodder should be without them. Many anglers accidentally discover the trough by stepping down into it while attempting to wade out.

Because the trough extends the length of the beach, there's plenty of it to explore. Like all edges, however, some portions of it are apt to be far more productive than others. Start by looking for the presence of feeding fish. If you see swirls, slicks, birds congregated, or bait leaping across the surface, move there immediately.

If there are no signs, try to locate the bait. The single most important type of prey, and the one that anglers can best see, is schools of forage fish. A large school may appear as a dark mass. It might be moving, or it could be fairly stationary. When moving near the top, it's apt to ripple the surface, creating what anglers refer to as nervous water.

A smaller school is not as visible, but nevertheless, you may see it cruise by as you wade. Other times, you may see a flash of silver as the school turns, their sides reflecting the sunlight. On occasion, you may see forage fish feeding on top, creating a dimpled surface that looks like it's caused by falling rain.

Seeing bait is not always easy. It may not be very abundant, and even when it is, conditions can make locating it difficult. Water depth or clarity is often an issue, and lighting conditions can be a significant factor as well. So if you're not certain where the bait is thickest, look for edges. Avoid the portion of the beach that runs straightest; focus on the portion that has the most shape. Next, cover the deepest sections of the shoreline, as indicated by their slope.

The depth of the trough is directly related to the amount of wave action a given shoreline sees over the year. On a highly protected beach, the depression might be less than a foot below the adjacent bottom, whereas on an exposed shoreline, the trough could well be a drop-off of 2 or more feet.

Given the trough's proximity to shore, anglers often fail to think of it as a good place to find fish. That's a mistake. Striped bass dine regularly in the trough, particularly in low-light conditions. And when they do so, you often see them swirling in the backwash of the waves. On a shallow beach, these bass are usually small, but they are fun to catch nonetheless. On deep, exposed beaches, even the largest of striped bass may cruise in and feed practically at your toes.

Although bluefish do feed here, too, they do so less often than bass. Hickory shad, windowpane flounder, and fluke can at times be found dining this close to the beach. Weakfish usually hang farther back. Though there are few beaches where Atlantic bonito and false albacore are caught from shore, in the locations where such action is possible, these two wonderful fish sometimes pass right through the trough. Don't expect them to hang there and leisurely munch as striped bass do. Rather, they will show up and be gone in flash, passing quickly down the shore.

Fishing the Trough on a Shallow Beach

On countless occasions, I've walked along Lobsterville Beach as the shadows lengthened into twilight. Terns wheel overhead in the fading light, while across the glassy surface of the sea, sand eels spray in their effort to leap free of bass. It's a thrill to see stripers right in the trough. I can think of no situation in saltwater fly fishing that I have enjoyed more.

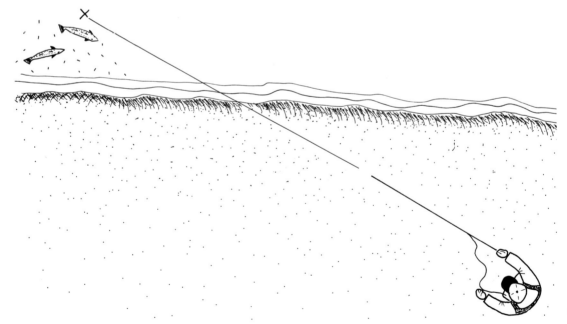

By moving back, you can retrieve right to the water's edge and still have enough line out to start a new cast.

To present a fly to those fish—or for that matter, to any fish feeding in close—it makes little sense to boom out 100-foot casts. Instead, use a relatively short throw of 20 to 50 feet. Besides shortening your cast, you might want to also try casting at an angle to the beach. The idea is to keep the fly as close to shore as long as possible during most of the retrieve.

These short, angled casts will do much of the work, but you may find it necessary to back up from the water before you loft a line. If the fish are feeding within 10 feet, and you stand at the water's edge, those fish are right under your rod. Standing farther back permits you to retrieve the fly all the way back to dry sand if necessary. If you stand back 20 feet or more, you can bring the fly right to the water's edge and still have enough line outside the rod tip to begin the next cast.

When striped bass are feeding right at the water's edge, it's also possible to present the fly to them from the side. Here's how. Walk 50 feet to the right or left of where the fish are visibly feeding, and then step quietly into the trough. Now turn toward the fish and make a cast parallel to the beach. From this position, you can work the fly right down the length of the edge. This keeps your offering in the strike zone for the entire retrieve, and for that reason, it can be a very effective presentation.

Nevertheless, I see few anglers use this tactic. For one thing, some anglers are hesitant to wade when fish are so close by. There is some merit to this

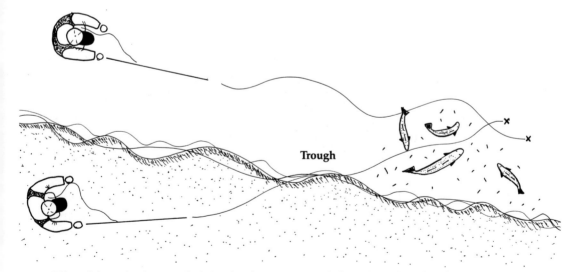

Trough

When fish are in the trough, it is often best to approach from the side, either from the beach or by wading.

thinking; undoubtedly, you may spook some fish. Still, if you wade slowly and quietly, it should not be a major problem. Don't be locked into the belief that wading through fish is always wrong. On shallow beaches, the fish in the trough may be pipsqueaks compared with the fish farther out. If that seems to be the case, by all means wade out and get the big guys.

Intermediate fly lines are usually an excellent choice for working in the trough. If the water is calm, a floating line can also be highly effective. Eight- or 9-foot leaders tapered to 12- or 15-pound-test are plenty long and strong enough. In fact, I recommend them for nearly all situations on the coast. The one exception is when you need to use a fast-sinking line. In those cases, a shorter leader of 4 or 5 feet in length is a better option.

While there are times when game fish herd large bait, such as menhaden, into the trough, usually the forage here is smaller, such as sand eels and silversides. Hence flies of 2 to 4 inches long riding hooks from size 2 to 1/0 are typically the order of the day. Given the size of those flies and the fact that distance casting is not part of the equation here, a light saltwater fly rod makes a lot of sense.

This is further bolstered by the fact that shallow shorelines are often protected from the strongest winds. Nine-weight rods certainly do the task, but in many locations, they may be more of a wand than you really want. Eight-weights seems a good compromise, although on highly sheltered shorelines where the fish are averaging 5 pounds or less, something in the 6- to 7-weight range could be great fun.

Unless you're asleep at the switch, hooking a fish this close to shore is pretty much a no-brainer. Still, a few tips are in order. Keep the rod tip pointed down at the water during the retrieve. This simple step reduces slack, thereby giving you better control and feel for the fly. Truth is, you should always do it when fishing, regardless of what type of edge you're covering. Though lifting the rod upward is the conventional method of setting a hook, I avoid it at all costs. First of all, the rod absorbs much of the force, and often that means a poor hook set. I retrieve the fly with the rod up under my casting arm, and then set the hook with the line, as detailed in the chapter on striped bass.

When fishing the trough, setting the hook with the rod has another drawback. Because you're standing near, and higher than, the fish, you could yank the fly upward and out of the fish's mouth, particularly when small fish are involved. Striking with the line causes no such problem. If you can't resist involving the rod, instead of lifting upward, sweep the rod to one side. At short range, it produces a more positive hook set.

Fishing the Trough on a Deep Beach

Beaches that face seaward bear the full force of the Atlantic. These are often wild places, with plenty of wind and waves. When they get revved up, they can really test your mettle. And yes, there are days when the surf is thundering and all you can do is sit on the dunes and watch. As a result, many saltwater fly rodders never visit these shorelines. Fine. That leaves more fish for you and me. Because on some days, they offer up mile after mile of calm, blue-green water—and some of the largest fish you'll ever see.

Not surprisingly, the troughs you encounter on these exposed beaches are deeper. Fact is, all the water you see before you likely is considerably deeper than on a sheltered shoreline. Though that limits or prevents wading, the good news is this: This increased depth encourages even the largest bass and blues to feed close to the beach. This is big-fish water.

Because you face considerably stronger wind and waves on these beaches, fishing the trough on a deep beach requires a slightly modified approach. For one thing, larger fly rods are in order. After over twenty years of coastal fly rodding, my favorite stick is still the 10-weight. It's large enough to handle the wind, throw a wide range of flies, and chuck some mighty heavy sinking lines. That said, the 9-weight is increasingly the rod of popular choice. It does a lot of things well in a lighter, easier-to-handle package. On these deeper beaches, lifting power is needed in a rod, another reason to avoid smaller sticks.

Beyond the size of your fly rod, the central issue is often how to control your fly in rough water or even surf. It is difficult work. When the waves are relatively mild, an intermediate line may work well. But when the waves build, it becomes exceedingly difficult to stay in touch with your fly, and you may miss a lot of strikes.

If this appears to be happening, go to extremes—switch to either a fast-sinking line or a floater. The fast-sinking line cuts down through the waves, thereby increasing your contact with the fly. Additionally, the fish feeding in these deep troughs are apt to be down several feet, and the sinking line delivers the fly right to them. When using a sinking line in these big waters, go with a short leader. A 5-footer tapered to 15-pound-test is typically all you need. If, however, the fish are very large and numerous or there are sharp objects in the water such as barnacle-covered rocks, a 20-pound-test tippet is more practical.

A popper or slider on a floating line is the other option. This rig works because you don't have to feel the strike—you can see it, making it easy for you to know when to set the hook. When there are weeds in the waves, the floater may be the better approach, since the bulk of the weeds hangs below the surface, and a sinking line will drag your fly right into it.

On a deep beach, larger forage fish are more apt to be in the trough. In the fall, mullet and herring may be found here. Even the sand eels that exist here are usually larger than on a shallow shoreline. Therefore, larger flies suit the situation. Another good reason also exists for using larger flies: It's often harder for fish to find your fly on these deep beaches. Not only is there more depth to cover, but in the trough there is considerably more turbulence and foam. Thus it pays to use a fly that has a fair-size profile, one a fish can see from a distance. Cover the water slowly and carefully, and don't give up quickly on any one spot. Easy does it. Give the fish an opportunity to find your fly.

Safety Tips for Deep Beaches

Many times over the years, I've fished beaches that held light to moderate surf. Though I've never been hurt, the potential does exist, particularly if you do not respect the power of the waves.

Always wear a wader belt, and if you're a weak swimmer, wear a PFD. The new inflatable models are lightweight and interfere little with your casting.

Because the surf can make fly rodding very difficult, you may be forced to pick stages of the tide when wave height is reduced. This is true to a degree regardless what type of edge you're fishing on these open beaches. The waves breaking against shore are usually largest on a flooding tide and smallest during the ebb. Wave height is also influenced by wind strength and direction, so pay attention to the marine weather forecasts. It's a mandatory part of coastal fishing anyway.

On some exposed beaches, after a wave breaks on shore, it washes up the slope of the beach with considerable force before draining back down. Anglers often find it convenient to stand in this wash of water and foam while they cast. This is understandable, but it must be done with care. If you fall or get knocked down in the wash, a retreating wave will try to pull you down the slope of the beach toward deeper water. Never stand so near the water that as a wave surges up the beach, it threatens to bowl you over. And never stand in the wash with your back to the sea; a rogue wave could take you by surprise.

If you want to cast near the water's edge, try this: As a wave retreats down the beach, move forward just behind it. When you near the water's edge, make your cast. Before the next wave breaks, back up to safe ground while allowing

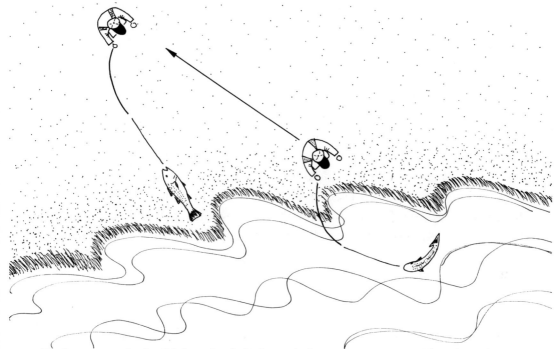

The best way to land a fish is to slowly back up, timing your movement with an incoming wave. Avoid going into the surf to land your fish.

additional fly line to exit through the guides. It may seem awkward at first, but you'll quickly learn the rhythm.

When standing in the wash, retreating waves tend to suck the sand from around your boots. If you feel your feet rapidly sinking, relocate to firmer ground before you become unstable.

It's a dangerous practice to walk parallel to the water's edge while in the wash. If a wave riding up the beach hits you as you're lifting the foot closest to the water, that wave can easily knock you over. I've seen it happen. It is far safer to first retreat away from the water, and then travel along the beach on dry sand to your next destination.

When unhooking a fish, if you kneel in the wash, you run the risk of a wave rolling right over you. Instead, drag your fish as high up the slope of the beach as possible. Wait for the wave to retreat, then walk forward, grab the leader, and slide your fish above the wash, where you can unhook it above the reach of the waves.

Dead Drift in the Trough

It's nice when you can see swirls, but bass feeding in the trough often have their heads down, looking for morsels to be uncovered by the force of the waves. Consequently, a fly moving overhead may not draw much fanfare. A sinking line or a sinking fly can be a real help for that reason, especially on deep shorelines. This will deliver the fly right to the fish.

Once you have the fly deep, don't be in a hurry to retrieve it. Numerous times, simply allowing a fly to hang stationary in the trough has proved deadly. What makes this tactic a killer is simply this: It leaves the fly indefinitely in the strike zone, and sooner or later fish find it. This trick is not hard to do. Tie on a streamer fly. Make a very short cast so the fly lands just beyond the breaking waves. Allow the fly a chance to sink, and then lift your rod up a bit so that there is very little fly line in the water. The idea is to dead drift the fly in the trough, much in the way a trout angler would present a nymph. You'll need relatively calm conditions to pull this off, but when you can do it, it works nicely.

You can add more life to the fly by twitching it occasionally, using your rod tip. This bit of extra action often sparks a strike. If, after a couple of minutes, the fly doesn't draw a fish, consider moving. Rather than take the fly out of the water, however, pull it in the trough behind you. This maneuver, aptly called beach trolling, can be a very effective way to search water. When you reach another good-looking spot, stop and again occasionally twitch the fly.

On a shallow beach, you may be able to see your fly and consequently the strike as well. But regardless of what type of beach you're on, when a fish takes, it often comes out of nowhere and nails the fly hard. So stay alert. And try to set the hook by either striking with the line or sweeping the hook to one side. Both are more effective than lifting the rod straight up.

When the Trough Is Prime

At times the trough can be swarming with fish. You'll see fish swirl, or bait spraying across the surface, or baitfish jumping right out of the water. The trough, generally speaking, fishes much better under certain conditions. Most notably, troughs become prime edges when turbulence or current is greatest along the water's edge. This typically means when the tide is rising, and therefore pushing hardest against the shore.

If forced to narrow it down further, I would select the last three hours of the flooding tide. Still, on any given day, wind is also a significant factor in the amount of turbulence and current near shore. A stiff onshore breeze certainly has its downside. It makes casting more difficult, and it may drive weeds in toward the beach and cloud the water. Nevertheless, such a wind increases wave height against the beach and therefore increases turbulence. From a game fish's perspective, that's desirable. Dead calm days, on the other hand, make casting easier, but they reduce turbulence in the trough, which draws fewer fish as a result.

If you ever see the waves striking the shore at an angle, walk over to investigate. When waves hit in this manner, they push water along the shoreline, producing what is known as a longshore current. This current attracts fish to feed, especially tight to the beach in the trough.

Light level is another factor. Expect trough fishing to be more productive during low-light periods than in the middle of the day, so give dawn, dusk, and even night fishing a try. Though it's harder to see feeding fish in the dark, it is still possible. In calm conditions, swirls can be seen, and even if you can't see the fish, you may well be able to hear them. Use your flashlight to look for bait in the water or lying on the beach. Also, the land is considerably darker than the water at night, and therefore you can still see the shape of the beach well.

HOW TO FISH SLOUGHS

Sloughs hold even more potential than troughs, particularly for big fish. A slough is a concave area in the bottom between a sandbar and the shore. Though not omnipresent like the trough, sloughs are still fairly common on the Atlantic coastline. The water they hold is of greater depth than in the trough, and hence this edge provides more of an opportunity for truly big fish to congregate close to the beach. Consequently, sloughs are excellent locations to hunt for big bass, big blues, and tiderunner weakfish.

Sloughs come in a few shapes and sizes. Typically, they are holes roughly 100 to 300 feet in diameter. Occasionally you'll come across one that is long and narrow, more of a trench or a chute. These are far from common and tend to be found more on open beaches or where longshore currents are strong near shore. Where they occur, these sloughs can run 50 yards or more.

Identifying a slough is rarely a problem. They're usually easy to see, especially for anglers with polarized sunglasses. For one thing, sloughs are associated with dramatic changes in water color. In clear water, a slough is markedly darker and bluer than the surrounding area. This contrast is particularly vivid where the slough joins the sandbar. Because it's shallower over a sandbar, the water there appears much lighter, tending to green or yellow. Even in places where the water is off- color, the position of a slough can usually be determined by studying the waves as they approach shore. Waves lift as they meet a sandbar, break while crossing over it, and then settle back down as they traverse a slough.

Sloughs tend to hold larger and more concentrated schools of bait than surrounding areas of the beach. Sand eels and silversides are important here, as they are nearly everywhere close to the beach. But in the fall, as schools of menhaden, herring, and mullet migrate down the shoreline, they stack up for periods in sloughs, especially those that lie close to an inlet.

When two or more sloughs exist on a particular beach, see if you can determine which is home to the most forage fish. Given the depth of the water, this may be no easy task. When in doubt, the biggest and deepest slough should get the nod. This is where the larger fish are more apt to reside. To figure out which slough is deepest, study the slope of the beach. The deepest slough is likely next to the steepest portion of beach.

Bass, blues, and weaks may be hiding anywhere in a slough, but there are often hot spots, which you'll discover over time. The deepest part of the slough is often a very productive area, especially for finding bruisers. Since the bottom of some sloughs is more or less a uniform bowl, the center is often the deepest portion. In many cases, however, the bottom is highly irregular. If that appears to be the case, try to figure out where the water is deepest, and give that section extra angling attention.

To learn the bottom of a slough, often all you need do is wade through it at low tide. There are sloughs, however, where the water depth never allows this type of investigation. In such cases, polarized sunglasses are invaluable, often allowing you to see changes in water depth, especially in calm conditions and strong sunlight. During your investigation of the bottom, should you discover a deep pocket where the slough joins the sandbar, make special note of it. In essence, this is an edge within an edge, and because of its location, it's especially attractive to truly big bass.

Because of its position behind a sandbar, a slough can, at times, have a considerable amount of turbulence and current, which further boosts its appeal to feeding game fish. Both the turbulence and the current are created as water forces its way over and around the ends of the bar. Granted, these currents are apt to be short-lived, but when they are there, the slough becomes a prime edge, a magnet for hungry game fish.

Striped bass, on occasion, tool back and forth in the slough hunting down food. If the bottom is light-colored sand, you'd think that the bass would be easy to spot. Sometimes they are, but bass that live over light-colored bottoms lighten in coloration to blend in with the habitat. Hence, bass in the clear surf of Cape Cod are usually very pale compared with a bass living in the muddy Hudson River. One has a pale green back and milk-colored sides; the other has a blackish back with silver and bronze flanks.

Current in the Slough

During the initial hours of the flood tide, the sandbar is in essence a wall, blocking the tide's progress into the slough. The tide then pushes around the ends of the bar. When this happens, currents may form. These currents will

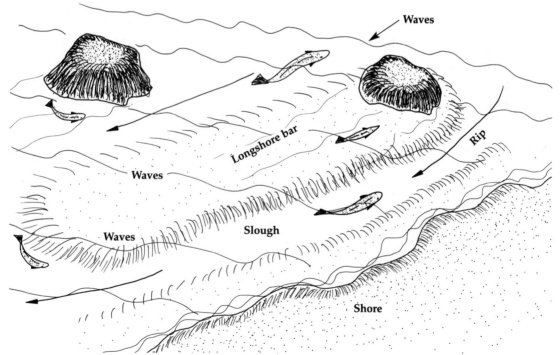

Sometimes a slough is shaped more like a trench than a hole This type of slough often has considerable current and very good fishing.

likely run for only a brief period, but while they are in gear, they create prime edges, drawing feeding fish. On the ebb, you may find currents as well, although these currents will be draining the slough rather than filling it.

Long and narrow, trenchlike sloughs tend to focus moving water. Consequently, when tidal current exists in this type of slough, it is usually considerably faster and more localized than the moving water you find in hole-shaped sloughs. In essence, these trenches are momentary rivers funneling tidal pressures down the beach.

Like the bottom of a hole-shaped slough, these trenches may well have deeper pockets. And when the current rolls, it is in these pockets that the fish frequently hold. Here again, polarized sunglasses are helpful. Study the color of the water for changes that indicate the greatest water depth. Walk to the end of the slough where the current is entering. Cast so the fly swings downcurrent in an arc. Then step and cast again, covering the water. As the water continues to fill in the slough, fish may begin feeding in the trough, right at your feet, so stay alert.

Fishing Sloughs on Shallow Beaches

When fishing a slough, you need to understand how forage fish and game fish move in relation to the tide. When the tide is dead low, forage fish, such as silversides and sand eels, bottle up in the slough seeking sanctuary. They do so knowing that as the water level lowers, striped bass and other predators are more or less forced to exit over the sandbar.

As the tide turns and starts to rise, the forage fish generally move toward the sandbar to feed on the fresh nutrients delivered by the rising water tide. At the same time, game fish begin to filter back into the slough. This is when the action gets under way.

The slough can be fished from the beach, but on a shallow shoreline, you may have the option of fishing it from the sandbar as well. This typically means wading out to the bar during the first hours of the flood. Simply strolling right through the slough on your way to the sandbar would spook the fish. Instead, find a path to either side of the slough that allows you to reach the bar without disturbing the water you intend to fish. Also keep in mind that you can't stay so long on the bar that the tide strands you out there. In short, use common sense.

Whether you fish the slough from the shore or from the bar, the tactic is similar. It's wise to assume that game fish feeding in the slough can be just about anywhere. Search the water by fan-casting, and use as long a cast as you can manage. Try to find the hot spots. For one thing, the slough's depth can vary. See if you can discover where the deepest areas are, and concentrate your effort there, especially during those hours when the tide isn't high.

On shallow beaches, the slough may be small enough that catching one fish can spook the others. I've seen this happen more times than I care to remember. You hook up, and as your fish runs, other wakes stream seaward. There's not much you can do about it.

As previously mentioned, if you find a pocket of deeper water up against the bar, this edge within an edge can be a honey hole for big bass. These pockets seem to be formed in spots where the turbulence and current coming across the bar are greatest as they enter the slough. Little wonder, then, that the biggest and strongest stripers like to set up camp here.

If you're lucky, you'll be able to reach this honey hole on a long cast from shore. If so, chuck your fly so it lands on the bar, and then retrieve so it drops into the slough. This is a killer tactic. Over the years, it has rewarded me with many fine striped bass. If a few casts bring no response, try changing your angle to the structure. You can do this easily by moving a short distance right or left on the beach and resuming casting.

During rising water, which is usually when this spot is hottest of all, your fly will be pushed back toward you by the tide. Unless you're careful, this causes slack to develop in the line, thereby reducing your chances of a solid hookup. The last thing you want is to have a big bass on for a second and then lose it. It's heartbreaking.

If you're fishing the slough from the bar, look for one of these honey holes. They often lean into the bar, producing a steep drop-off. Take care not to slip down this drop-off. To cover this spot, the best tactic is to back away from it and make a cast down the center axis of the bar in such a way that the tide or waves push the fly over the lip and into the hole.

When fishing sloughs where water depths are less than 10 feet, an intermediate or a floating fly line should get results, although I prefer the intermediate. If the water looks deeper, a sinking line may be in order. An 8- or 9-weight rod is good for fishing sloughs. Slim flies designed to match sand eels and silversides are good choices, especially in calm, clear conditions, but if large bait is present, a larger fly is the way to go. One of the predators crossing the bar to feed on the forage may well be squid. They can be imitated with a 2/0 white Deceiver-type fly. If squid are present, big bass will pound this large offering.

Fishing Sloughs on Deep Beaches
The sloughs you find on a deep beach have sufficient depth to hold fish at all stages of the tide. So don't be surprised if there are fish at low tide, even in the middle of a bright, sunny day. Their depth means it's quite possible that a good number of fish are holed up, and catching one rarely spooks the rest, as it often does in a shallow slough. So don't give up quickly. I'm never surprised to catch several nice fish from a slough on an exposed beach. Persevere.

Similar to a trough on a deep beach, larger flies and a more careful covering of the water are the way to go. You want to show the fly off, to make its presence known to any resident of this water. Poppers or sliders along the top or streamers dragged just under the surface are all useful means of covering this water. Don't consider a slough devoid of life until you've covered it with a sinking line and perhaps a weighted fly as well. Getting down is often key. I never fish on a deep beach without at least an intermediate fly line and a fast sinker. And for that reason, I like fly reels that allow you to quickly and easily change spools in the field.

When fishing these sloughs, you want to chuck some bigger offerings a fair distance, and pulling a 20-pound bass out of a deep slough requires some lifting power, so leave the small rods at home. A 9-weight will do the job, but I suggest a 10-weight if you can comfortably wield it. It will finish the fight sooner.

These sloughs may have areas of current, so it's important to keep an eye out for moving water. You might be able to find one of those honey holes, an edge within an edge, up against the bar. It could be very difficult or even impossible to reach from shore, even with your longest cast, but casting in that direction is always worth a try.

When the Slough Is Prime
Whether you're on a shallow, protected beach or a deep, exposed one, a flooding tide is a great time to fish the slough. During the first half of the flood, as waves cross the bar, they inject large amounts of water into the slough. This water is cool, well oxygenated, and rich in nutrients. And considerable

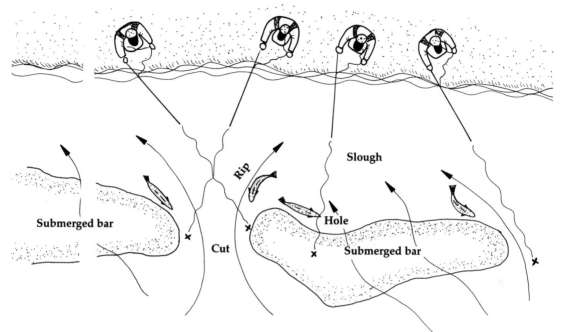

A slough can hold many fish, including big ones. Work the cut, the ends of the bar, and any holes up against the bar.

turbulence and current are created where the slough joins the bar. Forage in the slough moves to this location to feed, and so do the striped bass. In short, it becomes a prime edge. When this stage of the tide occurs in low light, the odds of meeting fish here are even higher.

The very best conditions are a rising tide, low light, and rough weather. Large waves move across the bar, crashing into the slough with authority. Granted, fishing with a fly rod in rough water is no picnic, but your chances of meeting up with a big fish are at their ultimate best. It's worth it.

Any stage of the tide that produces current in a slough is a good time to be there. These currents may only last for a couple hours, so planning is important. On deep beaches, because of the relative depth, there could be fish at all stages of the tide, even dead low. If you're looking specifically for larger striped bass—those 15 pounds and up—you should be more selective about when you fish. The higher stages of the tide are most likely to bring the bigger bass into the slough. Thus it's wise to hold your fire until the middle hours of the flood. By fishing earlier, you may hook other fish, but they're apt to be smaller than you want, and the commotion of the fight could discourage the big bass from coming within range. So be patient.

Wherever you find bass of mixed sizes feeding in the same vicinity, it's often the case that the largest stripers are the ones on the outside, farthest from the water's edge. Therefore, even though you have bass feeding close to you, longer casts may pay off. While you are making these casts, study the water for signs of a big bass, which generally make bigger, more powerful-looking swirls. If you see such a swirl, deliver the fly quickly.

HOW TO FISH SANDBARS

There is always something mysterious about sandbars, as if walking on one were a visit to a land waiting to be discovered. Little wonder that many of my fondest angling memories center around them, and in particular, the vast and beautiful reaches of Dogfish Bar. Bars allow you to move out from the beach and extend your range, but best of all, they offer a wealth of edges to explore. And these edges, in addition to the tide, have longshore currents and breaking waves.

Bars are convex structures rising up from the bottom. Most have sand bottoms and therefore are rightfully called sandbars. Still, anglers frequently used the term sandbar loosely to denote any bar, even those where the bottom is more rock or cobble than sand.

Bars characteristically are long and narrow, although some have a squarer shape. Some bars are small, with barely enough room for two anglers to work; others are quite large, capable of holding half a dozen or more; still others are so enormous that they can be seen in satellite photographs of the earth.

During lower stages of the tide, bars are usually easy to locate, for a couple reasons. Portions of the bar may lie exposed to view, particularly on moon tides. And the lower the water level, the more the waves are forced to break as they ride over the bar. The band of breaking waves associated with a bar can be seen for a long way off, even in relatively low-light conditions.

Even during higher stages of the tide, however, the waves traveling over a bar are still apt to look distinctive, even though they may not break. Typically, what happens is this: As a wave meets the seaward side of the bar, the wave suddenly grows in height. The wave continues to stand tall as it crosses the bar, but once it reaches the inside edge, it rapidly drops back down in size. You can quickly learn to spot this phenomenon.

Where the bottom is largely sand, the color of the water is a useful clue to determining the presence of a bar. A sandbar and a slough often display a vivid contrast of hues, the water over the bar being a lighter color, tending toward green or yellow, and the slough being a dark blue. Where wave action is not sufficient to outline the location of the bar, this change in water color is your best method of establishing the location of the bar and its size and shape. To do so, the water must be relatively clear, and it helps considerably if the sun is high in the sky and fairly bright.

Longshore Bars

The most common bars, the ones most anglers encounter, are called longshore bars. These bars run fairly parallel to the beach, from about 50 feet to 200 yards off the shore. Between them and the shore lies the slough. Most longshore bars have sand bottoms, although you'll find a few with firmer footing and fewer still where larger rock mixes in.

Longshore bars usually are solo structures, but at times two or more of them may exist together on the same shoreline. In those situations, they often sit end to end, each separated from the next by a channel of deeper water known as a cut. These cuts are usually easy to spot. They hold darker-looking water and have none of the breaking waves that march across the bar. There also are places where longshore bars are stacked back to back, running away from shore. The one nearest to the beach is referred to as the inner bar, and the others as outer bars. Between them are additional sloughs.

On a shallow beach, it's often possible to reach a longshore bar by wading through or around the slough at lower portions of the tide. Once you get to the bar, you can fish the bar and its edges for as long as the tide allows. On a deep beach, the bars usually can't be reached from shore, unless you're willing to swim out to them, something I don't recommend. Consequently, you would not be fishing the bar itself, but the area between the shore and the bar, as well as the slough.

Finger Bars

Instead of running parallel to the beach like longshore bars, finger bars run pretty much straight out to sea, often for a considerable distance, upward of a mile. Many anglers refer to them as long bars.

Finger bars typically originate right from the beach, although there may be a dip or depression that you'll have to wade through before reaching the bar itself. Further distinguishing them from longshore bars, they don't have sloughs associated with them, although there's sometimes a deep hole to either the right or left side of the bar where it joins the shore. Where it occurs, this deep hole is an edge that holds some good angling opportunities.

Finger bars are apt to have harder bottoms than longshore bars, with less sand. This in no way reduces their fishing potential; in fact, it improves things. When rock or cobble begins to dominate, it produces a richer habitat. Here the bottom hosts a good deal of life, including seaweed, algae, barnacles, green crabs, and even lobsters. In some cases, blue mussels colonize the bar as well. Anglers frequently call these mussel bars.

Though nowhere as common as longshore bars, where finger bars exist, they usually offer superb fishing. Finger bars are generally found where strong tidal rips sweep around the tip of a barrier beach or where tide exits the mouth of a bay or estuary. These bars seem more apt to be formed by tidal current, whereas the longshore bar is more likely to be a product of longshore current.

Unlike longshore bars, finger bars rarely occur in multiples. I do fish one location, however, where there are two such bars together. These particular bars are relatively short, about 120 feet long, and lie about 60 feet apart, with a deep trench or slough between them. These double finger bars hold excellent action; I wish I could find more pairs like them.

Fishing Longshore Bars

On deep beaches, you may not be able to wade out to a longshore bar, regardless of tide level. In those situations, you have to pretty much focus all your energies on the slough. If there appears to be a cut through the bar, however, this area deserves attention. Granted, this cut, like the bar, is probably out of range, but fish travel through the cut and then proceed toward shore, especially on a rising tide. For big bass and tiderunners, these cuts are the preferred entrance and exit routes to the slough. Simply by casting in the direction of the cut, you're placing your fly in the path of those fish. In addition, on a rising tide, there should be some current in the cut, and that may well reach the beach. This current holds fish and carries them toward you.

There are many shallow beaches where anglers regularly get on the bar. The usual scenario is to wade out during either the final hours of the ebb or the first hours of the flood, depending on the situation. But rather than simply wade out, I strongly suggest you fish your way out. Cast toward the bar, and then move forward gradually, covering the water before you as you wade.

A careful approach is warranted for this reason: Unless the bar is high and dry, there may well be fish on it, mainly bass and blues. Weakfish typically don't come up on a bar until late in the flooding tide, when wave action is reduced. If the fish on the bar are actively chasing bait, given the relatively shallow depths involved, you're likely to see swirls or other signs of commotion. Should that be the case, direct your cast accordingly. Sight fishing may even be possible—you may be able to see cruising fish and cast to them. It doesn't happen often, but never rule it out.

Given the skinny water up on the bar, don't be surprised if hooking one fish sends others scrambling for safety. For that reason, try to quickly land any fish you latch on to, and then release it behind you toward shore rather than directly back at the bar. When ready, proceed to the bar. Once you're up on the structure, assume that any portion of the bar you have yet to cover with the fly may have fish. Continue to fan-cast the water ahead as you move.

Although bars look highly uniform, typically there are some dips and depressions in the bottom. These variations may seem rather minor, but they are edges nonetheless, and fish use them. If you know where on the bar these edges exist, give them special attention. If you're new to the bar, you should be looking for them.

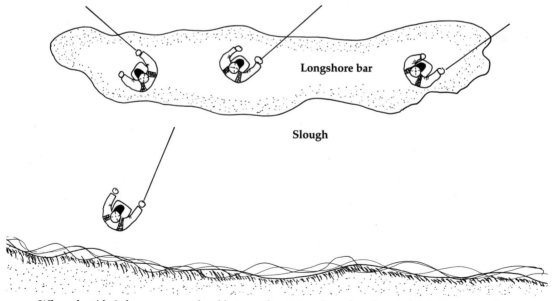

When the tide is low, you may be able to wade out to a longshore bar and fish the seaward edge.

Once you're fairly satisfied that there are no fish on the bar itself, it's time to shift gears. From the bar, you can fish back into the slough, but there's another option open to you as well. You can work the drop-off along the seaward side of the bar. This edge could be anything from a gentle gradient to a steep slope. Regardless, it is a productive location to wet a line. Expect striped bass, bluefish, and tiderunners to associate with it, often cruising along looking for a free lunch. On a few occasions, I've seen bonito and false albacore traveling this type of edge as well.

Expect the fish to be within 50 feet of the drop-off, and in bright light, also expect them to be deep, below the depth to which the sunlight penetrates. To reach them, don't stand right at the drop-off itself, but stay back 20 feet or more. Cast toward the drop-off, permit the fly to sink, and then retrieve it back up onto the bar. After several casts, move down the bar and cover new sections of the drop-off.

Casting straight out over the drop-off works, but there's an alternative that often works better. Try casting at an angle, the idea being to keep the fly as close to the edge for as long as possible. To do this properly, you'll likely have to move considerably closer to the drop-off. Then turn slightly and cast along the drop-off. This presents the fly along the edge during the retrieve, and therefore it remains in the strike zone longer than if you cast straight out.

Sinking flies are helpful here, but they're not the only game in town. If you wish to work on top, a popper can be very effective along a drop-off. Poppers not only draw fish from a distance, but they also have the ability to call fish up from the depths.

On a rising tide, expect some fish to cross the bar and feed in the slough. It's inevitable. As a result, you may at times have fish both in front of and behind you. It's impossible to know exactly when the fish will cross over, so periodically turn and throw an exploratory cast back toward shore. In low-light conditions, also listen for feeding fish in the slough. Striped bass, for example, make a popping sound as they suck bait from the surface.

The first fish to cross over the bar are usually the smaller ones, so concentrate on the front side of the bar rather than the slough, especially early in the flood. The one exception might be in a location where the slough has considerable depth and there is a deep cut at the end of the bar.

A cut supplies easy access to the slough, even for the big guys. Hence it's an important edge in its own right. Not only is it deep, but when the tide is under way, it has current as well. Fishing a cut is pretty straightforward. You move down the bar toward the cut and make a cast into it, allowing the available current to swing the fly. Pay particular attention to where the cut sweeps around the end of the bar. Fish—even very large ones—often hang right at this corner. You can also cover the cut from shore by chucking a fly toward it.

Fishing Finger Bars

When fishing a finger bar, if you arrive at the start of the ebb, you should fish your way out as the water level recedes. If you arrive at low tide, you should proceed as far out on the bar as safety allows, and then fish your way back to shore as the water level rises.

Just as with a longshore bar, if a finger bar has deep enough water over it to hold fish, you should work your way out, covering the water as you go. Check for a hole to one side or the other of where the bar joins the shore. It's worth investigating. Usually it fishes best on high water, but in low light, give it a try regardless.

It's common for one side of a finger bar to have a steeper slope and deeper adjacent water than the other. The difference may be subtle, but don't overlook

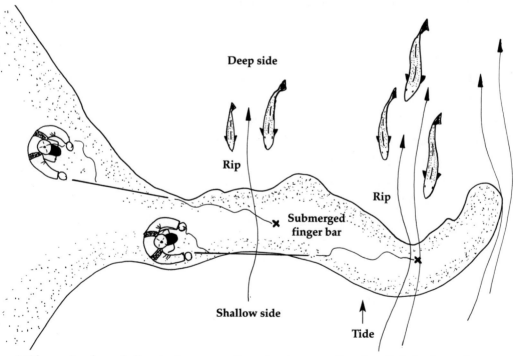

A tide moving from shallow to deep over a finger bar is an excellent bet. Fish the fastest lanes of current. Move out as water level allows.

it. Most often, this deeper edge provides the better fishing, so always make a serious effort to identify which side it is. Furthermore, these finger bars frequently have strong currents sweeping over them at certain stages of the tide. Try to determine which tide—ebb or flood—causes the water to move toward the deeper side of the bar. When the deeper side is downcurrent of the bar, the angling action sizzles.

As you move out onto the bar, look around you for signs of forage fish. At the same time, be on the lookout for dips or depressions in the bar itself, especially those that span the entire width of the structure. When the tide is in motion, these low spots may have considerable water pouring through them, making them in essence small rivers. These rips are prime edges. But don't expect the stripers to be in the depression itself. The bottom offers little place to hide from the current. Rather, expect the fish to be just off the edge of the bar, either on the upcurrent or the downcurrent side. And expect these fish to be sitting deep, well down out of the flow.

Because of the current, the fish on the upcurrent side are difficult to present a fly to. A heavily weighted fly on a sinking line may work, as long as you can get the fly down quickly and stay in contact with it. Another approach is to use a popper on a floating line. The fish on the downcurrent side, however, should be easy to reach. Cast into the rip, allowing the fly to swing over the edge of the bar. The strike should come at the end of the swing. If the water off the edge of the bar is very deep, a sinking line may be needed, even though the water up on the bar may be relatively shallow.

During a rising tide, some areas of the bar go underwater more quickly than others. As they do, they are washed over by broad bands of current. Don't expect the fish to be up on the bar itself; they are more likely holding either immediately uptide or downtide of the structure. Here again, the downcurrent fish are more accessible, so let the fly swing downcurrent over the edge of the bar.

When no current is crossing over the bar, focus most of your fishing effort on the deeper side, casting and moving along the bar until you find fish. If the bar exhibits even the slightest bend to the right or left, pay particular attention to this offset. Commonly this area will have additional bottom structure associated with it and more complex currents.

The tip of a finger bar often has the strongest currents of all and the deepest water nearby. It may also have considerable wave action as the tide rises. Put these elements together, and you can see why these outposts require caution. Nevertheless, they are red-hot fishing grounds, loaded with prime edges.

When fishing from the tip, methodically cover all the water before you, using whatever current is available. At the same time, study the surface of the water for the presence of submerged edges. You'll often find one or more additional bottom structures directly off the tip.

When to Fish Bars

The seaward edge of a longshore bar is often prime during the early hours of the flood tide. It may also produce well during the last of the ebb, but rarely is it as good. From the second or third hour of the flood until the middle of the ebb, the slough side of the bar is apt to host the better fishing. A bit of wave action is always desirable; it stirs things up and kicks feeding fish into gear. And low-light situations typically are more productive than broad daylight.

Low light and wave action pump up the fishing on finger bars as well, but frequently the defining agent is current. You want moving water, and best of all is water moving toward the deeper side of the bar. At low stages of the tide, fish at the tip, which will likely hold the deepest water and still have current. At high tide, the bar could well be submerged and therefore inaccessible, but there may be a hole to one side next to shore. This edge will be prime in higher water.

Exposed

Tide rips

Cut

Exposed dry

Tide rips

Cut

Exposed bar

As the tide rises, some areas of a finger bar may submerge much more quickly than others. Fish will sit on the rips formed by these cuts. But be sure not to allow rising water to strand you out at the tip.

Safety Tips

As soon as you wade away from shore, there is some inherent risk. Using common sense will lower that risk. A wader belt and even a PFD are good ideas, particular for weak swimmers.

Regardless of how good the fishing is, on a rising tide, remain aware that you have to return to shore before water levels get too high. As a basic rule, big bars—those that cover large areas—offer considerable resistance to the tide and therefore go underwater more slowly. Small bars offer little resistance and are apt to submerge far more quickly. Knowing exactly how long you can stay on any given bar is a matter of experience. The more you fish it, the better you know it. But even after you have some experience on a given bar, remember that moon tides, especially perigee moon tides, are substantially larger.

In addition, you have to factor in the wind. A strong onshore wind makes a flooding tide arrive sooner than scheduled. It could also make the tidal range greater than expected, increasing water depth over the bar and in the slough. Wind also produces waves. If, under calm conditions, you can barely cross a slough at a certain stage of the tide without shipping water over your waders, when waves build, your margin of safety quickly disappears.

Never assume that a sandbar has remained unchanged from year to year. Some may shift significantly with one big storm. And never attempt to learn a new sandbar at night. Do it when conditions allow you to see the terrain.

Finger bars require extra precautions, for several reasons: They can take you farther out from shore; the bottom may be rocky, making footing more difficult; and they often have powerful tidal currents and heavy surf. This is especially the case in locations where the tidal range between high and low tides is over 6 feet. You need to be very careful in such places. Also bear in mind that as the tide rises, the tip may stay exposed longer than other sections of the bar. Thus if you are fishing out on the tip, you could turn and find that large portions of the bar between you and the shore are underwater, making it difficult for you to return to shore.

HOW TO FISH SAND FLATS

Like a sandbar, a sand flat is an area of shallow water, but that's about where the similarity ends. Whereas bars tend to be narrow, longer than they are wide, flats typically are broad shoals that encompass many times the area of a bar. And whereas sandbars often reach their greatest size on open, fully exposed beaches, sand flats are usually found in highly protected coastal waters. Look for them on the lee sides of islands and barrier beaches, in the back of bays and coves, and in salt ponds.

Saltwater fly rodders jump at the chance to fish sand flats. Not only do these structures offer the pleasures of wading in a place of reduced wind and wave, but sand flats also allow anglers their greatest opportunity to sight fish—one of the most challenging and exciting aspects of our sport. Usually the quarry is striped bass, but bluefish and weakfish may be caught here as well.

When up on a flat, schools of game fish are less likely to spend time holding in ambush and more likely to be cruising about. The reason for this is twofold. First, a flat has a fairly uniform bottom without many strong edges. And few edges mean few places to hide. Second, given the shallow conditions, game fish can occupy the flat for only a short time during the tide; hence they must locate the bait relatively quickly by searching for it. Put these things together, and you see why flats fishing has its own unique flavor.

Even though flats generally have fairly uniform bottoms, they are never perfectly level, but contain some concave and convex structures, holes, depressions, and small ridges. Although these edges may be few in number and relatively minor in size, they are, nonetheless, a key ingredient in flats fishing. Fish do at times hang out near these locations, but more important, cruising fish frequently use edges as lanes of travel with which to visit various portions of the flat.

Fishing Flats

For the angler on foot, there are two basic methods of fishing a flat. You can set up camp and wait for the fish to come to you, or you can go off in search of the fish.

In the first approach, start by choosing a location that you feel has special promise. If you're highly experienced on a particular flat, that shouldn't be difficult. You should know places where the action is generally best. If you don't know the flat, look for the area with the heaviest concentration of bait. Given that flats usually have clear water, seeing the bait is often an easy proposition, even though the bait tends to be small. Polarized sunglasses are a must for this.

Should finding bait prove to be a problem or should the bait be spread out, slowly and quietly search for the strongest edge you can locate, especially one that is concave and thereby provides a pocket of greater depth. Such places are more likely to have fish around them during all stages of the tide. They're a good bet.

Once you've selected your spot, the next step is critical. Because you're sight fishing, it's imperative that you position yourself in such a way as to maximize your ability to see the bottom you intend to fish. This means placing the sun as much as possible to your back.

Once you've determined your angle, the next thing to consider is your distance to the target. This is another essential aspect of the sight-fishing game. If you stand too close, you may spook the fish before they enter the area. If you're too far back, you won't see the fish arrive. Generally, you want to be 40 to 50 feet back, 50 feet being about the farthest you can consistently see fish, even in extremely clear water.

Once you've staked out your position, peel line from the reel in preparation to make a few preliminary casts. Inspect the hook, and sharpen it if necessary. Then pick a portion of the bottom at about the farthest extent of your vision, and attempt to drop the fly there. You want to get a feel for things before fish actually show up. Make several additional casts to other areas. After practice casting, store most of the line in the stripping basket, leaving about 20 feet outside the rod tip ready to go. Most flats anglers prefer to hold this line in loose coils. When using a floating line, you have the option of simply dropping it on the water, but if you do so, occasionally check to be sure the line has not become tangled.

As striped bass have the ability to change their coloration to match the surrounding environment, they're not as easy to see as you might expect. On a sand flat, they will be quite pale, with only a hint of green on their backs. Consequently, more than anything else, you are looking for movement, something in motion across the bottom. Don't expect to see a striped bass or a bluefish sail completely into view; expect to see something subtle. Typically, these fish appear as a slowly moving object that is slightly darker than its surroundings. And don't expect to see that object by looking at the surface of the water; train your eyes on the bottom itself. Look through the water. It's the contrast between the moving object and the bottom that makes the fish visible.

You can't perfect this skill in one outing; it takes time. Fact is, your first attempt may prove frustrating, and quite possibly you'll walk away feeling like you couldn't spot a fish if it swam up your leg. Be patient; the rewards will come. Moreover, even if you've mastered this skill in the past, unless you sight-fish regularly, it will take time for you to get back in the groove. So even after you have some sight-fishing experience under your belt, don't expect instant success.

When you see a fish approaching, try to drop the fly ahead of it and directly in its path. With the exception of surface flies, such as sliders, you should let the fly sink a bit before you start the retrieve. With most baitfish imitations, middepth is fine. With a crab pattern, you may want to sink it right to the bottom. That requires additional time, and you must lead the fish accordingly. When the fish is within 3 feet of the fly, start your retrieve.

In the second method, the idea is to explore the flat in hopes of coming upon fish before they see you. Don't stay in constant motion; rather, observe a place for a few minutes, and if nothing shows up, wade a short distance and start over again. This stop-and-go method uses more stealth, and it's far easier to see and cast to fish from a stationary position. During all of this, you must be ready to cast on a moment's notice. Keep enough line outside the rod tip so that you can react with little warning.

While wading, move in a direction that permits you the greatest possible visibility. Wading directly into the sun is a poor choice, since the reflected light will be at its strongest, reducing your ability to see the bottom. If possible, wade with the sun to your back. Second best is to have the sun off to one side.

Whether you choose to lie in wait or go off hunting, occasionally look up from the bottom and glance off in the distance. When schools of game fish cruise the flats, they usually do so with no commotion. Still, at times a large school moving near the top may cause a rippling effect on the surface, what anglers call nervous water. On a calm day, this nervous water can be seen for some distance. If you see such a disturbance and it's headed toward you, you're about to get a shot at some fish. And since the fish are moving in a pack, they're apt to be quite competitive, eager to hit your fly. If the nervous water doesn't appear to be coming toward you, try to gauge an intercepting course, one that will place you in casting range. Move with as much stealth as possible.

Another warning sign of impending action is a school of baitfish suddenly hustling into view. Get ready—this school may well be running from trouble, exactly the kind of trouble you want to find. Not every school of bait has predators in close pursuit, but certain signs bode well. Pay particular attention to schools of bait that are extremely concentrated or milling about nervously. And if a school of bait swarms around you, they likely are using you as cover.

Tackle and Gear

Floating fly lines are very useful on a flat, and I highly recommend you have one with you. Intermediate fly lines are also effective. Of those, I suggest you pick a clear one, such as the Airflo. These transparent lines provide an extra measure of stealth.

On the fly front, the key words are small and sparse. Sand eel patterns and Clouser Deep Minnows are musts in your fly box. Small sliders are very good, and crab patterns can be useful, although they are the hardest to use properly, as they need to be twitched on the bottom.

As the fish you hook on a flat rarely have any place to dive deep, you don't need a rod with a lot of lifting power. Moreover, you don't need a rod capable of lofting the entire fly line; rather, you need something that is highly accurate in the 30- to 70-foot range. Hence, on the flats, 10-weight rods are overkill. Nines are okay, but 8-weights seem even better, and 7-weights should not be ruled out unless you know that some heavyweight fish are around. These lighter rods are also better for presentation. A lighter-weight fly line creates less disturbance when cast upon the water. The typical 8- or 9-foot leader works well here, although some may want to lengthen it a foot or so. That's fine, but never make the leader so long that you can't accurately place the fly. As far as tippet strength goes, 15-pound-test seems excessive, particularly given the lack of sharp objects on a flat. Ten-pound-test is strong enough for this work, and its smaller diameter may give you an extra margin in fooling the fish.

On the flats, avoid wearing brightly colored clothing, especially hats. Such clothing increases the odds that the fish will see you coming. Instead, pick a neutral tone, particularly light blue.

Your height above the water has a huge effect on how far you can see, and for that reason an angler standing on the deck of a boat has a major advantage when it comes to spotting fish. If you're a wading angler and plan to establish a camp, consider taking along a small ladder. I know it sounds unorthodox, and it is a bit cumbersome. And if you're not careful, there's a chance of falling off. Nevertheless, where it can be used, a ladder greatly expands your range of vision and quickly becomes an ally.

When to Fish a Flat

There is a seasonal aspect to this brand of fishing. Northeast flats fishing is usually best in the spring, while water temperatures near shore are still relatively cool. This typically means from late May to mid-July, not a huge window. After that, water temperatures get too high in these shallows to host fish of any size. Skinny water environs are very sensitive to other weather conditions as well. Cold fronts quickly shut the action down, and strong winds can roil the water, making sight fishing impossible. Heavy rains also may affect the fishing on flats by lowering the salinity.

Sunny days with little or no wind are ideal for sight fishing. Clear blue skies are a real help too. As nice as puffy clouds look overhead, they are reflected in the surface of the water, reducing visibility.

Time of day can be important, too. When the sun's rays are on a slant, they produce more contrast, which in turn helps you spot fish traveling across the flat. Therefore, plan to fish from roughly 8:00 to 10:30 in the morning, and then again from 2:00 to 4:30 in the afternoon.

Given a choice, I prefer to fish a flat as the water first starts rising. I find that it tends to bring the fish toward you, and that makes seeing them and casting to them easier. Ebbing tides can be productive, too, although the fish are typically falling away from shore and consequently away from you. This can make seeing them and casting to them harder. During the ebb, you must also follow the fish as they drop back. Expect the fish to concentrate in the remaining deep water, especially in any nearby channel.

Though I do like the flooding portion of the tide, if the water is discolored, I would opt for a different stage of the tide. In such circumstances, sight fishing is limited, and whatever opportunities exist are likely best when the water is quite low—the last two hours of the ebb and the first two of the flood.

Some of the really big flats, such as those found on the bay side of Cape Cod, are best fished by wading out as far as possible at low tide, and then waiting for the fish to come at you as the tide turns. Pulling a canoe behind you on a rope is not as crazy as it may sound. Should the tide take you by surprise, you have the canoe to ride home in, and it allows you to stay on the flat longer then you could otherwise.

HOW TO FISH MUDFLATS

A mudflat is a flat where the bottom is mud rather than sand. Like sand flats, mudflats are found in highly protected places. Look for them in the rear of bays and salt ponds, around salt marshes, and especially in the lower ends of coastal rivers.

Given the shallow depth, wading is likely possible, although you need to take care, as the bottom could be very soft in spots. As a general rule, mudflats hold small fish, although where a mudflat joins a deep channel, bigger bass, blues, and weakfish are certainly possible.

The dark bottom of a mudflat is in essence a solar energy panel, rapidly absorbing the heat of the sun. Therefore, this type of flat is one of the first places to warm in the spring, making it an excellent spot to look for early-season striped bass. This is particularly true of the mudflats located inside coastal rivers. In many locations, such flats hold the earliest and best spring action. And they may be equally productive late in the season as well.

Mudflats, unlike sand flats, do not usually have clear water. As a consequence, sight fishing is far less likely to be part of the angling picture. Still, there are opportunities to see fish and cast to them. These opportunities usually are best when the water is at its lowest levels—the last hours of the ebb and first hours of the flood. Even when you can't see the fish, you can often see evidence of their presence, given the shallow water. Swirls may appear, or you may see the wakes of cruising fish or jumping baitfish.

Small, schooling baitfish such as mummichogs and silversides call mudflats home. Shrimp may be a large part of the forage base, and along the banks, there are apt to be a variety of crabs. None of this, however, rules out using larger flies. Poppers on a mudflat can be very effective for cruising bluefish, and they will at times be deadly on school bass as well. Large streamer flies have their place, too, especially in the spring, when coastal rivers host runs of herring. And overall, large flies are easier for fish to find in these discolored waters.

When to Fish a Mudflat

Fish move on and off a mudflat in much the same way as on a sand flat. A rising tide is usually a good bet, and you should expect the fish to be coming toward you from deeper water. On the ebb, the fish fall back, and you must follow. In a river, at low tide you may be able to wade a mudflat out to the channel and fish that edge as well.

At high tide, wading could be out of the question, but angling opportunities can still exist. Consider walking the shoreline and casting over the flat from the bank. Often on high water, fish come right to the banks to feed on crabs and shrimp. These opportunities typically exist during the higher stages of the tide. In such situations, expect some fish to be within 10 feet of the bank. Move along the bank while casting at an angle to the shoreline, retrieving the fly close to the bank. Marsh banks are often undercut, especially those touched by tidal current or subject to boat wakes, so you should stand back a bit, lest the bank collapse under your weight.

Moon high tides may be a problem. As the water rises well above its normal level, it will back up into marsh areas and float mountains of loose stuff such as logs, sticks, leaves, grass, weeds, and debris. On the ebb, all of this flotsam will be carried out onto the mudflat, making fishing very difficult.

Safety Tips

On some mudflats, the bottom can be very soft, and it's possible to sink in considerably while wading. Avoid those situations by backing out of any area where you sink in over ankle-deep. As a general rule, areas of a mudflat close to a river channel will be very firm because of the nearby current, whereas areas of the flat where the current never reaches are likely to be quite soft.

Since mudflats are often associated with salt marsh environs, mosquitoes, horseflies, and other biting insects can be a very real problem, especially as the weather warms. So take along bug repellent. This is especially important wherever mosquito-borne diseases like West Nile virus or eastern equine encephalitis are known to exist. If you have to walk through a marsh in order to reach the flats, you may run into ticks as well. Generally these are not the ticks that carry Lyme disease, but it's wise to check yourself when you get back home.

HOW TO FISH CHANNELS

Channels are lanes of deep water. Some channels occur naturally, but frequently they either have been dredged or are entirely man-made as a means of safe passage for boat traffic.

Channels typically occur in coastal rivers, harbors, embayments, and salt ponds. Where they exist, rarely are channels hard to find. They often are clearly identified on nautical charts, and even if you don't have a chart handy, buoys or other types of navigation markers often mark channels in an effort to make them plainly visible to boaters. In clear water, you should be able to spot a channel by its color. The shallow areas look lighter in color—more green and yellow—while the deeper places, such as the channel, look darker and bluer.

Often channels hold not only deep water, but considerable current as well. This combination makes them prime edges and ideal habitat for striped bass, bluefish, and weakfish. Given their significant depth, channels hold big fish; they're edges fully capable of providing the fish of a lifetime. Atlantic bonito and false albacore are caught in channels too, especially those in harbors and salt ponds.

When fish congregate in a channel, generally they are either along the drop-off or sitting in the deepest portions. Overall, however, channels are not equally productive along their entire length; some stretches are noticeably better than others. To a large degree, this has to do with the fact that water depth and current speed in a channel vary from location to location. Often you can see where the current is greatest simply by studying the surface of the water for rip lines. Pay particular attention to any rip where the surface of the water shows considerable turbulence. Most likely the channel bottom here undergoes some type of significant change, either rising or falling rapidly. This is a hot spot—an edge within an edge.

Channel bends are hot spots as well. Here you find complex currents and bottom structure. Along the outside of the bend, depth and current increase, while on the inside of the bend, depth decreases as currents slow and back eddies form. As a result, you have many changes in water speed and changes in depth, resulting in many potential edges to fish. All of this causes nutrients

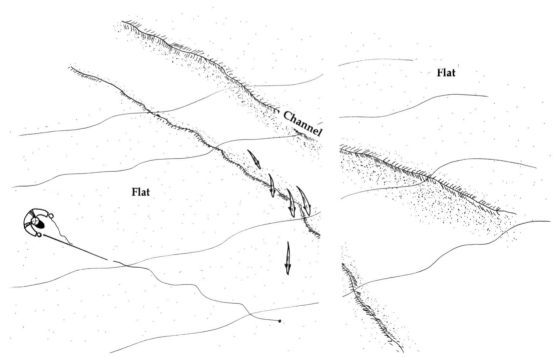

When fishing a flat, pay special attention to the edge of any drop-off or channel during the first hours of the flood and the last of the ebb.

to settle out, and that in turn draws forage fish to feed. Altogether, it's an attractive package.

Another hot spot to consider is where the channel ends. After passing through an extensive shallow area, a channel may suddenly terminate as it reaches deep water. Like the channel bend, complex currents are apt to be here, as well as complex bottom structure. As with the channel bend, this complexity holds fish, often some of the biggest ones around.

Fishing a Channel

No question, boat-based anglers get in more channel fishing than anyone else, but those on foot get a crack at them too. Occasionally you'll find a location where a channel swings in tight to shore. Commonly these situations occur in salt ponds and coastal rivers, especially where a river takes a sharp bend on its way to sea. In both instances, the shoreline is often not a sandy beach, but a marsh bank. By walking that bank, you can cast into the channel as you go. If

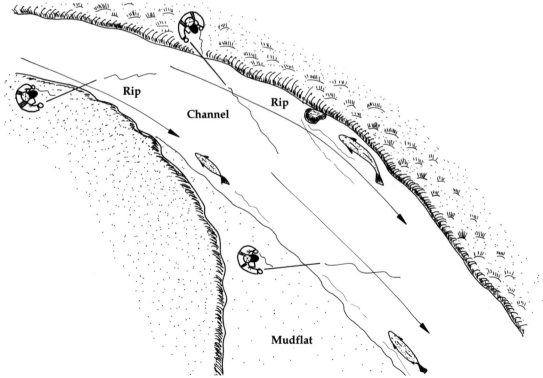

Where the channel bends, you're apt to find rips, bars, and plenty of edges that hold fish.

you see signs of feeding fish, move within casting range if possible. The depth of the channel is likely to hide baitfish from view, but look for rip lines, turbulence, and signs of bottom structure.

As you cast, let the fly sink a long way before retrieving; the fish are apt to be fairly deep, and you must get the fly to them. Some fish may be practically under your feet, right where the current brushes the bank. Therefore, place some casts to present the fly along the shoreline. After covering one area, move on, but be careful where you step; some marsh banks are loaded with ankle-twisting holes. Remember, too, that there is deep, swift water nearby; this is a bad place to fall in. Avoid that possibility by keeping back from the water's edge. Often these marsh banks are undercut by the current, and standing at the edge of the bank may cause it to collapse, launching you into the water.

Another means of accessing a channel on foot is by wading out to it. Channels frequently wind through and around flats. Where this occurs, the channel is an important part of your flats strategy. The channel will not supply additional sight-fishing opportunities, but it will complement the action by offering you a chance to blind-cast into an area where fish may be highly concentrated. During lower stages of the tide, many fish boogie off the flat and drop back into the channel. The water there is deeper and cooler, making it an ideal hangout for fish as they await the return of the flood tide. Furthermore, the channel is essentially an artery by which the tide fills and drains the neighboring flat. Consequently, there is often current in the channel, even near dead low tide. This, too, attracts game fish to reside here.

When fish sit in the channel, they are frequently schooled up into a few key locations. You'll have to search a bit to locate the action, but it's worth it. The fish are concentrated and apt to be aggressive to the fly. As you already know, the hot spots are typically where the channel has either greater depth or increased current. So look for rip lines, complex currents, turbulence, and channel bends.

Wherever you find the fish, expect them to be down, below the depth to which the light penetrates the water. So sinking lines and possibly sinking flies are in order. If you were just sight-fishing the flats, that means swapping spools, assuming you had the foresight to bring a sinking line with you.

To work the channel, move toward the drop-off, but take care. A channel can have a very steep lip, especially where dredging has taken place. If there is moving water, cast upcurrent so as to allow the fly an opportunity to sink. As the fly line starts to pass, take up the slack so the fly can swing down and across on a fairly tight line. Expect the strike on the swing. Where there is no current, cast into the channel and allow the fly to sink well out of sight before starting your retrieve. Expect the strike as the fly begins to climb the drop-off. At slack tide, a floating line and popper may do some damage. You'll want to work the fly just inside the lip of the channel. That may mean getting a bit closer and casting at an angle rather than straight out into the channel.

Given the depth of a channel and the potential for huge fish, a strong rod with plenty of lifting power is in order. Nine-weights make the grade, and 10-weights do it even better, as long as you feel comfortable casting them. But don't use more rod than you can physically handle, as injuries may result.

Flies for channel fishing can run the gamut from slim to supersize. When working a channel that is connected to a flat, I assume that the bait in the channel is the same type of bait that's on the flat. Therefore, I tend to stick with smaller patterns, such as sand eel flies. When fishing a channel in a river, especially one where the water is discolored, I use bigger patterns. They will be easy for fish to find, and rivers are home to large forage fish, such as herring.

When to Fish Channels
A channel often fishes best during the last hours of the ebb through the first hours of the flood. During the second half of a rising tide, game fish are more likely to move out of the channel and into shallower areas to feed. But as the tide lowers, they are more inclined to return to the safety of the channel.

Light level is a factor too. Striped bass and weakfish like to feed in shallow water from dusk through the night to dawn. As the sun rises, they frequently drop back to deeper water. Where a channel supplies that needed depth, it can be a hot spot in early morning.

Safety Tips
Whether you wade or use a boat, fishing a channel requires some care. If you wade near a channel, take care not to step too close to the edge, as the lip of the channel can be fairly steep. Many channels have a lot of boat traffic. If you're in a boat, avoid anchoring it so that you impede that traffic, especially at night. When wading, you must also be careful of boat traffic. A large boat traveling in the channel can send a considerable wake across the adjacent shallows. If you're already up to your waist in water, that wave could ship over the top of

your waders. Even worse, it's possible for a captain to wander off course, and it's even possible in low light for an inexperienced captain to mistake your silhouette for a channel marker.

HOW TO FISH ROCK PILES

One of the key ingredients in any marine habitat is the composition of the bottom, be it sand, mud, cobble, or large rock. In fact, it's such an important factor that some marine species are pretty much found only over certain types of bottoms. Not surprisingly, then, the composition of the bottom plays a role in angling as well.

Coarser bottoms—gravel or rock—provide richer habitats than finer materials such as sand. The coarse stuff simply provides more places for life to hide and hold on to. Vegetation counts as coarse material too. For instance, where you find eelgrass growing on the bottom, you have found an important edge. Eelgrass provides a foothold for many forms of life—far more than a bare sand bottom could.

Another aspect is the presence of current or turbulence. Moving water has a tendency to lift sand and transport it away, and in the process expose harder substrate. It's erosion, pure and simple. Consequently, when you find a patch of hard bottom surrounded by softer material such as sand or mud, you may have found a place where a rip, or at least considerable wave action, exists at some stage of the tide. And these things draw feeding fish.

Even on a shoreline that has a bottom entirely composed of rock, some of those rocks provide better habitat than others. You should spend the least amount of time on areas where the rock bottom is fairly level, and instead concentrate on spots where one or more large rocks form a convex mass rising up from the bottom. This is an edge, and you can expect striped bass and bluefish to visit this structure.

There are a great many variations on this theme, too many to fully cover here. Instead, we will look at two prime examples of this type of edge: rock piles that lie close to the water's edge, and large boulders that sit back from the beach in deeper water.

By rock piles, I'm referring to rocks at least 2 or 3 feet in diameter on up to boulders. In essence, the pile of rocks on the beach is a small point running out underwater. That alone makes it an edge. As waves approach the beach, they

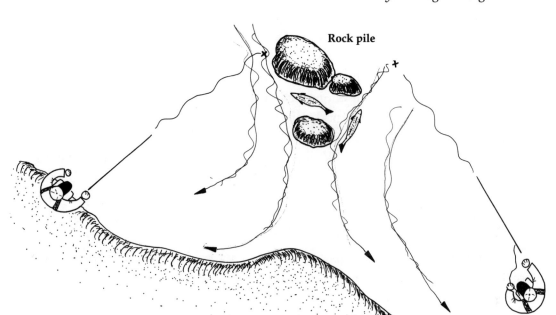

As tide and waves approach a beach, they cause currents to form around rock piles. These piles quickly become prime edges. Work the rip and foam lines.

course through and around this pile, creating complex current between the rocks. Even as a wave retreats back down the beach, it may cause reverse currents back through the rocks. That makes this pile a prime edge.

When the rocks are fully submerged, they may be hard to see at first. In clear water, however, the large rocks stand out as dark masses when encircled by a lighter-colored bottom. Often there is a mix—some submerged rocks and others that break the surface. That makes things easier. And in a few cases, the rocks lie not only in the water, but extend right up onto the beach into plain view. That makes thing even easier yet.

As with so many other edges, waves are valuable clues in locating these rock piles. Where the rocks stick through the surface, the waves will break as they pass over them. Such breaks can have considerable whitewater and foam associated with them and therefore are visible for quite a distance. Even when the rocks are submerged, waves may still help you out. If the rock's height brings it near the surface, as the wave passes over, the water wells up, producing a boil mark in the surface. On calm days, these marks can be easily seen, although you may be fooled for a moment into thinking one of them is the swirl of a large bass. It has happened to me plenty of times.

The other kind of edge is one or two huge boulders sitting well off the beach in deeper water. Time and again, experience has shown me that large boulders surrounded by deep water are ideal habitat for huge bass. If I could refine things further, I would like to see those rocks breaking the surface, with surf and foam pouring around them. That would be perfect. Another highly desirable situation is where a tidal current runs parallel to the beach. As that current courses around the boulders, rips form. And if the rips are swift, you will have whitewater and foam.

Granted, in some locations, such deep-lying boulders are outside of fly-casting range. Heartbreaking, but it happens. Still, there are times when they are reachable, especially if you know how to throw a long line. Where that is the case, that edge could well give you the striper of a lifetime, especially in low light. And if it does, you'll know why in some regions stripers are called rockfish.

Fishing Rock Piles

When fishing a pile of rocks next to shore, start by working both sides of the structure. In many cases, you can do this from the beach, although other times, some wading is required. Bring the fly along one perimeter of the rocks, and after a few casts, walk to the far side and do the same there. If no strikes come, cast directly into the rocks. Allow a bit of time for the fly to settle.

In some situations, you may be able to climb out on the rocks and fish off the front of the structure. This can be a very productive tactic, but one that requires a good deal of care. Rocks are often overgrown with algae and sea-weed and can be slick. Cleats and a wading staff can be a real help and provide a measure of safety. As you move forward, look for a flat rock that will provide a safe casting platform. Remain conscious of waves as they approach the beach. You don't want to get knocked down.

Although rocks sitting back from the beach may be out of fly range, you can try throwing a popper as near to the rocks as possible. The idea behind this strategy is that frequently a popper will call a curious fish a considerable ways. This tactic requires multiple casts to accomplish, but it's worth a try.

Some of these large rocks off the beach are near enough to drop a fly close by. Where that's the case, a good-size bass could be anywhere around the

Lisa Blalock with a 28-inch striper taken off a rock pile east of Watch Hill, Rhode Island, on a white Deceiver. PHIL FARNSWORTH

structure. It might be sitting on the seaward side, the one facing away from the beach; on the beach side, the one facing the shore; or to the right or the left.

Begin by trying to show the fly to any fish on the seaward side of the structure. Granted, this is apt to be difficult, but at least make an attempt. It may mean moving well to one side or perhaps wading out a bit. Once you've tried that, work the right and left sides of the structure. Then place a few casts right down the middle, toward the center of the edge.

If there is a current chugging parallel to the beach, however, you can bet that any bass by the rocks is facing into the flow. Position yourself on the beach well upcurrent of the rocks, and swing a fly as tight to the rocks as possible. Move in front of the rocks and do the same. Then move downcurrent of the rocks and try again.

Keep your eyes peeled at all times. You may well see a fish follow or swirl behind the fly. Unless the fish are feeding aggressively, that fish is not likely to take your fly, even on subsequent casts to the same spot. But don't give up. Rest the spot for five to ten minutes. Then make additional casts using a

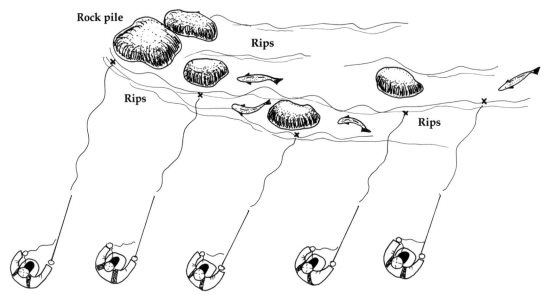

A rock pile in heavy current quickly becomes a prime edge. Work the rip lines and lines of surface foam.

different fly. If you initially chucked a small streamer fly, try throwing something larger, or vice versa. You might even opt for a popper.

In all cases, when working these edges, a slow retrieve is best. The bass are apt to be feeding very close to the rocks and perhaps even with their heads down. They need time to sense and locate the fly, especially in places where there is a good deal of wave and foam. But a slow retrieve is only half of the picture; the other half is line control.

As waves and current pass through or around rocks, they may tend to push the fly toward you, creating slack in the line. It's imperative to stay in contact with your fly or risk missing strikes. You need to be able to feel the weight of the fly at all times during the retrieve. In part, that's accomplished by keeping the rod tip low to the water. But when a wave lifts the fly, it also means speeding up the retrieve until you once again feel the fly. Stay alert.

When working around clusters of rocks, as long as there's at least a bit of sunlight on the water, a big, white streamer in the 7-inch range on a 3/0 hook is excellent. A 9-weight rod can handle it, but a 10-weight chucks it better. Perhaps the white stands out strongly underwater against the dark mass of the rock, but whatever it is, believe me, it works. After dark, a black fly of the same size would be a better choice.

Given the barnacles, shells, and other sharp objects in this type of habitat, you need to use a fairly stout leader. No 12-pound tippets here; 15-pound is a minimum, and a 20-pound tippet if often better. After you land a fish, run your fingers along the entire leader, checking for signs of abrasion. Where found, replace it with fresh mono. On rare occasions, you'll nick the coating on the fly line. Unfortunately, there's little you can do to repair this.

When to Fish a Rock Pile

Rock piles hold a lot of food, and bass and even bluefish could be nosing around at any time of day. Still, it's fair to point out that whenever wave or currents are strongest, the fishing is likely to be best. And low-light conditions always bring bass and blues closer to the beach.

At low tide, particularly a low moon tide, it may be possible to wade out and work rock piles that are at other times impossible to reach. This may seem like a small opportunity, but it's been productive for me on numerous occasions.

HOW TO FISH ESTUARIES

Perhaps the single most complex piece of water anglers face—and the single most productive, too—is found where fresh and salt water meet. These places are called estuaries, and they come in a raft of shapes and sizes, from tiny tidal creeks to salt ponds, inlets, and large coastal rivers. But in every case, there is good action to be found.

Estuaries have strong currents, and therefore rips abound. These currents carve out the bottom in the mouth of the estuary and along the adjacent beaches as well. The result is a myriad of edges. Expect to find longshore bars, finger bars, sloughs, flats, channels, and deltas.

All these edges hold schools of forage fish. The sheer number of baitfish in an estuary is sometimes truly astounding, due to the tremendous amount of nutrients that fresh water transports to the brine. These nutrients encourage forage fish to spawn and grow in these waters. In addition, estuaries are frequently gateways for anadromous runs of herring, which are important attractors of striped bass. Even tidal creeks small enough to jump over can be home to alewife runs. It's amazing how little water it takes.

This wealth of current, forage, and edges not only is found in the mouth of the estuary, but extends to the beaches on either side, making them rich fishing

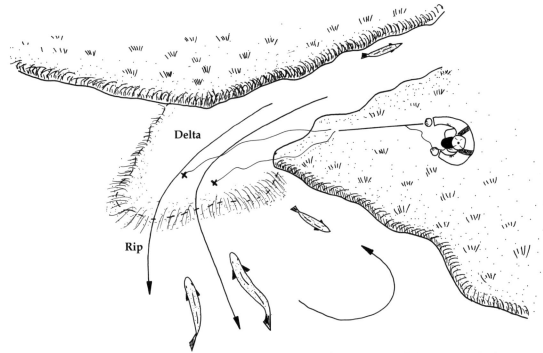

On an ebbing tide, a creek mouth can be a hot spot. Look for the biggest fish just outside the mouth, along the steepest drop-off.

grounds. Little wonder these areas host many varieties of fish, including bonito, false albacore, bass, blues, weakfish, and hickory shad. In fact, beaches adjoining the mouth of an estuary are some of the most productive shorelines you'll ever fish.

When to Fish Estuaries

When working the mouth of an estuary, an ebbing tide is almost always best. It draws the forage fish down toward the mouth, and the currents and rips near an estuary are invariably strongest on the ebb. That combo pretty much ensures results.

Though the first half of the ebb may give you the best shot at a big fish, the final hours have fine fishing too. Toward the end of the ebb, the game fish tend to concentrate in the few remaining areas of current and depth. In some cases, you may have to wade out to reach them, but when game fish are concentrated like that, the bite can be fast and furious.

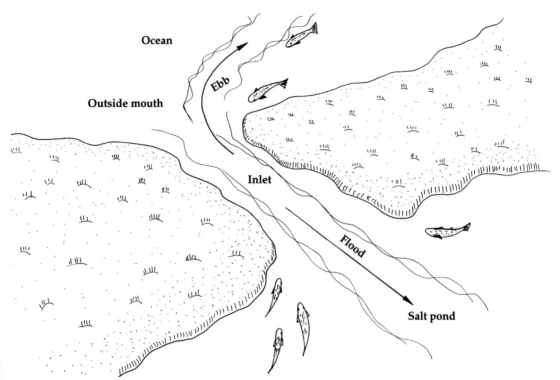

When fishing inlets and estuaries, expect the best bite to be outside the mouth on the ebb and up inside on the flood.

In estuaries large enough for game fish to enter, the flood tide is productive too. On this tide, the predator and prey are farther up inside the mouth. If you're trying to catch a member of the tuna tribe from shore, this is exactly what you want. If the channel is deep, expect some game fish, especially freshwater-tolerant ones like striped bass, to ascend a long way upstream. Look for them in holes, by undercut banks, and at bends.

In a tiny tidal creek, all of the action is at the lower end. Out in the mouth, look for a delta or shoal over which the creek flows as it exits to the sea. These structures typically have a steep drop-off where the edge joins deeper water. Swinging a fly through here can pay consistent dividends, especially in low light.

The fishing you find where fresh and salt water meet is a bit sensitive to the seasons. In the spring, these edges often hold the first striped bass of the year, here to hound spawning runs of herring. Still, autumn is the hottest time to fish

Wherever fresh and salt water meet, the fishing is apt to be very good. This holds true not only for large coastal rivers, but for small tidal creeks like this one.

in and around estuaries. During this season, many species of forage fish stage near the mouth in large numbers, preparing to migrate for the winter months. At first they may hole up inside an inlet or river, but as colder weather approaches, they drop out to the coast. This sparks many a blitz.

In the larger inlets and rivers, it is the current you seek, not the tide. The hours of current may not exactly match the hours of tide. This may sound strange, but it's true. For example, in an inlet, an ebbing current does not necessarily start immediately after slack high tide. Rather, it may start one to three hours later. Likewise, the ebbing current may continue to ebb for one to three hours beyond the time of dead low. The good news is that once you have determined the difference between the time of tide and the time of current for a given inlet, it always remains pretty much the same.

CHAPTER SIX

Forage and Flies

The extent to which forage affects your fishing is not fully apparent the first few times you hit the salt. Sure, anglers know that forage attracts game fish and that some flies are designed to imitate certain baits. Yet beyond those two things, initially at least, knowledge of the impact of forage is a little vague.

You'll learn quickly, however, that the relative abundance of forage along any beach determines to a fair degree the quality of the fishing you'll find there. And the character of that forage—the species involved and their diversity—is a significant factor, too.

You will also discover that, year in and year out, some beaches always hold more food than others. But even in those locations where bait is the thickest, it rarely sits still, coming and going with the seasons, the light, and the tides. Game fish are tuned in to these trends; they return year after year to the places where the forage is most abundant, and then track the prey as it moves.

Most predator fish are opportunists, capable of feeding on a wide array of different forage. A big bass, for instance, can sip in a slender sand eel or gulp down a lobster. Having a wide palate is a useful strategy, one that helps wild creatures survive. As a consequence, game fish, at times, hit a variety of different flies. That's good news. This willingness is especially evident in locations where forage is not in great abundance, although when food is very scarce, game fish generally go elsewhere.

Game fish likely have favored foods and travel great distances to find them. In fact, there is a good chance that the migratory paths of many game fish are, in essence, routes to specific foods. When game fish find their favored bait, they seem to key in on it to the exclusion of other forage, even when that other food is close at hand.

Oily schooling baits rank highest on the menu. Most notable in that regard are the members of the herring family, especially menhaden. Every species of game fish covered in this book loves to swallow menhaden. Some take them small, some take them big, and some take them in all sizes. So you can bet your favorite rod that wherever menhaden roam, so goes the fishing.

If herring are not available, the fish turn to other oily baitfish that are, for the most part, smaller in size but apparently still delectable. These include sand eels, bay anchovies, mullet, and butterfish. Where none of those are present, the focus may switch to less oily forage such as squid—a large boneless fillet if ever there was one—and the omnipresent silversides, a bait as common as sand.

FUSSY FISH

When game fish single out a school of prey and attack it, some flies may far out-perform others. I've seen it hundreds of times—the fish just get fussy. And when that happens, not surprisingly, some anglers far outperform others. These successful anglers have some idea what flies are going to work based on previous experiences with the same type of bait. In addition, these anglers had the forethought to bring the right flies with them for the location and time of year. And they know how to present those flies so they have the best chance of being taken.

When faced with fussy fish, many fly rodders assume that the right fly is one that closely matches the size, shape, and color of the prey. Such thinking makes intuitive sense, and often it is effective. After all, practicality dictates that during the heat of the hunt, game fish visually lock on to a specific size and shape target for the duration of the blitz. Hence, flies that mimic that target are also apt to draw attention and therefore a strike.

It doesn't always work that way, however. If the water is discolored, a brighter fly—perhaps chartreuse—could be more visible and thus produce more strikes than a fly that better matches the natural coloration of the bait. On occasion, matching the size and shape of the prey can actually end up reducing your catch. This is especially true in situations where the schools of bait are extremely thick, composed of hundreds or thousands of individuals, as is often the case with juvenile menhaden and bay anchovies. In this circumstance, a matching fly becomes lost in the crowd, but a fly larger than the prey stands out, perhaps even boldly. If you know the size of a bait that schools thickly, tie the fly slightly larger. So where 1½-inch sand eels roam, for instance, use a fly of 2 inches or even a bit larger.

This bigger-is-better routine can also be taken to extremes. Instead of throwing something 20 or 30 percent larger, I sometimes chuck a fly four or five times longer than the prey. This is possible only with small baits, but it does work. This jumbo fly mixed in with the prey may well represent a second predator moving in to feed and may provoke a territorial response in game fish, which move to kill the intruder. Whatever the actual reasons, when bait is numerous and concentrated, a fly that's bigger than the prey may well catch the most fish, and possibly the biggest.

ACTION

Some spinning lures, especially lipped swimmers and certain soft plastic ones with fluttering tails, will at times outfish flies. The reason is action. These artificials squirm and wiggle, and that action not only helps catch a game fish's eye, but also sends out vibrations that help a predator locate it in dark or discolored waters.

Though flies have far less of this built-in action, there are some exceptions, such as Bob Popovics's Pop Lip and Jack Gartside's Gurglers. Other patterns gain action by using soft materials such as marabou or strips of rabbit fur. Fly design also helps. A streamer tied with bulky shoulders and a long, thin tail is one example. When pulled through the water, the wide head of the fly creates a disturbance around the fly that causes the tail to wiggle. Another example is a fly weighted at the head in order to cause it to jig, such as Bob Popovics's Jiggy.

Wiggle is not everything, however. Size, shape, and flash are the central issues, and flies constructed with mainly rigid materials, such as Gartside's Corsair Sand Eel, can be dynamite. Nevertheless, built-in action is something that innovative fly tiers should experiment with.

PRESENTATION

Choosing a fly is one thing, but properly presenting it is another. When confronted with a blitz, most anglers simply cast directly into it. This sometimes works well, but often you have to decide whether the fly should be on top or on the bottom, or in front of the action or to the side. It matters.

A fly presented under the school of bait or to the side is more quickly found. Not only does the fly stand out better, but it likely appears to be highly vulnerable prey—one that has become wounded or disoriented. If the blitz is moving, a fly presented slightly ahead of the action is a killer; a fly dropped behind the school is typically a dud.

Knowing where to cast the fly is only half the problem of presentation. Using the right retrieve speed is also important. As a general rule, a good starting point is a slow to moderate pace, moving the fly at roughly a foot every one to three seconds. If that doesn't work, try going slower, especially if the bite is in low light. Now the fly might be traveling a foot every five to ten seconds, and in the middle of the night, it might even be much slower. A fast to very fast retrieve, one where the fly travels more than a foot per second, is a last resort, but it can be important at times. In daylight, when bluefish strike short, a fly zipping by can be the best ticket. And there are moments when a fly on the fast track scores more consistently with false albacore.

DROPPER RIGS

In freshwater fly fishing, droppers have been around since I can remember, but in the salt, few fly rodders use them. Surf casters, on the other hand, have long reaped the rewards of casting two things at a time. Sometimes called a teaser rig, a typical combo for a surf caster might be a swimming plug on the end of the line, along with a smaller offering, usually a fly or a soft-plastic bait such as the Red Gill. If you wonder about the wisdom of serving up dual offerings, consider this: In 1981, Tony Stetzgo caught a world-record 73-pound striper on Cape Cod using a 6-inch dropper fly ahead of a live eel. By the way, the big bass picked the fly.

So why don't saltwater fly rodders use droppers? Nearly every fly rodder knows intuitively that droppers are not trouble-free. They're right; no question, droppers can be a pain. Still, I think few saltwater fly rodders understand why and where droppers can be a real help. There are actually several situations in which you might want to try using a dropper next time you're on the coast.

Often you'll be searching a large expanse of open water where there are no visible signs of activity. Faced with this, pick a searching pattern, something

DECEIVERS

Black & White Deceiver, tied by Mark Lewchik

Sand Eel Deceivers, tied by Bob Ververka

Large Black Deceiver, tied by the author

Large White Deceiver, tied by the author

Bucktail Deceiver, tied by Bob Popovics

Blue & White Deceiver on circle hook, tied by Mark Lewchik; Sparkling Deceiver, tied by Chris Windram

Small Deceiver, Baby Bunker Deceiver, both on circle hooks, tied by Mark Lewchik

Siliclone, tied by
Bob Popovics

Pogy, tied by
Bill Catherwood

Pop Lip, tied by
Bob Popovics

Razzle Dazzle
Herring, tied by
Mark Lewchik

Razzle Dazzle Eel,
tied by Mark
Lewchik

CREASE FLIES

Silverside Crease Flies, tied by Bob Veverka

Baby Bunker Crease Flies, tied by Mark Lewchik

Articulated Crease Flies, tied by John Timmermann

Yellow & Orange Crease Fly, Peacock & Chrome Crease Fly, tied by Capt. Joe Blados

Black & Chrome Crease Fly, Striped Crease Fly, tied by Capt. Joe Blados

Gartside Gurgler, tied
by Jack Gartside

Owens Silver Shiner
Popper, tied by
Brian Owens

Sand Eel Slider, tied
by the author

Chrome Slider, tied
by Mark Lewchik

Chrome Bob's
Banger, tied by
Bob Popovics

Ka Boom Boom
Popper, tied by
"Terp" Terpenning

Brian's Baby Bunker
Popper, tied by
Brian Owens

Chartreuse Bob's
Banger, tied by
Bob Popovics

Blue & Chrome
Slider, tied by
Mark Lewchik

Mark's Floating Worm, tied by Mark Lewchik; Windram's Cinder Worm, tied by Chris Windram

Presto Felt Worm Fly, tied by Phil Farnsworth; Eric's Cinder Worm, tied by Eric Peterson

Mark's EZ-Body Squid, tied by Mark Lewchik; Chris' Squid White, tied by Chris Windram

Sparkling Grass Shrimp, Chris' Squid Orange, both tied by Chris Windram

Mark's Soft Hackle Shrimp, tied by Mark Lewchik; Ultra Shrimp, tied by Bob Popovics

Pheasant Crab, tied by Jack Gartside; Mark's Floating Crab, tied by Mark Lewchik.

WEIGHTED FLIES

Weighted Deceiver,
Mark's Bunny Fly,
tied by Mark
Lewchik

Yellow & White
Clouser, Tan & White
Clouser, tied by Mark
Lewchik

White Cone Head
Jiggy, Yellow & White
Cone Head Jiggy, tied
by Bob Popovics

Black & White Jiggy,
Blue & White Jiggy,
tied by Bob Popovics

Chartreuse & White
Jiggy, Olive & White
Jiggy, tied by
Bob Popovics

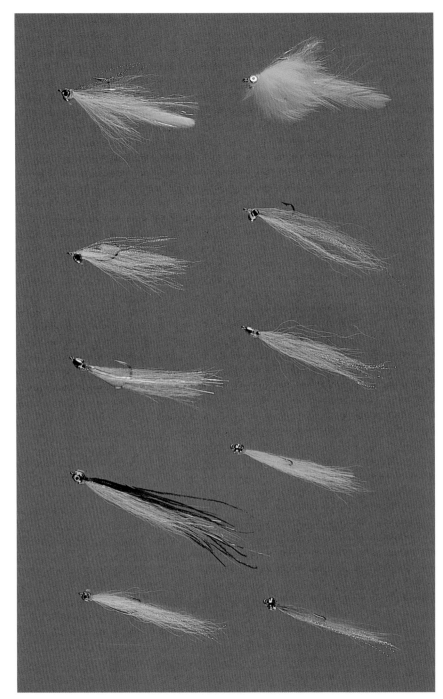

Fish Head Sand Eel, tied by Jack Gartside; Sparkling Sand Eel, tied by Chris Windram

Epoxy Sand Eel, tied by the author; Sand Eel, tied by Phil Farnsworth

Secret Soft Hackle Streamer, Soft Hackle Streamer, tied by Jack Gartside

Epoxy Minnow, tied by Chris Windram

Synthetic Sand Eel, tied by Bob Veverka; Baby Butterfish, tied by Mark Lewchik

Diet Candy
Silverside, Diet
Candy Bay Anchovy,
tied by Bob Popovics

Deep Candy, Surf
Candy Silverside,
tied by Bob Popovics

Lazer Tinker
Mackerel, Peanut
Bunker, tied by
Bob Veverka

Lazer Bay Anchovy,
Holographic
Silverside, both tied
by Bob Veverka

D.L's Glass Minnow,
tied by D.L.Goddard;
Hi-Tie Epoxy Baitfish,
tied by Chris
Windram

relatively large and easy for fish to find such as Kenney Abrames's Razzle Dazzle. This has worked well for me. Adding a second fly as a dropper should improve your odds of hooking up. After all, two flies should be easier for fish to find than one. Even if it gets you only one extra fish per trip, it's worth it.

Another advantage of searching with two flies is that you give the fish a choice. When covering open water, frequently it's difficult to identify what the fish are feeding on. By using two dissimilar flies, you can better cover the bases. For instance, try a 2/0 Lefty's Deceiver on the tippet and a slim #1 sand eel pattern as a dropper. As soon as the fish show a preference for one fly over the other, use that fly alone.

Many species of forage fish are plankton feeders, and plankton tends to concentrate in certain spots because of wind and tide. Thus it's possible to have two schools of bait feeding very close together. Here you might be able to identify the forage, but the question becomes which bait to imitate. With a dropper, you can match both.

When you use a single fly, in effect you are also deciding what part of the water column to fish. You pick a popper or slider to work the top, a streamer to work subsurface, or a weighted fly to work deeper. A dropper rig allows you to fish two levels at once. Using a sinking-tip line, you can have an unweighted dropper up near the fly line and a weighted fly on the end of a long tippet. A floating fly and a subsurface one make a useful combination. Think of it as an over-and-under rig. Striped bass love a popper, but at times they can be picky, swirling under the popper yet refusing to hit it. One solution is to tie a small fly, such as a streamer or a shrimp pattern, off the bend of the popper. The popper is still what attracts the bass, yet the dangling streamer may induce the fish to strike. Try it. I think you will like the results.

Eric Petersen, one of the best tiers in the Northeast, recently told me of a trick that worked well for him during a worm hatch. Use a floating line with a slider on the end of the tippet and a worm fly up the leader as a dropper. The slider is easy to see and allows you, even in very low light, to gauge where the worm fly is. By making adjustments in your presentation, you can position the worm fly in the exact zone where the fish are feeding most actively.

Problems

Using droppers also has its problems. A two-fly rig is harder to cast. The difficulty depends on the size of your flies, their bulk or wind resistance, the size of your rod, and your casting ability. You have to use a bit of common sense in selecting your rig. Here is a starting point: For an experienced caster, two sparsely dressed flies are not a problem to chuck on a 9-weight, especially if neither fly is larger than 1/0. A 10-weight makes things even easier.

Without a doubt, the single biggest problem with dropper rigs is that they tend to tangle. To minimize that problem, use a very stiff leader. If you use 12-pound-test tippets with a single fly, use 20-pound-test with two flies.

How you attach the dropper fly has a major effect on tangling, too. Many anglers dangle the dropper fly off the leader on a short stub of mono. One way to create this short stub is to leave one of the tag ends of a barrel knot untrimmed. While this dangling method does work, it tangles often, and it also makes a weak spot in the leader.

Here's a better method for rigging droppers: Take the fly that you want to use as a dropper, and bend the hook eye up at a 45-degree angle. With stainless steel hooks, the bending process is easily done with pliers, but carbon steel hooks are much harder and apt to snap if you go too fast. The leader is constructed in three sections: A 40-pound butt is barrel knotted to a 25- or 30-pound midsection with a surgeon's loop in the end. The tippet also has a surgeon's loop, and the two are connected loop to loop. Cut the surgeon's loop knot off the midsection, and slide the fly with the bent eye up the leader. Reform the surgeon's loop, and reattach the tippet. Now the dropper rides on the midsection. As you retrieve, the dropper slides back against the surgeon's loop, which is too large to pass through the eye. This is a relatively tangle-free rig, and it's very strong.

But no matter how you rig things, some tangles are inevitable, and therefore you should come prepared. Always carry spare leaders ready to roll. When a tangle arises, simply swap the old leader for a new one. Even when the existing leader looks fine, after a few fish, it's probably getting weak or ready to tangle. Change it before you get broken off or messed up. Also carry a conventional leader straightener (a piece of rubber inner tube), the type used by freshwater fly rodders. It's a help in straightening your leaders.

Two Fish at a Time

At times you may hook two fish on a cast. This sounds like a bonus, but it may end in a broken leader. Furthermore, two fish twisting on the end of your line can produce a nasty snarl. Therefore, droppers should be avoided wherever fish are numerous and aggressive. If you do get a double hookup, consider changing leaders unless both fish were very small.

Safety Tips

Droppers require you be to extra careful. When using a dropper rig, never forget that you have two hooks to contend with. It's imperative that both flies be barbless. Take your time when landing and releasing a fish, especially in the dark. If the fish is on the point fly, there is a hook dangling off the leader between you and the fish. If the fish is on the dropper, things are less problematic, but care is still in order. When using a dropper, I prefer to beach a fish if possible. Then I can put my rod down, turn on my light, and find both hooks before proceeding. Play it safe.

You also need to be careful when transporting a rod rigged with two flies. Anglers using a dropper rig for the first time tend to stick the point fly in the keeper or reel seat and then move off. But there's still a second fly up the rod someplace dancing around. If you take a rod rigged this way and stick it in the back of your car or in the roof rack, or even if you walk with it in your hand, the free hook is likely to eventually grab something or somebody. Thus you should cut the dropper off when transporting or storing the rod. It will save you a lot of grief.

BAY ANCHOVIES

Anchovies are some of the most numerous fish on earth, inhabiting tropical and temperate waters, both inshore and offshore. As such, they are an enormous biomass and play a critical role as forage for many fish and birds around the planet. Of the roughly 150 different species, two get a special tip of the hat from fly rodders along the Atlantic coast. They are the striped anchovy, found most often from the Chesapeake Bay southward, and the bay anchovy, found from Cape Cod to Florida.

When abundant, bay anchovies are a key ingredient in the fall fishing along the southern New England coast and at Montauk. And for that reason, fly rodders increasingly prepare to meet the challenge of fishing over this tiny, bite-size bait. As adults, bay anchovies are silvery fish that reach a maximum size of close to 4 inches, although 3-inch adults are far more common. It's the smaller and lesser-known juvenile, however, that's responsible for the excellent near-shore fall fishing in the Northeast. This is a very important distinction to make, since the young of the year is quite different from its parents in size and coloration.

The immature bay anchovy varies in length from location to location, and even from year to year. In some years, the ones I saw along the Rhode Island coast were up to $1^1/4$ inches, but in other years, some were closer to 2 inches. Such changes are likely the result of weather patterns and the ability of these fish to spawn over many months of the year.

These immature anchovies are pale and translucent, with a hint of yellow brown. A closer inspection reveals small, black dots along the perimeter of the body and out onto the fins. Contrasting with the subdued coloration of the body, the head and gut are opaque, and there may be a hint of a silver lateral line, especially as the juvenile gets bigger. The striped anchovy, the bay anchovy's cousin, is similar in appearance but has a very distinct silver lateral line and is considerably larger. Its size and stripe make it easy to confuse with the silversides.

While knowing the size and coloration of any baitfish is always helpful, knowing when and where to find them is even more essential. The baby anchovy bite occurs in my waters during a roughly six-week window each fall. That window first opens during September, as the immature bay anchovies start to stage around the mouths of the salt ponds on the Rhode Island coast. Usually a strong blow or a series of moon tides seems to trigger their arrival.

In these locations, they often form long lines, parading slowly back and forth along the length of a jetty wall within inches of the rocks. These streams of bait produce some exciting fishing for a wide range of predators, and it's usually at point-blank range. Because of the bait's diminutive size, some of its enemies are small as well, such as snapper blues. Three years ago, I caught two relatively rare fish, at least for my waters, working a school of bay anchovies: a banded rudderfish and a pilot fish. The sheer volume of bait makes these anchovies an attractive meal for much bigger predators too, including large bass and bluefish. They are also, at times, the fish du jour for bonito and false albacore.

Sometime between late September and early October, the anchovies leave the estuary mouths and start moving along the shore. During this journey, the slow-moving schools initially stay close to the beach, giving shore-based anglers a reason to smile. But nothing good lasts forever. By early November, these schools are usually well away from shore, headed to deeper water.

At close range, spotting these schools is not a difficult task. The little guys often swim on top in plain view, and you can easily see them in the curl of a wave when the light is right. From a distance, things get harder. Still, there are clues to look for. First, scout for birds. Cormorants regularly hound these schools, sometimes forming a line to herd the anchovies toward the beach. Once they have the school pinned in against the shore, they dive under for an attack. Also keep an eye on the color of the water. Bay anchovies are so numerous that they can make the water look a yellowish brown. And when things get really crammed together, such as in a blitz, I've seen them turn the water dark red.

At times, bay anchovies may be so abundant that they cover several miles of shorefront. This happens along the southwestern coast of Rhode Island because of the close proximity of several salt ponds. As a result, in October, there are times when stripers simultaneously blitz long stretches of shore in a single day. They drive the anchovies against the shore, right into the trough. This action usually peaks in early morning and again in late afternoon. During those periods, it often goes on for hours, and rarely does the action move a great deal once it gets under way.

Fishing over Bay Anchovies

Fish feeding on baby bay anchovies can be terrible finicky, and the volume and small size of the bait are to blame. One of the best solutions, at least in southern New England waters, is a small epoxy-type fly between 1 and 2 inches overall. This fly does an excellent job of imitating the natural. Farther south, where immature striped anchovies roam, a larger fly is needed.

Many of these epoxy patterns appear to spring from the original Pop Fleyes concept created by Bob Popovics. D. L. Goddard and Page Rogers have also created effective anchovy flies, as has Mark Lewchik. Still, as good as epoxy flies are, they not mandatory. Small silicone flies, such as the one tied by Capt. Johnny Glenn, Jim Slater's new Easy Prey, and Bob Veverka's Lazer Bay Anchovy are excellent choices. And an appropriate-size Deceiver can also be expected to take fish.

Baby bay anchovy flies can be constructed on size 1 or 2 hooks, although some anglers go down to size 4. All of these hooks are capable of holding on to your prize, but be careful about making an extremely lightweight fly. True, they are easy to cast, yet once in the water, they may be difficult to keep a tight line to, especially where there is turbulence. One solution is to use a

Bay anchovies are a small, but plentiful forage source along the coast.

larger-than-normal, heavy wire hook with a short shank. Live bait hooks are a good example. This keeps the body length the same but gives the fly a little additional weight, making it easier to control. Bob Popovics's Deep Candy takes an innovative approach, incorporating a beadhead to give the fly Clouserlike jigging action.

Regardless of how convincing your bay anchovy imitation is, expect there to be times when it doesn't seem to work. This frequently is the case when big stripers get a school of bay anchovies pinned down inside a tight bay, slough, or bowl. Here they seem to practically wallow in the bait, sucking them in by the pint. It's an incredible sight: backs, dorsal fins, and tails milling around and through the bait. Yet because the bass are targeting them by the mouthful rather than keying on individual fish, a single small fly easily goes unnoticed. And with the adrenaline pumping, some anglers will continue to cast the same offering, hoping their tiny imitation eventually finds a taker.

In such a situation, stop, take a deep breath, and rethink things. Frequently the solution lies in using a fly larger than the natural. For instance, something 50 percent bigger will stand out. Taking it one step further, an 8-inch blue and white Deceiver with prominent eyes has worked well for me.

It's not a question of simply throwing out the fly and pulling it back; there is a trick to it. Once you cast the fly into the battle zone, creep it back as slowly as possible, just fast enough to maintain tension on the line. Given the mayhem in front of you, this snail's pace may feel absurd, but it seems to greatly increase the fly's appeal. Likely with so much food in front of them, stripers have zero incentive to chase something zipped past their faces. But a big, slow-moving meal is another story, one much harder to resist. Still, it may pass in front of several fish before one decides to give it a chew. Even then, expect the strike to be relatively soft, so stay alert.

SAND EELS

Sand eels, more properly called sand lances, live both inshore and offshore along the Atlantic coast, with a range extending from North Carolina to the Canadian Maritimes. Throughout the region, they are essential members of our marine ecosystem, supplying a valuable forage base for fish and birds. They can grow to over 8 inches in length, but sand eels that large are rare. Most often you see them in the 2- to 4-inch range, although along the outer reaches of Cape Cod, sand eels to 5 or 6 inches are regularly seen. Unlike the wide-bodied baits

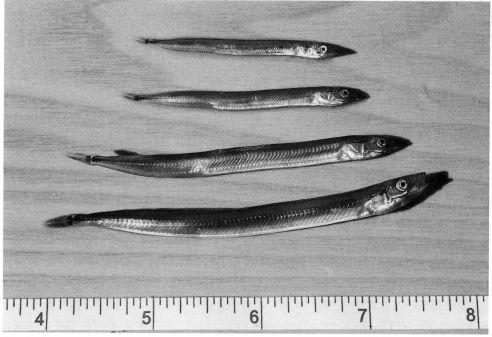

Sand eels are typically 2 to 4 inches long, but in some locations grow to 6 inches or more.

such as menhaden, these slender guys are a snap to imitate with a fly. Just lash a small clump of bucktail to a hook, and you're already most of the way there.

Like many marine fish, sand eels can change their coloration to match different habitats and thereby better camouflage themselves. Where the water is discolored by freshwater estuaries, such as you see in Long Island Sound, sand eels have darker backs, often leaning to brown or black. In clear ocean water, sand eels are considerably lighter, with backs of a pale mint green.

Coloration is not as critical as some fly tiers might think, however. When viewed from a distance underwater, the primary thing you see is the sand eel's silhouette—its size and shape—not its color. Second in importance is reflectivity. In all locations, sand eels have silvery sides. When schools are feeding near the surface during the day, these bright-plated flanks emit flashes of light as the fish twist and turn. Therefore, sand eel patterns intended to be used topside between dusk to dawn benefit from the addition of reflective materials.

The sand eels you see living along the beaches during the summer move offshore in late fall, where they spawn during early winter. The success of the spawn varies from year to year, and there is some evidence that water temperatures in December play a key role. Surviving adults and young of the year move back inshore in May and are often seen in the same locations where schools resided the prior year. At this time of year, sand eels are one of only a few forage fish available in any number.

Finding sand eels shouldn't be much of a problem. As a general rule, terns nest near sand eel populations. Consequently, any shoreline with a population of nesting terns is apt to have plenty of sand eels nearby. Coastal river mouths, salt ponds, inlets of all kinds, bays that face the prevailing wind, and warm-water releases from coastal power plants are also likely places to look. All of these spots hold plenty of plankton, the sand eel's primary food. Current tends to concentrate plankton, so sand eels often feed near rips, especially those formed where the exiting flow of an estuary funnels over a bar.

Though it's possible to find sand eels of varying lengths mixed together on the same beach, generally sand eels segregate by size. The biggest—those 4 inches and longer—typically inhabit exposed beaches or locations where currents are swift. Smaller sand eels—those 4 inches and under—are more likely to be found in sounds, bights, bays, and protected waters in general. These sheltered sites also hold young-of-the-year sand eels. These tiny creatures can be barely 1 to $1^{1}/_{2}$ inches in length.

Schooling is a defensive tactic that many baitfish employ to confuse preda-tors. Sand eels do it, but they also use another trick. When threatened, sand eels are capable of burying themselves up to 6 inches deep into soft sand. Not surprisingly, then, sand eels are found primarily over sand bottoms, although at times they can be found over soft mud and will swim through areas of mixed sand and rock.

Dusk and Dawn

Sand eels exhibit one of the most dependable diurnal patterns of any forage fish you'll come across. As the light begins to wane in late afternoon, sand eel schools begin to swim closer to shore in search of a place to bed down for the evening. Terns are quick to take advantage of this migration into shallow water, ceaselessly cruising the beach after the schools, occasionally diving for a mouthful.

If you walk one of these beaches, by all means follow the terns. Where they are busiest and most concentrated, so are the sand eels, and so will be the bass. When there are few terns aloft and the fishing is slow, I've even watched indi-vidual terns work the beach. Wherever a tern dives into the water, I move quickly and drop the fly as close as I can. Often I'm rewarded with a striper for my efforts.

When the bass get rolling, they push the sand eels to the surface, so expect to see swirls. Another sure sign is sand eels leaping for their lives. Most of the time, this bite is well within fly-casting range, and on occasion, the bass drive sand eels into the trough and the action is right at your feet. Nice.

In June, this action gets under way slowly around 5 or 6 P.M. and builds in intensity as the light lowers, with a flurry of action right at sunset. All told, there could be three hours of fishing. A brief lull follows, perhaps an hour or so, and then the fishing returns, building slowly into the night. The night bite can be fantastic, with bass throwing caution to the wind. On Lobsterville Beach, it's possible to hook and release five or more stripers before sunset, and then hook and release another thirty during the night.

Unlike the afternoon bite, dawn fishing is red hot but ever so brief. If you're lucky, it might last an hour or so, but it might only be twenty minutes at best. For that reason, the dawn bite requires you to plan carefully or risk miss-ing the fishing. Set your alarm so that you are in place and casting at least an hour before the scheduled sunrise; an hour and a half ahead is even better. The other alternative is to fish right through the entire night. My friends and I at times have fished from 6 P.M. to 6 A.M., twelve hours in the saddle. You'll be weary, but when the bass are big and numerous, it's worth the effort.

Expect things to get cooking with the first hint of light, what anglers call false dawn. This takes place while the sun is still fully hidden from view; all you see is a faint glow on the eastern horizon. Look for swirls and cast right to them. Work hard, for the fish often get fussier as the light rises. As soon as the sun has fully shown its face, the bait and the bass move. Instantly the game is over.

Fishing over Sand Eels

The usual approach when fishing over sand eels is to tie on a sand eel pattern that roughly matches in size the local bait. But if the sheer volume of sand eels is enormous, things can get difficult. In that situation, the key is often to throw something much bigger. I've had wonderful success chucking a 6-inch-long 3/0 white Deceiver. I like to use a very slow retrieve, although occasionally a faster pace works too. The bass pound the fly. I believe there are frequently squid feeding on the sand eels and that the large, white fly imitates a squid reasonably well. But for whatever reason, the bass love it.

When the schools are extraordinarily thick—so packed that they darken the water—you may see a tremendous number of stunned or dead sand eels lying about. Some may be moving weakly near the surface or simply hanging in the water column, and a great many may wash up along the beach. The first time I saw this phenomenon on the Vineyard, the sand eels were scattered along the water's edge for a mile or more at a stretch. You could stop anywhere and quickly pick up a dozen or more dead sand eels. The total kill surely was in the tens of thousands.

At first I thought a violent storm or a lightning strike must have been responsible, but it became clear that the cause was simply relentless attacks by terns and bass slamming into the schools. Given the sheer volume of bait and the fragile nature of sand eels, terns diving into a thick school of sand eels and bass blasting through the schools can wound a good many by their sheer force. The net result was stunned and wounded sand eels.

Sand eels were littered on the beach at the water's edge, where greedy gulls picked them up. Out in the water directly in front of me, dozens of injured sand eels swam weakly at the surface, their bodies rather stiff as they tried to propel themselves along. Later, I saw dead sand eels on the beach being picked up by a rising tide and then sucked back into the wash, where stripers could easily grab them. This helped me understand why stripers take a lone sand eel fly in the midst of thousands. If it barely moves and otherwise acts unlike the crowd around it, bass probably see it as dead or wounded—an easy meal. This is true with a subsurface fly as well as a floating pattern. A small foam slider dropped in the vicinity of feeding bass will sometimes work, even though it's dead in the water.

Typically, subsurface fly patterns in the 3- to 5-inch range do most of the work. Still, in some locations, small flies to match young-of-the-year-size sand eels are important. When fishing exposed ocean beaches such as one finds on the outer shores of Cape Cod, where there are big sand eels, longer flies upward of 6 or 7 inches may be useful. While long-shank hooks lend themselves perfectly for these flies, I tend to avoid using them, at least in stainless. Long-shank stainless steel hooks have a habit of opening up on big bass, especially if you play the fish hard, as you should do.

While most sand eel patterns are subsurface flies, few are ever weighted. Nevertheless, a weighted sand eel fly can be an important addition to your fly box, especially where currents are strong or striped bass are grubbing for sand eels on the bottom. You don't need anything special for this task; a sparsely tied Clouser Deep Minnow or a Popovics Jiggy does the job admirably. If you want a fly that more closely matches the bait, try Chris Windram's Deep Sparkling Sand Eel. Floating sand eel flies are effective at times, too; in fact, on calm nights, they can be killers. A floating fly line makes the best delivery rig. Applying fly floatant to the fly and the leader will keep the whole deal on top where it belongs.

These surface flies are in essence small sliders, and they can be quickly made in a variety of ways. Perhaps the fastest method is to cut a slot in a cylinder of foam and then superglue it to a hook. If you'd like a small tail, before attaching the foam, tie a sparse bit of bucktail to the rear of the hook shank. If you don't have any foam, make the body with spun deer hair or a piece of balsa wood. And the tail need not be bucktail. Synthetic hair or hackle works too.

Whether or not you use a floating fly, the retrieve speed must be at a snail's crawl. Start it immediately after the cast, as some fish hit almost as soon as the fly lands. The only exception to this slow pace is where you find current. Here you can let the fly swing on a tight line, and then retrieve it back. You can also try dead drifting the fly on a short line. It's challenging, but it does work.

Larger sliders worked right in the film can be deadly, too. In fact, I never fish these bites without a couple in my fly box. These babies are in excess of 4 inches long and have consistently proven themselves over the years, especially on the bigger bass. This type of fly can be made in several different ways, depending on what material is handy. These sliders also require a slow retrieve.

SILVERSIDES

Along with sand eels and bay anchovies, Atlantic silversides are one of the most common forage fish along the coast. They inhabit a wide range of different habitats, including salt ponds, inlets, sandy beaches, rocky beaches, and the lower reaches of coastal rivers. They are called spearing or sperling on some parts of the coast and are referred to as glass minnows as well.

The silversides' most distinguishing feature—and the one from which it gets its name—is a wide silver stripe running down the midline of the body. Otherwise, the silversides is translucent for the most part, lacking any strong markings or coloration, although the body may take on a yellow or perhaps olive green tinge, particularly on older, larger fish.

In overall shape, the silversides is more robust than the sand eel, and it's a faster swimmer to boot. Silversides are rarely seen in schools as large as those of the sand eel. They're more apt to be found by the dozens rather than the thousands that typically make up a sand eel school. At night, a flashlight beam passed over a school of silversides frequently causes them to jump into the light.

Like sand eels, silversides migrate offshore in cold weather and then return in the spring. The returning fish are small in number but capable of reproducing several times during the warmer months. Consequently, their numbers are often low in June but jump quickly by late summer to early fall.

Silversides grow to about half a foot in length but are more commonly between 2 and 4 inches. It's typical for many different sizes to mix together in the same location. Hence, the fish feeding on silversides are rarely fussy about size.

Fishing over Silversides
Where silversides are the central component of the forage base, the fishing is usually not terribly difficult. A 1/0 Lefty's Deceiver constructed in olive over white is a good match. Epoxy flies, however, more closely mimic the

Atlantic silversides are very common near-shore baitfish. They can reach 5 inches.

translucent look of this baitfish and are especially effective where bonito and false albacore are the main target.

MENHADEN

During my seasons in the salt, no forage fish has had a larger impact on the quality of the fishing than has the menhaden. Simply put, in years when menhaden are abundant in an area, the fishing is apt to be excellent. In years when menhaden are not present, the fishing suffers for it.

The Atlantic menhaden is a member of the herring family that moves seasonally along nearly the entire Atlantic coast from Nova Scotia to southeastern Florida. Commonly called bunker or pogy, adult menhaden run close to a foot in length, although they can reach a maximum size of 18 or 20 inches and ten years of age. Seen from the side, they have broad, paddle-shaped flanks similar to those of their sportier cousin the shad. Expect a foot-long bunker to be about 4 inches from belly to back. It's not the easiest thing to match with a fly, as many a coastal veteran will attest.

Menhaden have bright, silvery sides, although in murky water, they take on a bronze sheen. The back is dark, varying from a rich blue to green or even brown, again depending on location. Behind the gill plate and above the midline is a single large, dark spot characteristic of many members of the herring family. In addition, you're apt to see a group of smaller dots loosely arranged through the center of the fish below the dorsal fin. The menhaden can be separated from other herrings by two characteristics. First, it has a very large head, taking up nearly one-third of the total body length. By comparison, the head of an alewife or shad is only one-fourth to one-fifth of its length. Second, the dorsal fin, unlike in other herring, starts directly over the ventral fin.

In a school of menhaden, the members are all pretty much the same size. This is true of baby bunker, also known as peanut bunker, as well. But menhaden spawn several times a year, and therefore there can be several different sizes of juvenile menhaden living in the same area, especially by late fall. There might be schools of 3- or 4-inch peanuts and, farther up inside protected waters, schools of 1-inch peanuts.

Menhaden spend considerable time near shore, and they draw game fish within casting range, including bass and bluefish, which follow schools of menhaden. And a large school of menhaden is usually easy to spot on the surface.

Menhaden move a considerable distance along the Atlantic coast each year. Northern waters, from Long Island Sound to the Gulf of Maine, are cool

Adult menhaden can reach 18 inches or more, but most are closer to a foot.

enough that only the older, larger adults are willing to migrate into those waters. Generally speaking, these would be adults age three or four on up. Even in years when adult menhaden populations are low in these northern waters, large numbers of juveniles may appear. These young of the year are the result of successful spawning. When environmental conditions are right, even a small number of adults can result in a huge number of offspring. But when conditions are wrong, large numbers of spawners may not succeed in producing a good year class.

As the storms of late winter subside along the south Atlantic coast, menhaden regroup and begin moving rapidly northward from their winter grounds south of Cape Hatteras. Schools are made up of individuals of similar size, a pattern that holds true throughout the season. By April, they have reached southern New England, moving into the quiet bays and harbors of Long Island Sound. By mid-May, some menhaden have found their way up into Massachusetts Bay, and by June, others have reached the Gulf of Maine.

The fall return migration begins in the Gulf of Maine in September. Many years, the schools travel along the Rhode Island and Connecticut coast

Juvenile menhaden are often called peanut or baby bunker. By fall most of the juveniles are 3 to 4 inches long.

sometime between late October and mid-November, depending on the prevailing weather. The exact schedule varies with weather, but overall, both the northward and southward migrations are remarkably similar to the annual movements of striped bass. I've never seen menhaden after the water temperature drops below 50 degrees. As they travel southward, they are constantly hounded, especially by striped bass and blues. Sometimes these processions travel at the water's edge, causing unforgettable blitzes right at your feet.

Given their size, adult menhaden are difficult for fly rodders to match. Peanut bunker, on the hand, are fairly easy. They are about 3 to 4 inches long by autumn, not a difficult size to imitate. Even their wide profile is manageable.

Thick schools of peanut bunker draw plenty of predators. And when those predators blast through the school, the feeding frenzy can be wild. But when peanut bunker are extremely numerous, it may be quite difficult to persuade fish to take your imitation. Surprisingly, you can cast the fly right into the melee and bring it back untouched. In such cases, your fly is simply lost in the crowd.

Rather than casting directly into the blitz, try working the outside edges of the school. This often works. If the blitz appears to be moving, however, avoid casting behind the school. Instead, try to get ahead of it or to one side. If working the edges of the school does not quickly pay off, switch to one of two strategies: Either go directly over the top of the school with a popper or a slider, or go under the school with a fast-sinking line and perhaps a weighted fly.

Going under the school is apt to produce the better bass, but the surface strategy is far more fun, as you get to see the fish chase and blast the fly. If the predators are school stripers, some cartwheel across the top in their pursuit of the fly. If the bass are less than 24 inches, they may be difficult to hook and hold on a standard 2/0 popper, so a few small poppers in your box can be very valuable.

While Atlantic menhaden are prolific, able to spawn someplace along the coast nearly every month of the year, their abundance varies from year to year. Stocks reached record size in the late 1950s but dropped suddenly thereafter and have never totally recovered. Still, bunker can be found in good quantity. When and where they are abundant, fishing is excellent. So direct seems this connection that commercial and recreational anglers have occasionally been at loggerheads over the netting of menhaden. A couple summers ago, the Maine chapter of the Coastal Conservation Association had to handle one such situation. And a similar issue is ongoing in Narragansett Bay. The problem arises when commercial fisherman net bunker in areas heavily used by sportfisher-men. Once the bait is removed, rod-and-reel angling can come to a screeching halt. Then tempers flare.

Fishing over Adult Menhaden

Although adult menhaden are occasionally seen in open water, they seem most at home in bays, coves, and especially the lower ends of estuaries. Here in these nutrient-rich waters, menhaden form large, tightly packed schools, often swimming near the surface feeding on their sole food: plankton. On calm days, you can locate a school from a considerable distance by the splashy surface dis-turbance they create. During these warm months, menhaden may stay for weeks or even months in the same general area, although the passage of a front or several days of high wind momentarily sends them deep.

When menhaden are under attack, the ruckus is hard to miss; swirls and crashes abound. Things can get so hot that menhaden actually jump on the beach to avoid being eaten. Even when the action is deep and away from shore, the surface of the water marks the slaughter. Oil released from the bunker as they are consumed rises to the top, forming slicks. On a clear day, these glassy patches of water are visible for quite a distance.

Most schools of menhaden appear to be totally unmolested. They'll feed quietly as if without a care in the world. Don't be fooled. More than half the time, predators are close by. So no matter how tranquil things look, work the area intently. Casting into the middle of the bait is counterproductive, as your fly will be largely hidden from view. Instead, always work along the edges of the school. If the water is 10 feet or deeper, also get a fly underneath. Pay spe-cial attention to any school of menhaden that steadily moves. This often indi-cates that one or more large predators are pushing the school. Big bass are usually the culprits. They will silently follow menhaden for a considerable dis-tance, waiting for the right opportunity.

Fish feeding on adult bunker are usually 10 pounds or better, but rarely are they easy to fool. For one thing, the common garden-variety 3- or 4-inch streamer, so effective in most surf situations, goes largely ignored. This produces some frus-trating moments, particularly when you're surrounded by feeding fish. Jumbo flies are in part the answer, but even the biggest fly does not guarantee instant success. Some tiers have developed menhaden flies over 10 inches in length in order to match the natural more closely. They work, but flies of 6 or 7 inches, such as large Razzle Dazzles, are nearly as effective and more practical.

Bait fishermen use an extremely effective technique that involves casting out a weighted treble and drawing it rapidly through a school of menhaden. When a bunker is snagged, it immediately starts to struggle, broadcasting its vulnerability. Any striped bass or bluefish in the vicinity quickly homes in on this one fish, disregarding the rest of the school. Likewise, flies that disturb the water around them are often better producers. For that reason, many experienced saltwater fly rodders like to use large poppers or sliders when working near adult menhaden.

Conventional, 4-inch-long, 2/0 saltwater poppers, such as Bob's Banger by Bob Popovics, do work. But jumbo poppers, while the devil to cast, are often better at attracting attention. This is particularly the case with the final push of big blues each fall. With water temperatures low, these guys are noticeably more sluggish, and only a banquet passing by lights their fuse. In early November, I've used 7-inch-long poppers suitable for sailfish. You need a 12-weight to chuck them, and even then you can't throw them far, but frequently you don't have to. Extralong sliders, sometimes called megasliders, do the same thing. They push water and throw a wide wake. Seen from underneath, they make a long, thin silhouette that closely resembles a menhaden moving overhead. Believe me, they work.

Fishing over Baby Bunker

Though adult menhaden create some great fishing opportunities, in the fall, young-of-the-year menhaden are an even better bet. They attract just as many fish yet are much easier to match with a fly. In the Northeast, these juveniles are the result of an offshore spawn that takes place mainly in late spring and early summer. The larvae depend on onshore winds and currents to push them into the quiet estuaries critical for early growth. By late summer, baby menhaden can be found feasting in the coastal rivers and salt ponds from Cape Cod southward. These young of the year can be anywhere from 2 to 7 inches long, depending on local conditions. You can expect baby bunker along the Connecticut and Rhode Island coast to be 3 inches or better by mid-September. A month later, they grow another full inch. Therefore, it makes sense to carry increasingly longer flies as the season progresses.

As the summer wanes, young-of-the-year bunker begin dropping down to open water. In southern New England, this begins around the time of the first frost, generally in early October, as water temperatures fall through the middle sixties, although the exact timing fluctuates from year to year. Upon entering the ocean, they travel in dense schools, often close to the water's edge. Everything from bass to bonito show up to feast on these bite-size bunker, guaranteeing superb fall fly fishing. Look for these small menhaden near inlets, points of land, rips, along breakwaters, and wherever plankton accumulates due to wind and tide.

Just about any 3- or 4-inch white or silver streamer works, but a wide-profile fly gets the most attention. Mark Lewchik's Baby Bunker is a fine fly for that reason, as is Bob Popovics's Inner-Flash Baby Bunker. And one of the finest flies to come along in many years is Capt. Joe Blados's Crease Fly. It's a killer. While these schools are frequently near the top, they do not create the large surface disturbance of their adult kin. Instead, they only dimple the water as they feed. Still, finding these schools is usually easy, because large numbers of birds such as gulls, cormorants, and loons follow these youngsters along the shore.

MULLET

Mullet. The word alone can make anglers do some heavy breathing. After all, when schools of mullet move along the Atlantic coast, their presence in the surf ignites some of the finest fishing of all.

Mullet are a significant forage base along the Atlantic coast, especially from New Jersey southward. There are two species of concern, the striped mullet and the white mullet, but they are similar enough for fly rodders to deal with them as one. In the south, these mullet grow big, upward of 2 feet or more in length, but the farther north you go, the smaller they become. Along the southern shore of Long Island, mullet max out around a foot; in Long Island Sound, 8 inches is a giant, and most are 5 inches or well under.

These mullet have bright silvery sides and dark backs that tend toward dark olive or black. They are a robust prey—much studier looking than a silversides or a sand eel—with a round, cigar-shaped body. Further distinguishing them from the silversides, mullet are heavily scaled and lack the single broad, silver lateral line. Mullet have forked tails and appear to be powerful swimmers. They are capable of leaping out of the water when attacked, hence the nickname jumping mullet.

In early fall, they stack up in the breachways of Rhode Island and occasionally in Long Island Sound, especially near the warm-water release of power

Mullet are a very important baitfish along the coast, especially in the fall. This one is 5 inches, but they can grow much larger, especially in the southern part of their range.

plants. These schools are not huge, perhaps two hundred or more fish, but that's only because this is at the northern extent of their range. Farther south, the schools can be enormous.

The key with mullet everywhere is to determine when the schools leave protected water. The mullet in the salt ponds of southwestern Rhode Island move to the coast sometime in late September. The exact timing of the run is typically between the last moon of September and the first frost, which in this region occurs around October 10. Warm stable weather tends to delay the run, while strong north winds spur the mullet to move.

Mullet are meaty, and your fly should echo that. Bulky streamers, such as Bob Popovics's Siliclone, are a good match. Given the chrome sides of a mullet, flash would be helpful, too. Retrieve speed can be moderate to fast, given that the mullet is a strong swimmer. When the schools are thick at the surface, try working your fly underneath on a fast-sinking line.

CRAB HATCHES

In Long Island Sound, crab hatches occur when water temperatures are near their seasonal high, which is from August to September. These clouds of baby crabs are most often found near estuaries or immediately outside bays and coves. The hatches seem to be primarily visible only on an ebbing current. The individual members are loosely grouped together by the thousands, just under the surface to 2 feet or more below the surface. They struggle to swim but are drawn along with the tide. The crabs I have seen are dark brown to black on top and pale white underneath. In your hand, they move about vigorously. That coupled with their swimming motion leads me to believe they are either immature blue crabs or lady crabs, likely the former.

It's usually difficult to see a crab hatch, even in broad daylight. For one thing, it's unlikely to attract gulls the way a school of baitfish near the surface would. The crabs are tiny and drab colored. From tip to tip, the shell might be roughly $^1/_8$ inch wide, and the entire crab with legs outspread would fit inside a circle of $^5/_8$ inch in diameter. And crabs drift silently with the tide. They do not jump, flash sunlight, or cause nervous water. So unless you're deliberately looking for a crab hatch, you may never notice one. In fact, you may have already been near one and never even known it.

I've seen striped bass feeding in a crab hatch, and I have no doubt bluefish—including the young of the year—do too. What's more, I'm fairly certain that crab hatches are in large part responsible for the slow rolling behavior of bonito and false albacore.

During late-summer crab hatches in southern New England, thousands of these tiny creatures drift in clouds just below the surface.

When any of these game fish feed on the juvenile crabs, you can't expect to see the kind of surface eruptions caused when they hunt down a school of baitfish. Rather, all you generally see are fish feeding in an unhurried manner near the surface, gentle swirls, and a few backs and tails breaking the surface. Such behavior, particularly in late summer or early fall, should prompt you to look into the water for signs of a crab hatch.

In all cases, it's a very fussy bite, and there is currently no proven fly pattern or presentation tactic to use in these situations. The fish regularly refuse streamers of all kinds, although bass feeding in a crab hatch may whack a popper. The best solution might be a small crab fly dead drifted, hanging under a strike indicator.

SQUID

Squid are both predators and prey. They eat a wide range of small fish, from young cod and mackerel offshore to silversides and sand eels and immature herring near shore. Their fondness for these baits brings them into direct contact with other, larger predators that are in the same area.

In southern New England, squid begin to appear in late April and early May. Many of Connecticut's harbors and bays have runs. The same holds true

Striped bass and bluefish love to eat squid. Here, a small blue regurgitates one.

in Rhode Island, where squid runs are expected by anglers in the lower end of Narragansett Bay. From Watch Hill Reef to Woods Hole, and over to the island of Martha's Vineyard, it's June when the squid are in.

In the spring, both bluefish and striped bass feed upon adult squid. Even a relatively small 6-pound blue can swallow a foot-long squid. Bass love squid. I often rely on a large white Deceiver to imitate them, but if you want to more closely match squid there are some good patterns around. Bob Ververka's 3-D Shimmering Squid is one. Mark Lewchik's E-Z Body Squid and Chris Windram's Squid fly are two others. Cast out a large, white streamer, and let it sink slowly. A variety of retrieves seem to work, from high-speed dashes to long pulls with pauses in between to ones at a snail's pace. If you see swirling bass, however, cast the fly directly to them, let it sink for a second, then retrieve at a fairly high rate. It often results in a vicious strike.

WORM HATCHES

Perhaps the most intriguing forage item on the entire coast is the lowly annelid—the marine worm. When I started out in the salt, I spent a lot of time trying to figure out how to predict when good fishing would take place. That has never proven to be an easy task, but forecasting worm hatches seemed to be an exception. The ones I fished proved to be so reliable that it was possible to pinpoint the date of a hatch a year in advance, based on the time of the new moon. And like clockwork, striped bass would appear out of nowhere to feast on this soft flesh. Given that level of predictability, I made the mistake of assuming that worm hatches in neighboring areas along the southern New England coast followed the same pattern. Turned out I was wrong.

The big worms that tackle shops box up as bait are not the same worms. That worm, *Nereis virens*, seems to spawn during the colder months, at least in southern New England, when there are no striped bass around. Too bad.

The worms that do spawn in May and June, and sometimes into July and August, are related to *N. virens* but are considerably smaller. These worms are marine annelids of the genus *Nereis*, although pinpointing the exact species is not easy. (For further reading, see George Roberts, Jr., *Salt Water Naturals*, Ragged Mountain Press, 1994.) And that's likely part of the problem; there may be more than one species involved, with different spawning behaviors.

Worm hatches in southern New England often take place in the spring of the year. The worms in this photo are 1 to 2 inches long.

To simplify matters, I think of worm hatches as coming in three kinds: those in tidal creeks, those in salt ponds, and those you cannot fully predict. At the same time, I realize that in the seasons ahead, new places may bring further information to light. So plan on using what I say here as a guide only, and expect that the worm hatches in your area could be significantly different. You need to become familiar with the hatches on your own waters.

Hatches in Tidal Creeks

Many, if not most, worm hatches take place at the lower ends of tidal creeks. Not every creek has a worm hatch, but those with a bottom of mud and broken shells are prime candidates. Where hatches occur, they are closely linked to the period around the new and full moon. The new moon is generally better, although some creeks produce on both. The initial hatch of the season happens as early as May, especially if temperatures have been above normal. Expect additional hatches in the same creek on the subsequent moons of June, July, and August. Usually the first couple hatches of the year are the strongest. The size and frequency of the hatch in any location may vary widely from year to year.

Typically, the hatch kicks off as high tide crests in darkness and continues for the entire six hours of the ebb. Along the Connecticut coast on a new or full moon, this roughly translates into a midnight to dawn bite. And this is not a one-night stand. Expect the fishing to boot up a night or two before the moon and last a night or two after.

At the top of the tide, the worms emerge from the bottom farther up the creek. Then, as the current ebbs, the worms are drawn downstream toward open water. Striped bass will ascend to meet them, but in many cases, these creeks are too shallow to permit stripers far upstream. Therefore, most fishing can be found in the deeper parts of the channel at the creek mouth. It's common for one side of the mouth to have a faster current, and consequently the better fishing. Regardless of which side you fish, be sure to thoroughly cover any spot where the current flows over a deep hole. The biggest bass are apt to reside there.

As the tide continues to lower, the worm and the fish drop back farther outside the mouth to the final lanes of fast current. So it's conceivable that you might begin fishing up inside a creek at the crest of the tide and finish up six hours later 100 or more yards outside the mouth.

Since the action is connected to moving water, you must always figure into your plans the difference between the time of tide and the time of current. If you're fishing a small tidal creek, there may be hardly any difference. On a larger creek or river, however, it's another story. Here the tide may flow upstream for one or more hours after the scheduled time of high tide. Thus the ebbing current may not start until one to three hours after the scheduled time of high tide. Plan accordingly.

Hatches in Salt Ponds

In some salt ponds, the timing of the hatch is similar to that in tidal creeks, coming off in low light at the crest of high tide. It could occur on the full or new moon, although the latter is more common. In other salt ponds, however, some hatches occur in broad daylight, often during early afternoon, and then tapering down toward dusk. These daylight hatches can be found in the larger salt ponds along the Rhode Island coast, as well as in the sounds of North Carolina. My guess is that these daytime hatches involve a slightly different worm, but it's only a guess.

Once under way, the daytime hatches may repeat every day for two or more weeks, although their exact location is apt to move daily. In Rhode Island they begin in mid-May. In North Carolina they can occur in April and May. Unlike the nighttime hatches, which repeat several times a year, these daytime hatches are often a one-shot deal. Once they're over, they're done for the year. In Rhode Island the water temperature in the ponds is in the low to mid-sixties during the hatch. This is borderline for really good striper fishing. Sixty is fine, but anything over 65 or approaching 70 degrees seems to send big bass scrambling for cooler climes.

At least 60-degree water seems to be necessary for the hatch to start. Consequently, you should look toward the shallow areas in the back of the pond to host the initial few days of action, since they are the first to warm. The hatch seems to wax and wane daily, with warm, bright weather producing the better action. Each day, things kick off around 2:30 P.M. and then slowly build. Since both gulls and mallard ducks enjoy the worms, be on the lookout for spots where these birds congregate.

During the initial weeks of the hatch, look for the worms tight to the shorelines, often within a foot of land. Likely there are worms living in the bottom throughout the pond, but the shallows are the first places to sufficiently warm, and hence the first to have activity. Usually the action starts in mid- to late afternoon and continues until dark. A flooding tide that occurs after noon is a problem, since the incoming water chills things down somewhat. This can result in a weak hatch or none at all.

Gradually, as the weeks pass, the hatch along the edges of the pond wanes, but don't give up. Slowly but surely, the deeper areas are reaching the required warmth, and there will be hatches in those locations too. When this happens, the action on a given day begins in the deeper, center portions of the pond. At first, the worms stay deep, and so you don't see busting bass. But gradually the worms come nearer to the top, and then swirling bass can be seen. As the sun lowers, the worms slowly move closer to the shore. Soon the cruising bass are evident. As darkness approaches, the worms cover the water, particularly in coves, where bass feed on them with soft, slow rises—much like the sipping of trout during a spinner fall. By nightfall, things are quiet.

Fishing over a Worm Hatch

Stripers feeding in any type of worm hatch can be pretty picky eaters. The right fly is a real help, but no matter what's on the end of the line, presentation is equally important. As a rule, a worm fly should be retrieved very slowly or dead drifted if possible. Yes, the worms can swim, but they rarely get up much speed, and at times they seem to slowly circle in an area. Thus it's difficult to match their motion with a fly. You'll see this swimming behavior most often in areas without current, such as the bays of a large salt pond. A slow, steady retrieve is about as good as you can do and will draw its fair share of strikes.

In these salt pond situations, you frequently face cruising fish gulping worms in still water. Where there is sufficient light, you can cast directly in the path of a feeding fish. A floating line is very effective. You may also want to put floatant on the leader and the fly to help keep your offering right on top. A strike indicator may work here, too. It will allow you to cast a fly out to feeding fish and simply wait for one to find it.

Where you have current, it's a different game. The worm hatch in a tidal creek is often fished best at the creek mouth, where it joins the salt. Here there are swift currents during the ebb. The worms are weak swimmers, and once caught in the current, they more or less drift straight out with the current. In this situation, you can either dead drift a worm fly or present it wet-fly style— down and across. To dead drift a fly, try casting upcurrent and stripping back at the speed of the water. Or you can use a floating line, cast across current and mended. Another useful trick with a floating line is to suspend a worm fly under a strike indicator. Cut your indicator from a block of foam. Make it large enough that so you can spot it in low light and fat enough that it does not resemble a worm. And it should not be red.

The overwhelming majority of the worms you see seem to be males. They are short—1 to maybe 3 inches—and vary in color from brick red to pink, often tipped on one end in black. Most flies are made to mimic these worms. Occasionally in the salt ponds, however, I've seen a big solo female slowly hovering about, looking for her male harem. The females are considerably larger, 4 inches and up, and in the water are paler in color, ranging from a sickly milk white to a weak yellow or green. Their presence probably explains why a larger dead-drifted fly sometimes works so well.

In any case, worm flies are usually constructed of a soft material such as marabou or fabric. There are plenty of such patterns around, but the easiest fly to tie is Phil Farnsworth's Presto Felt fly. Most of the time, you want an unweighted fly or, better yet, one that floats. Here, foam or deer hair comes into play. Eric Peterson's Cinder Worm is an excellent deer-hair fly. Still, a sinking fly can be useful when fish are holding deep. When using a weighted fly, try lifting the rod tip toward the end of the retrieve so the fly rises to the top. Now and then, this provokes a strike.

At times, none of these things seem to work. When this happens, go against the grain. Cut the worm fly off, and try something totally different. A huge streamer fly, for instance, may turn the tide. Cast it out, and move it slowly through the hatch. The idea here is to imitate a fish feeding on the worms. Sometimes the largest bass in the bunch will see this tempting hulk as just the right thing to round out its meal.

With the majority of coastal migratory stock between 20 and 26 inches, it should come as no surprise that bass you catch in worm hatches today tend to be in that size range. But this was not true years ago, nor is it true today in all locations. Some places still offer a shot at big bass, 20 pounds or better. In some situations, the bigger bass seem to skip over a worm hatch. This happens where thick schools of meatier forage exist nearby. The presence of a large school of herring or sand eels, for example, may draw off the bigger striped bass, leaving only the small schoolies to show for the worms.

As I discovered one night out in front of the Connecticut River, there are unpredictable times and places where worm hatches come off sporadically during the spring and summer. These hatches may be so sparse as to largely go unseen, but their presence can affect your fishing. The bottom line here is this: It pays to carry a few worm flies whenever you go afield during the warmer months. If you run into fussy fish, those small, red flies may well prove to be powerful medicine.

CHAPTER SEVEN

Fishing the Migrations

On the opposite side of the channel, a northern harrier glided over the marsh grass, the white spot on its rump stark in the October sun. From its dark brown coloration, I figured it be to a female. Slowly she headed upwind, an effortless journey on long, still, outstretched wings. Pushed down from the north country by the ebbing of summer, she was a visitor on the Rhode Island coast, migrating through with the cycle of the seasons—a sure indication that winter was not far off.

Around me, the salt marsh displayed further signs of the time of year. With the coming of the first frost, the tall grass had begun to gray, and in the gusty breeze, it now rattled thin and hollow. At the surface of the inlet, schools of silversides, juvenile menhaden, and mullet herded in the current—walls of living silver riding a turquoise tide. Like the harrier, these tiny fish were on the move. To reach their wintering grounds, however, they had to run a gauntlet. For nearby in the shadows, striped bass and bonito awaited, looking to fuel up for their own migratory trail.

The annual spring and fall migration of fish along the Atlantic coast is a fascinating spectacle. And, as any angler experienced in the ways of the brine knows, it is around these migrations that the finest fishing of the year revolves. So great is the intensity that during these two periods, most anglers consistently catch more and larger fish than they do during the rest of the year. Little wonder, then, that coastal anglers eagerly wait for these runs. They are the best of times.

Perhaps the first thing that comes to the mind of an angler is which time of year is best for the species he or she prefers. The season for bonito and false albacore is so short that you simply fish for them while they're here. With weakfish, no doubt the finest fishing occurs in the spring. Granted, records show good September runs in southern New England and elsewhere, but even in those golden years for weaks, the spring was king. With bluefish, however, though spring can light a fire in your eyes, autumn is where the real action is. With striped bass, the jury is out. In some locations, it's the spring run that grabs the applause, whereas in other areas, fall is better by far.

Regardless of species, in order to take full advantage of seasonal movements of game fish, you need to know when spring fishing starts in your area, and what species to expect. You also need to know what happens to the fishing as summer rolls around. And finally, you need to know when late-season fishing usually begins and ends for the various species.

To help out, at the end of this chapter is a coastal planner that gives some general shape to the seasonal movements along the Atlantic of striped bass, bluefish, weakfish, bonito, and false albacore. This should get you into the ball-park, but realize that this planner is not definitive. Rather, it is a starting point, one that must be augmented with local knowledge such as can be obtained from tackle shops, guides, veteran anglers, or experience.

Environmental Factors
These seasonal migrations appear to have no sole trigger, but rather to be controlled by the interplay of several environmental factors, including day length, water temperature, weather, tides, and the availability of forage. That there should be more than one factor involved is understandable when you consider that fish migrate for more than one reason. They migrate to spawn, to feed, and to avoid threatening water temperatures. Moreover, the issues affecting any species' survival are multifaceted, and to base a migration on a single element would therefore be risky.

Two of the environmental factors, day length and tides, are chronologically fixed and can be predicted long in advance. The others factors, however, vary from year to year. So overall, game fish migrations are built around both static and dynamic elements, and as result, you should expect these migrations to be predictable to a degree, but never totally.

Each year's fishing is slightly different, its own special vintage; any experienced saltwater fly rodder will tell you so. The action may begin early, or on time, or be delayed for several weeks. And variations occur as well at the other end of the season. The migration of a particular species may build smoothly over the course of weeks or be a series of starts and stops, retreating and advancing from day to day, from week to week.

MAKING A MIGRATION LOG

An angler who has some knowledge of how the various environmental factors influence the migration and feeding behavior of game fish is better prepared to take advantage of angling opportunities. So with that in mind, I strongly recommend that you make an annual log for your own home waters. In order for this log to be effective, you must keep it up for at least five years. Now that requires some work—no question. But if you're willing to do it, this log should make you a more successful angler, as well as one of the most knowledgeable people in your area.

Enter into your log the day or week when various species of game fish show up in your area. Your own experiences on the water are best, but information from friends, tackle shops, and local fishing journals will do. Also record the dates when the fishing was hottest for each species and when that fishing ended for the year.

With this basic information alone, over the course of several seasons, you'll build a useful log. Still, it can be greatly fine-tuned if you record other elements as well. To get some idea of the effect daylight has, mark the following dates in your log: March 21, June 21, September 23, and December 21. These are the dates of the vernal equinox, the summer solstice, the autumnal equinox, and the winter solstice.

Day Length

Nothing chronicles the time of year more accurately than day length. Wildlife innately understands that, as do our own bodies. As the light level increases, we all get busier. Striped bass shake off their winter stupor and begin heading to spawning grounds as we pass through the vernal equinox. And they quickly end their migratory push northward into New England waters as we hit the summer solstice. At that same time, I believe some bonito typically are arriving in offshore New England waters to spawn. About a month later, they move inshore to feed through the long days of summer. As the autumnal equinox approaches, the fall migration of bass, bluefish, bonito, and false albacore begins in southern New England. They'll all eat hearty for a month or more, but one by one they will be on the road long before the winter solstice.

Water Temperature

Water temperature is perhaps the single strongest environmental stimulus for fish. And therefore it plays a major role in their migratory and feeding behavior. Because the sun provides the warmth, water temperatures are greatly affected by day length. Water temperature is not, however, controlled by season alone; it's also affected by weather. So there is no guarantee that the water temperatures on October 1 this year will be the same on October 1 next year. Such variations are likely one of the key reasons why migrations are subtly different from year to year.

In your log, track weekly water temperatures as well as you can. Newspapers, local weather reports, and tackle shops may be useful in this regard. Try to determine the approximate temperature at which various species of game fish arrive and depart in your locale, and the temperatures at which fishing was best. Also record when these water temperatures were reached.

If you do this for several years, you'll start to see trends. In years when water temperatures are running behind their normal calendar schedule, often so does the fishing. And conversely, in years when water temperatures are advanced, the fishing is likewise ahead of schedule.

Autumn fishing is often considered the finest of the year. Because of this, you will want to determine at what temperature this bite usually begins. Recognize that fall fishing commences well ahead of the time when fish depart for the season, for several reasons. The fish need a fairly long period of intense feeding in order to prepare for the trip and the lean winter months ahead. Along with this is the fact that the baitfish are also migrating at this time of year. So striped bass, or any other game fish for that matter, must rev up while the forage is still available.

It's risky for fish to wait until water temperatures sound the final bell before starting to migrate. A powerful storm could push colder water in from offshore, or a sudden snap of cold weather might arrive, either one of which could surround the fish with a wall of cold water. Furthermore, migration requires an immense expenditure of energy. Doing it at low temperatures makes things even more difficult, so it's far better for any migrating fish to anticipate things and get going while conditions are still in their favor.

Fish Size

Clearly, each species has its own thermal niche, but inside each group, size seems to count. Regardless of the species, the older, larger members are better able to tolerate cold water. Therefore, the first bluefish to arrive in southern New England in the spring and the last blues to leave in the fall are generally larger fish. The same concept holds with striped bass, although spawning is also a factor. In the spring, bigger bass are the last to leave the spawning grounds, and as a result, they are not in the lead coming up the coast. Still, come autumn, the jumbo stripers are able to tough it out considerably longer than their smaller brethren. This does not imply that bigger bass are easy to find as the season goes on. Larger bass tend to feed and migrate in deeper water away from shore and therefore rarely are as visible as schoolie stripers.

Marking the Moons and Tides

Years ago, I began looking at the tides more closely in an effort to see if there was any seasonal pattern to them. In my home waters of Long Island Sound, I discovered a subtle structure across the seasons. It was not evident every year, but it existed more years than not. Beginning in March, the tides start to strengthen, rising slightly higher than in January or February. The tides strengthen further into April and May, often peaking in a series of very strong tides in mid- to late June. During July and August, the tides dissipate a bit. Beginning in September, the stronger tides return. They increase in October, which often has the single strongest moon tide of the year. They may reoccur in November, but after that they taper away into the winter months.

When I matched up this cycle of tides with the migration of stripers, the correlation was clear. The seasonal movements of striper bass appear to be scheduled in a manner that allows them to travel during the periods of strongest tides. And why not? Clearly, for any species planning to move long distances, it would be necessary to conserve energy—it makes survival sense to do so. And riding the strongest tides would do just that. This would be especially true for species, such as striped bass, that travel near shore, where tidal currents are strong.

This relationship was also borne out in my striper fishing experiences; often the best bites occurred in June and October around the time of the moon tides. Furthermore, strong moon tides in the fall frequently also held the best action for bluefish, bonito, and false albacore. I now firmly believe that game fish tend to migrate in and out of regions on moon tides and to feed heavily during these same periods.

Consequently, beyond noting day length and water temperature in your log, you should mark the new and full moons. Then look for any connection between those moons and the arrival and departure of species from your area. Note, too, any connection between moon tides and good fishing. My guess is that you'll find some association on both counts, and that this information will improve your angling.

Forage

The seasonal schedule of game fish is also clearly linked to another fundamental environmental factor: food. The spring migration of striped bass, for instance, is neatly timed to coincide with the spring migrations of river herring and menhaden. In autumn, the link is the same. In southern New England, game fish leave as forage fish migrate out of the region. Furthermore, I believe that game fish sense where and when forage is available, and then travel to meet it. And conversely, they move away from areas if forage is scarce in an effort to find more abundant food.

Because of this link, any major change in the availability of forage in an area, especially as it pertains to important oily baits like herring, is apt to have a major effect on how game fish plan their moves—and on your fishing.

Some species of forage fish are more important than others. And when they undergo a population change, it can have a major effect on their predators. In my waters of Long Island Sound, for instance, adult menhaden largely disappeared around 1990 and to this day they have never fully reestablished themselves. Shortly after their decline, the movements of bluefish and striped bass also underwent a radical change. Striped bass immediately began a run up the Connecticut River in the spring, likely to pursue different forage such as herring and shad. That run became a yearly event and continues to this day. By 1993 bluefish had for the most part disappeared from the Sound, many of these fish likely moving offshore to feed.

Here in southern New England, it has long been apparent to me that the availability of forage plays a key role in how long game fish hang around in the fall. When forage is scarce, the fish hit the road; when it is abundant, they hang in, regardless of tide and water temperature. Predators apparently have the ability to adjust their water temperature tolerance to meet the water temperature preference of the prevailing forage. Therefore, when bait is abundant, even though the water is colder than the predators would like, they may stay around to take advantage of the situation. The clearest example of this I have seen involves false albacore. When the prevailing bait in southern New England is bay anchovies, the false albacore tend to leave for the year on the same timetable as the anchovies; both are gone by the middle of October. In other years, when the same waters are filled with baby menhaden, things are quite different. The menhaden stay well into November, and a few false albacore will too. I have seen small pods of these tuna in Long Island Sound into the second week of November with water temperatures in the low to mid fifties.

Weather

Weather affects water temperature and therefore the overall timing of the spring and fall migrations. But weather can also have a marked effect on your fishing from day to day. At first this may seem counterintuitive. Wouldn't it take several weeks of inclement weather to have any noticeable effect on water temperature? The answer is yes if you consider only the effect of air temperature on the sea, but you have to figure in the wind too. I'm not talking about windchill; I'm referring to the wind's ability to move water. A strong wind can drive in a serious amount of cold water from offshore, especially if the tide is also moving toward land.

In June, I've seen a day of 25-knot northeast winds drop the water temperature in Menemsha Bight by 3 degrees. Three degrees may not seem like much, but in the spring, when water temperatures are already borderline, a 3-degree drop is a significant change to a striped bass. A slow-moving bottom fish, such as a flounder, may respond to a sudden unfavorable change by becoming dormant—it may try to wait it out. Faced with the same situation, however, a strong-swimming predatory fish such as a striped bass can be expected to do exactly the opposite. In response to the change, these fish seek more comfortable waters. So strong is this desire to avoid being caught in unfavorable conditions that bass may actually reverse their migration temporarily.

I think that fish in relatively shallow water can sense an approaching front via the change in barometric pressure. Furthermore, I think they react by eating and running, falling back to deep water, where they wait for conditions to stabilize. And it's likely that the sharper the barometric change, the greater the rapidity with which the bass leave town. I've observed bass going on a feeding frenzy in the hours just prior to a front's arrival. Immediately after, they raced out of the bay. The fishing was dead for two days afterward.

The relationship between weather and migration has long been a factor. Many years ago, commercial striped bass fishermen in Rhode Island reported that weather patterns, especially strong winds, affected their autumn catch. If the wind stayed in the southwest, the bass lingered along the Rhode Island coast and then headed into Long Island Sound. Landings were good. But if the wind went around the compass, trouble was brewing. Powerful and persistent winds from the north apparently caused the bass to take a shortcut, leaving the Rhode Island coast and shooting directly across to Montauk.

If you fish the Connecticut and Rhode Island coastlines, you can see the same thing happen today. In October, southwest winds prolong the striped bass season, and I believe that's true for bluefish, bonito, and false albacore as well. North winds, on the other hand, prompt the fish to push away from shore. For a short time, boat anglers in the area continue to do well, but overall fishing rapidly deteriorates. Meanwhile, anglers on the North and South Forks of Long Island see their fishing kick into high gear.

So as a rule, stable weather, in either the spring or fall, produces the most consistent fishing and often the longest season. A storm can create fabulous fishing, but the bottom is apt to drop out just as quickly. Moreover, a stormy spring or fall usually produces less predictable fishing overall and shortens the season.

Migration Paths

By now your log book is getting fairly fat, but if you have the room, there is one more thing you should take note of: location. As game fish migrate in and out of areas, they frequently follow a particular route. And it is along this route that the finest fishing takes place. Let me give you a good example.

Using 1966 to 1972 as a database, the state of New York conducted a study of striped bass movements in Long Island Sound. That study was then published in 1977. The study showed that in the spring, striped bass entered Long Island Sound from both the eastern and western ends. The largest quantity of fish came through the two areas of strong current on the eastern end. One was Plum Gut, a tidal rip between Plum Island and Orient Point, New York. The other was in an area of tidal current on the western end of Fishers Island, New York, known as the Race. Once striped bass were in the sound, they spread out along the shores of Long Island and Connecticut, and some continued on to Rhode Island and farther north.

When autumn rolled around, a return migration of striped bass entered the sound on the eastern end from points north and east: Massachusetts and Rhode Island. The study documented an interesting pattern in the fall along the north shore of the sound, one that anglers can learn a good deal from. Striped bass from Rhode Island, Massachusetts, and other New England states enter the sound from the east end in the fall and then move along the Connecticut shore. No surprise there. But upon reaching roughly the center of the Connecticut coast, roughly the mouth of the Connecticut River, a large number turn and head south, crossing the sound back through the Race and Plum Glut. These fish are the ones likely headed back to the Chesapeake Bay.

That indicates two things about striped bass migration. First, the routes taken during the spring and autumn migrations overlap to a fair degree. Second, it seems that the striped bass use the areas of the coast that have the largest, and often strongest, tidal rips. Plum Gut and the Race in essence are highways over to Montauk and the rips around it.

There is even some speculation that striped bass search for, and even know from experience, the location of preferred water temperatures. Such locations may well be built into their migration routes. This could help them in their migration. Certainly, colder ocean currents would be avoided, and large shallow portions like Nantucket Shoal, which are the first to warm in the spring, would be preferred.

Striped bass are not alone in using the strongest tidal rips as migration routes. False albacore make a distinct autumn migration through the sound, exiting out the Race and Plum Gut, and eventually passing by Montauk. Bluefish like this route, too. I'm a bit less certain with Atlantic bonito, but the first place we see them in the sound during the spring is the Race.

COASTAL CALENDAR

Note that I've written this calendar as if it took place in the best of times, and the species were all plentiful along their historic ranges. In reality, however, that is not presently the case. Bluefish and weakfish, for example, are not

abundant in the Northeast, although weakfish are definitely building in number. Nevertheless, I did it this way because I thought it would have more value.
And between the time I write these lines and you read them, a given species'
population size could have conceivably increased or decreased.

Also note that I've written this as if the season were legally open for all
species every month. That may or may not be the case, depending on changing
fisheries management regulations. For instance, the striped bass season may
not be year-round, even though there are striped bass to be caught in some
states even in winter. Always check the latest local regulations.

Maritime Provinces

Sport fishing for striped bass became popular in the Maritimes right after
World War II, just when it did in the United States. Fishing camps were established around the Bay of Fundy and an annual striped bass fishing tournament
was even held in Quebec. About thirty years ago, however, the striped bass
population waned, and the fishery went into decline. Present data indicates
that it takes a Maritime angler roughly fifty hours to catch a striper; obviously
the fishing is not red-hot. Nevertheless, this fishery is intriguing and could
bounce back at any time. If you go, be sure to check local fishing regulations.

At this writing, Canadian striped bass fishing is largely concentrated into
two regions: the Gulf of St. Lawrence and the Bay of Fundy.

Bay of Fundy

Tagging records prove beyond a doubt that some of the bass here are migrants
from the Chesapeake Bay and the Hudson River, and it seems safe to assume
that a few bass make the journey from the Delaware and the Kennebec River
systems as well. Bass also move in the other direction. One tagged in New
Brunswick was recaptured about a month later in Rhode Island, having trav-
eled over 500 miles in thirty-six days.

On the New Brunswick side of the Bay of Fundy, there are several rivers
where striped bass have been reported over the years. The most famous is the
St. Johns, where a 62-pound bass was caught in August 1979. Stripers used to
spawn in the St. Johns until a dam was built about thirty years ago. Anglers
here concentrate on Reversing Falls in St. Johns Harbor, and various tributaries
of the main river. Nearby are two other rivers that have seen striped bass in

The cliffs of Aquinnah on Martha's Vineyard's west end. During the seasonal migrations of game fish, points of land like this are frequently angling hot spots, especially in the fall.

their lower reaches: the St. Croix and the Magaguadavic. Both empty into Passamaquoddy Bay just south of the St. Johns.

On the Nova Scotia side of the Bay of Fundy, striped bass are found in the Shubenacadie River, which empties into the rear of Cobequid Bay near the city of Truro, and in the Stewiacke River, a tributary of the Shubenacadie. Another important river is the Annapolis, which runs southwest toward the Bay of Fundy and widens into Annapolis Basin below the town of Annapolis Royal. Although some spawning occurs in these rivers during May and June, no one is sure how many of these fish are actually permanent residents of the Maritimes. Many may be coastal migrants who simply use the rivers as a place to winter over. Stripers descend these rivers in late spring and then head out to feed in the Bay of Fundy. In September they run back upriver. In the Truro area, fishing centers around the north shore of Minas Basin and Cobequid Bay, and in particular, the mouths of the Harrington, Five Island, Economy, and Bass Rivers.

Gulf of St. Lawrence

Most striper fishing is concentrated between Chaleur Bay down through Northumberland Strait, which lies between Prince Edward Island and the mainland of New Brunswick and Nova Scotia. Stripers spawn in rivers of this region, and most of the bass here are thought to be permanent residents of the Maritimes.

While there are no known spawning populations of striped bass on Prince Edward Island, the New Brunswick mainland has several important rivers, including the Kouchibouguac and Richibucto. The best fishing in these two rivers occurs in August and September. Farther north, the Miramichi and the Tabusintac Rivers, both of which flow into the Gulf of St. Lawrence, have runs of bass, but I believe the bass are protected by regulation. Continuing north to Chaleur Bay, the hot spot is Bathurst Harbor, which lies at the mouth of the Nepisiguit River. September is the best season.

Atlantic mackerel are plentiful beginning in August. These cousins of the bonito are a blast on a light fly rod. A fast retrieve and a flashy fly do the trick, and they can be caught from shore or a boat. They average 8 to 12 inches in August, but bigger fish from 2 to 3 pounds move in during September and October.

Bluefish are rare this far north, but in recent years their numbers have been on the upswing in the waters off southwestern Nova Scotia. Fishing is best in late July and August.

Maine

Like the Canadian Maritimes, Maine has both migrating striped bass and some resident stock. Stripers winter over in Maine waters, and some spawning also takes place in the state's rivers. Overall, the season here in northern waters is shorter than its counterpart to the south, but the combination of picturesque coastline and numerous coastal rivers makes for some fine saltwater fly fishing.

When weather allows, the first migrating bass arrive in the southern rivers of the Pine Tree State by the last few days of April, although the serious striper action doesn't start until the second moon of May. For the first bass of the season, most anglers look to the mouth of the Mousam River and the adjoining Parsons Beach in Kennebunk. Gradually, as the weeks go by, the bass work well up inside the rivers.

Other early-season spots include the Saco, York, Scarborough, and Presumpscot Rivers. On the Saco, you'll find public access to a jetty at Camp Ellis. Farther north along the state's coastline, the season is delayed a couple weeks by colder water. But by May, the bass are in the lower Kennebec River.

In June, striper fishing reaches a high point. Once again, it's the rivers that supply the action. The Kennebec River from Merrying Meeting Bay downstream to the mouth is famous for striped bass. This is a boat fishery, for the most part, and care must be taken because of 10-foot tides and swift currents. By July, however, the river fishing has hit its peak, and now stripers filter back down the rivers to the cooler surf. Popham Beach is a popular spot. The water is clear, and some sight fishing may be possible on the coast, although night fishing can be very productive.

For several years in the mid 1990s, the Kennebec River had a fantastic run of big bass in June. This run drew many avid anglers to Maine in pursuit of jumbo stripers, some of which were in excess of 40 inches long. Unfortunately, that big bass fishery has cooled down considerably in the intervening years, and now the Kennebec is more apt to give up schoolies.

When the August doldrums hit, wise striped bass anglers head afield at night on both the rivers and the surf. But the action may be slim. Bluefishing can be excellent in August some years, but bluefish do not always make it this far north. The blues that do are true "gators," the larger members of the coastal migratory stock. Look for them in the southern part of the state, between Kittery Point and Old Orchard Beach. Even if the blues don't make it, by the end of August the bass fishing is starting to pick up again as cool nights return. The history books mention bonito being caught in August in Casco Bay, which lies to the immediate north of Portland, but I know of no such reports in recent times.

Fall fishing kicks into gear during September and may last until Columbus Day in some years. There may be some fishing on the coast, but you'd do better focusing on the rivers. By October, the striper fishing is rapidly diminishing as water temperatures drop and the bass drop back.

New Hampshire

Striped bass pop up in the Granite State around the middle weeks of May. This seems a bit late, given that schoolies are already busy in southern Maine, but that's the way it works. As in most coastal areas, it's the rivers that host the finest spring fishing. In New Hampshire, that means the mighty Piscataquis River. This is a large, swift river, and not easy to fly-rod. Boats and fast-sinking lines are best. Farther upstream, the river joins forces with half a dozen other smaller rivers as it works its way inland. Little Bay is good, as is Great Bay.

As in Maine, June is an excellent time to cast a fly for striped bass. Larger bass have moved in by this month. For boaters, the Piscataquis River, which has a record of giving up jumbo stripers, continues to be the major focus. The turbulent currents near the General Sullivan Bridge also hold some of these big bass. The striper action continues into July, but as the Piscataqua River warms, many bass drop back to the cooler waters near the mouth. Increasingly, the action is best on night tides.

The ocean beaches have bass, too, and sometimes bluefish. In many locations, it's a rocky world, so have your cleats. Odiorne Point State Park on the southern entrance to Portsmouth Harbor is a good spot. Farther south along Route 1A is Rye Harbor State Park. Continuing south on 1A, you come to Hampton Beach State Park. Here the Hampton River joins the open Atlantic. There is fishing both on the exposed front side and in the protected backwaters of the Hampton River.

The heat of August allows for some daytime striper bites, but nighttime is the right time for the better bass action. If bluefish show, this is the month. Like Maine waters, New Hampshire sees bluefish only during certain years when the population is abundant. Those years, boaters find plenty of bluefish by working the shores around the Isles of Shoals during the summer. And there are some large bass here, too. The Isles of Shoals is less than 10 miles outside Portsmouth Harbor.

The cooling days of September stir stripers to feed heavily both in the rivers and along the open coast. This month is the peak of the fall season, especially around the moon tides. Early October still holds some occasional good fishing for striped bass, but it will not last long. The bass are heading south. Anglers looking to extend their salt season may want to turn to sea-run trout. Berry Brook near Portsmouth is a good choice, although this sea-run game demands plenty of patience. Berry Brook exits into the southeast corner of Little Harbor, behind Odiorne Point State Park. Look for the sea-runs to enter the brook on the moon tides of October and November.

Massachusetts

With stunningly beautiful water, a history of large fish—especially striped bass—and a fairly long season, the Bay State has the finest saltwater fly fishing in New England. Truth is, these waters may well be the finest from Maine to North Carolina. So if you've never cast a fly here, you owe it to yourself to come take a look.

There are six different regions in which to wet a line: Buzzards Bay; the south shore of the Cape from Woods Hole over to Chatham; the islands—Martha's Vineyard, Nantucket, and the Elizabeth chain; the Outer Beaches of the Cape from Chatham north to Provincetown; Cape Cod Canal and Cape Cod Bay; and Massachusetts Bay. The season lasts from May through October, and public access is fairly good.

A few overwintering stripers are caught as early as March, but the action is not very predictable, and the striper season is far from in gear. Scorton Creek on the Cape is known to hold stripers through the winter. Scorton has some sea-run trout in the colder months, too. If you want to try fly-rodding for white perch, late March into April should be a good bet.

Unless the winter has been very cold, the first bass pop up around the second week of April. The rivers and harbors on the west side of Buzzards Bay are good locations to try. Both Nantucket and Martha's Vineyard will have small schoolies, too. In both cases, the fish are found on the south side of the island; don't expect action on the north side for a few more weeks. By the third week of the month, some bass are entering the Cape Cod Canal and filtering eastward along the south shore of the Cape.

By the first week of May, the south shore has plenty of schoolies. Here there's a series of salt ponds and rivers that the bass find mighty attractive. This stretch extends from Falmouth over to Yarmouth and includes Bourne Pond, Great Pond, Waquoit Bay, Popponnesset Bay, and Cotuit Bay. This first action may be spotty, but by midmonth, rods are bending more frequently.

In all locations, expect these early bass to be small. The only exception is around the annual opening of Edgartown Great Pond. There, a few large bass may be caught toward the end of April. Larger bass come to the islands in early to mid-May. On the south shore of the Cape, they arrive in mid- to late May. The water in Cape Cod Bay is still too cold for any bass action.

Bluefish begin to pop up around the second week of May, especially out on Martha's Vineyard and the South Cape from Woods Hole to Chatham. Look for these early blues in the warm shallows. Out on the Vineyard's eastern end, from Cape Pogue around to Wasque Point, there should be some pretty big ones, but as elsewhere, they are long and lean at this time of year. Anglers call them racers. In most locations in the Bay State, predictable bluefishing is still at least a month away.

The month of May sees the striper fishing improve on the Cape and the islands. The shores of Buzzards Bay are also hot with bass by now. The East and West Branches of the Westport River near the Rhode Island line are good producers, especially if you have a boat. There should be fish a little farther north in the Weweantic River, too. Herring are running in the canal, and bass follow, including a few big ones.

By midmonth, bass are spreading out in the cool waters of Cape Cod Bay and on up into Massachusetts Bay, including Boston Harbor, and up to New-buryport. On the inside of the Cape, Barnstable Harbor and the Brewster Flats are popular destinations with fly rodders. And along the south shore, the chances of catching a bigger bass are increasing rapidly. By late May, the bass have surrounded both islands, and the bite will build into June.

When the Bay State sees a run of weakfish in the spring, which unfortunately is not that often, it's in June and July. In the Buzzards Bay region, the Lee River in Swansea and the Wareham River are good places to look for weaks. Along the south arm of the Cape, the salt ponds and their openings, from Woods Hole over to Cotuit, are good bets, too. Weakfish are known out on the islands as well, in locations such as Cape Pogue and Menemsha Pond. Some weakfish snake through the canal to Cape Cod Bay and even as far north as Massachusetts Bay, but only in those few years when the population is very abundant.

By June, the bluefish population builds further, and the fishing is more con-sistent. Dawn often holds the best bite. By July, some blues are moving into the bay side of the Cape, but it's August before action is steady there. The Wellfleet area, including Billingsgate Shoal, is an excellent place to look for big blues.

From late May into June, worm hatches start to occur around the times of the new and full moons. Known hatches occur in Lake Tashmoo on Martha's Vineyard and along the south shore of the Cape in the salt ponds near Fal-mouth. Other hatches are probably as yet undiscovered by fly rodders.

June holds the finest striped bass fishing of the entire year. And considering that the Bay State has much of the finest striped bass fishing on the entire coast, especially for big bass, June is a great time to be here. Look for moon tides to host the hottest bass action. Chatham and Nauset are prime at this time of year,

Anglers flock to Martha's Vineyard's north shore for the spring run of striped bass.

and so are the waters around the islands of Martha's Vineyard, Nantucket, and the Elizabeth chain. The Elizabeth chain is legendary at this season, especially the fast rips between the various islands. Locally, they are known as holes. Robinson's Hole and Quick's Hole are two. Cuttyhunk produced a 73-pounder, taken by Charley Cinto in June 1976. There are plenty of fine bass in the canal as well, and this is a good month to get them, as the herring are dropping back down to the sea.

Bay-side bass fishing is heading toward a peak this month too, particularly in places such as Barnstable Harbor. Wherever you fish from shore, expect bass at dusk and dawn, with more and bigger fish to catch in the middle of the night. Boaters can do well in low light too, but since boaters can reach the deeper edges, they catch bass through the bright hours of the day. Middle Ground in Vineyard Sound should have both bass and blues. Farther north, there is excellent fishing in the mouth of the Merrimack and all along Plum Island. And from shore you might hook a couple unexpected species: hickory shad and fluke.

By June, bait is plentiful on the Monomoy Flats, and the bass are there to feed on it. So besides the big bass mania that sends anglers afield from dusk to dawn, June also holds some of the best sight fishing for bass during the daylight hours on the Chatham Rhodes Flats near Monomoy. Summer fishing on the outer Cape can be very good into July before the summer doldrums hit. And by July, the striped bass have spread out all along the Cape and are available in a range of sizes. But now the action is best in low light—dusk, dawn, and through the night. Weakfish are still around in better years.

Come July, bass fishing from shore on the Vineyard tapers off. But the bonito will appear about the time of the first moon tides this month. The early bonito fishing is best for boaters, but gradually the "greenies" work their way into shore. Their cousins the false albacore won't be here until the third week of August. By mid-August, however, the bite for bonito is on in earnest. The reefs in Vineyard Sound are a fine bet, including Hedge Fence. Bonito are in the rips around Woods Hole, too, and from Nobska Point and the pond openings to the east. False albacore also like these same spots.

Massachusetts is the northern extent of an established fishery for both bonito and false albacore. Focus your efforts for these tunas on the southern portion of the state. It's a rare occasion when false albacore and bonito are found in Cape Cod Bay. Of the two species, bonito are more tolerant of cool water, but only in the warmest years are there any real number of them as far north as Provincetown.

Spanish mackerel may come to the Cape in the beginning of August. Martha's Vineyard and Nantucket are good places to look for them. Usually they are found in the same locations that the bonito and false albacore frequent.

For bass anglers, however, night tides rule along much of the Cape, although Provincetown's Race Point may be an exception. Here, there may be daytime feeding frenzies of striped bass in the heat of August. Also take a look farther around the horn at the outside beaches down to Highland Light. Some of the biggest bass ever caught on the Cape were landed on these lower ocean beaches in midsummer. These fish, however, were taken off the beach well out of fly-rod range. There can be plenty of surf to contend with here, and at times mung weed clogs the water's edge.

August is a fine month for bluefish everywhere. The warmer waters of August allow these fish to make their way around the Cape and into Massachusetts Bay, and it will be on the backside of the Cape where some of the finest bluefishing takes place. Blues are found on the outer Cape beaches as well. There are bluefish on the islands, too, but as in most locations, the bigger ones are off the beach in deeper, cooler water.

September supplies a lot of striper action, on both day and night tides. The Plum Island area up near Newburyport should be red hot with bass. This far north, they are getting ready to move soon. Around the islands of Martha's Vineyard, Nantucket, and the Elizabeth chain, by early September the bass start to feed close to shore again, but look to the night tides and dawn to provide the most hookups. During the day, bluefish are chewing hard. It's best to get one now, because by late October, they will be hard to find, although the ones you come across may be huge.

Between the last moon of September and the first moon of October, some of the biggest bass ever landed were taken on Cuttyhunk. Big bass are also to be sought in the Chatham and Nauset areas of the Cape at this time. This is also when bonito and false albacore fishing are at their fall peak. One of the most famous places is the inlet to Cape Pogue Gut, a narrow inlet that feeds Cape Pogue Bay. This hot spot is commonly referred to at this time of year as Albie Alley. Here, great blitzes of false albacore blast inside on the flooding tide.

By the middle of October, the false albacore have hit the road south, but truly big bonito may linger for a few weeks around the islands. Striper fishing is hot for the first half of October, but it soon trails away, especially if the wind stays north. The Outer Beaches of the Cape can be excellent in the early part of this month. Herring Cove and Race Point Beach, both just outside Provincetown, beckon many anglers. Head of the Meadow Beach in Truro is a beautiful spot as long as the surf is down. October is great on the islands, too. Some of the best action is on the reefs of Devils Bridge off Gay Head or Sow and Pigs, but there's plenty of action right from shore.

In November, the striper game slows to nearly a standstill. A few large to very large bass may be caught till around Thanksgiving by hard-core anglers, especially around Martha's Vineyard and Cuttyhunk at the end of the Elizabeth chain. Look for these late-season bruisers to be caught around the last moon of the month.

Rhode Island

The Ocean State has a variety of different types of water and plenty of public access. All in all, it's a fine mix for salty fly rodders. Truth is, the full fly-rod potential of Rhode Island waters is just starting to be discovered.

In March and April, there isn't a lot going on. As in the Bay State, some white perch action may be available. The southwest corner of the state, from Point Judith over to Watch Hill, typically has schoolie fishing under way by the first week of May. Some years, the schoolies show as early as the second moon of April. Whenever they first arrive, it doesn't take long before they head eastward up into Narragansett Bay. There you'll find them in places like the Providence and Seekonk Rivers. On the southwest coast, the West Wall in Point Judith is one of best-known early bass spots. Another early-season hot spot is the Pawcatuck River on the Connecticut–Rhode Island line. In Narragansett Bay, you can try Easton's Beach on Memorial Boulevard in Newport.

By the second moon of May, Rhode Island's striped bass fishing is kicking into high gear. Around this time, a new slug of bass is entering these waters as well. These are bigger striped bass that have finally left the spawning grounds. The fishing should be good all along the southwest coast, including Napatree Point.

Bluefish are checking in, too; usually by the middle of the month, a few are caught. As elsewhere, these early blues are found in the warmer areas of shallow water first. Narragansett Bay is one place to look for that reason. Along with the blues, some weakfish may appear in late May. Like the Bay State, Rhode Island sees weakfish only in those years when the population is robust. When they do come to Rhode Island, Narragansett Bay is a hot spot for them. There are numerous places to check out, but Greenwich Bay, Greenwich Cove, Conimicut Point in Warwick, and Nayatt Point in Barrington have good records.

Worm hatches start in early May and can last into June, depending on which of the many salt ponds along the southwest coast you are dealing with. These hatches, unlike the ones generally found in Long Island Sound, are often daytime events. The best action is usually from roughly 2:00 in the afternoon until dark, and sunny, warm days are prime. Cold spells delay the hatch. A boat may be required to stay on top of the action.

As elsewhere in southern New England, June is a super time to fish for big striped bass in the Ocean State. The points in the lower end of Narragansett Bay and the inlets to the various salt ponds are all excellent choices. Look to the low-light tides to be the most productive, although daytime bites are possible. One of the finest fly-rod bites at this time of year happens near Watch Hill Light, where hordes of hungry bass chase squid over the reefs. This action is in the bright light of day and is usually accompanied by large flocks of gulls. The days around the moon tides are often the hottest.

In June, there is fine striped bass action on Block Island, well worth the ride over in the ferry. The mouth of New Harbor on the ebb is one good bet. Blue-fishing in Narragansett Bay also picks up this month. The bluefish go every-where in the bay, all the way into the Providence River.

July brings increasing warmth, and wise striped bass anglers focus their efforts more on night fishing, although boaters still do well during the day. If May saw some weakfish, they should still be on the bite, but expect the action to taper off into the summer doldrums. Atlantic bonito appear this month. Look for these speedsters around the first set of moon tides. Don't expect a steady bite until August, however, especially near shore. The mouth of Narra-gansett Bay is a good place to check out, as are the inlets from Point Judith over to Watch Hill.

In August, striper fishing is slow from shore; it's pretty much a darkness game now. Some places many still hold plenty of small bass on a summer night. Narragansett Town Beach is a productive spot, and a good walk up the beach takes you to another fine fishing spot, the mouth of the Pettaquamsett River, sometimes called the Narrow River. If night fishing is not your game, try for bonito. They are closer to shore now and more aggressive. Check around Point Judith or in Watch Hill passage. Blues please many anglers right through the daylight hours. Weakfish have fallen away with the heat. Look for some return action for this fish next month. By the end of August, false albacore join the bonito. The two often feed in the same locales. The best fishing for these two guys is often in early to midmorning, say from sunrise to 11:00.

September sees the fishing slowly pick up for all species. For bass and blues, try casting along the shorelines under Point Judith Light, or go out on the East Wall jetty, which lies to your immediate right, if you dare. It can be very tricky. False albacore and Atlantic bonito are really busting bait hard now. Look for them all along the coast, especially in rips and at the mouths of salt ponds. They are around Block Island, too. During this month, striped bass and bluefish pick up as well. Night tides are still excellent for bass, but by month's end, some schoolies are in the surf all day long. This is particularly true around the salt ponds, where bay anchovy are migrating out. Soon mullet, silversides, and eventually juvenile menhaden will follow.

October typically holds the finest fishing of the entire year. Bass are coming down the coast into Rhode Island waters to join their brethren already here. Bonito and false albacore action is at its peak during the first two weeks of the month. The false albacore are usually gone by midmonth, so if you're looking to catch one, this is the time. From shore, try Weekapaug Inlet, Quonochontaug Inlet, Charlestown Breachway—especially the beach—and the West Wall at Point Judith. Some bonito will hang around until the first week of November. Expect them to be hard to find and to hook. But they are usually very large, well worth the effort.

In the first half of October, there are still plenty of bluefish around, but as with the tunas, the bluefishing declines sharply as the month wears on. The inlets spill baitfish onto the coast, where they migrate either south or out to deeper water. They will attract a lot of feeding fish.

The first week of early November may see a quick blast of big blues chasing herring along the southwest shore. Dawn is the time to find them from shore, and East Beach is a known spot. During the day, the blues move out a ways, roughly about a quarter mile. Boaters can catch them, but the ground bite ends. By the second week of the month, this bite usually evaporates entirely. November fishing for schoolie bass can be excellent along these same beaches, but as with late-season fishing anywhere, weather plays a big role. If the wind blows hard from the north day after day, the season ends quickly. When things stay settled or, better yet, the wind stays southwest, the fishing continues. There was a time nearly thirty years ago when the peak action for jumbo bass came in the first part of November. It happened in many spots along the Rhode Island coast, but Watch Hill is one that comes to mind. This late-season striper bite was also hot out on Block Island. Dusk and dawn often saw the action. Today, this late-season striper run is a slim deal. But either way, the bass are going to be shutting the door by month's end.

Connecticut

Connecticut anglers fish Long Island Sound, Fishers Island Sound, and the tidal rivers on the mainland. All these waters are protected and relatively shallow, ideally suited to the fly rod. Though it's generally not thought of as big-fish country, some exceptionally large striped bass and bluefish have been caught in state waters. And the Nutmeg State also has a longer season than any place discussed so far. On the downside, the coastline is heavily developed, and as a result, public access to the shore is quite limited. Nevertheless, knowledgeable fly rodders catch plenty of fish from shore just the same. Numerous boat ramps are located in the harbors and rivers throughout the state.

The Thames River is famous for its overwintering population of striped bass. These fish stack up on the bottom of Norwich Harbor, but they are typically too deep for fly-rod work, especially during the colder part of the winter. In April, these bass become more active and begin to track herring entering the river. Fishing improves rapidly into May, and then the fly fishing really begins. There are some overwintering bass in Niantic River as well, and a few may be caught as early as late March if the weather is especially mild.

If the winter has not been colder than normal, April sees a fair amount of migrating stripers arrive, mainly from the Hudson River. Typically, the western end of the state sees the fish first, and then they spread eastward as the weeks go by. The two best hot spots are the lower Housatonic River and the lower Connecticut River. The tides around the second moon of April are a good time to go afield in search of these immigrants. For public access to the lower Housatonic, try Short Beach Park or McKinney National Wildlife Refuge. To the east, in the Connecticut River, the first bite favors the east side, from Griswold Point up along Great Island all the way to Calves Island above the I-95 bridge. Boaters do best, but there is some public access from the ground. Ferry Landing State Park is popular with fly rodders. The last of the ebb or the first of the flood tide is best, because you must wade out to the channel. Watch the local anglers.

In the Connecticut River, the fish used to hang around in the lower end for some time, but now many bass travel quickly upstream, some going 50 miles to Hartford. This upriver migration has produced a relatively new fishery for striped bass, from Portland to the Enfield Dam. Much of the fishing is done with live herring, but some fly-rod opportunities do exist, especially for boaters. Along the way, bass enter the larger tributaries and coves, following the herring.

By late May, a second pulse of bass enters Long Island Sound, but this time from the eastern end. Unlike the early fish from the western end, these new arrivals are more likely of Chesapeake Bay origin. These fish usually appear first in the fast waters of the Race or Plum Gut, producing fine fishing for boaters in both locations. Some blues may be mixed in. At roughly this time, bigger bass start prowling the sound, too. Some hang in the lower end of both the Housatonic and the Connecticut Rivers, but many stay out in the deeper rips of the sound.

Like the rest of southern New England, Connecticut rarely sees a decent run of weakfish. The region seems to get them only every twenty-five years or so. When they do come, they begin showing up during the last weeks of May. Look for them at the West Haven sandbar, which is called Sandy Point on the map. They are found in the Norwalk and Branford areas, too. Weakfish also take up residence in the lower end of the coastal rivers, including the Housatonic, the Connecticut, and the Mystic. Don't bother looking very far upstream, as these fish are not tolerant of fresh water. This fishing lasts into June as the weakfish spread eastward, and then fades quickly as water temperatures climb near shore in summer.

Bluefish are around in late May, too, although it's usually another month before the action gets locked in good. By July, bluefishing is in high gear, especially in the Race. Boaters are doing very well during the daylight hours, but as with bass, the best blues along the shore are now caught during low-light hours.

July sees the water temperature near shore starting to soar. Weakfish are no longer as easy to find. Bass fishing from the beach switches to night tides. But blues are around and often feed heavily in the day, especially around dawn. The stronger moon tides of the month bring the first Atlantic bonito to Long Island Sound as water temperatures reach the midsixties. Unfortunately for shore anglers, these early arrivals are well off the beach, often popping up in the Race or around the south side of Fishers Island. These early "bones" stay well off the beach and tend to be extremely shy. While little is known about their reproduction rites in these waters, these fish are probably in a pre- or postspawn mode. What makes me think so? I caught a 9-inch bonito on a fly in mid-September on the Connecticut coast. Since young-of-the-year bonito grow at the astonishing rate of an inch every ten days, this baby bonito was likely born ninety days prior. Counting backward, I figure the spawn to be in mid- to late June, probably offshore.

These first bonito are spread out and difficult to catch, and even boaters will have a difficult time. Be patient; as the summer wears on, things improve. The bite in the Race should pick up, and some of these "greenies" come in close as they work the mainland side of Fishers Island Sound. Morning tides are often best.

In general, August fishing is slow, especially from the beach. If nothing else is biting, try for hickory shad. In places like Niantic Bay, they should be busy pounding silversides. This small, tarponlike fish is a blast on a 4-weight rod. For blues from the beach, running tides at daybreak are best; for bass, fish the night tides. By now, Fishers Island Sound and the Race should have some bonito and bluefish action during the day. Bass are apt to be deeper than fly rodders usually fish, but some surface action may occur around Big and Little Gull Islands. Spanish mackerel are infrequent visitors to Long Island Sound, but in years when they do arrive, August is the month. The season is short, however, and they will pull up stakes by the end of the following month. Try the warm-water release at Millstone Nuclear Plant in Waterford.

By the end of August, false albacore join the ranks, although in cool years, it could be Labor Day before they are here in any number. September sees weakfish picking up, after the slow days of midsummer. Some of them may last into October, but in general, come September, expect weaks to be dropping back south fairly fast.

This month, bluefishing gets into high gear, and the action lasts until at least midway through the following month. Traditionally, some of the biggest choppers are found in the harbors of the western end of the sound, if adult menhaden are present. A good public-access point down this way is Penfield Reef in Fairfield. But Sherwood Island State Park and Compo Beach, both in Westport, should have action for the beach angler, too. Farther east, in Madison, try the point at Hammonasett State Park. Rocky Neck State Park in East Lyme can be good at times. And there is often fine fishing at Harkness Memorial State Park in Waterford.

Atlantic bonito and false albacore are revving up in September, too, especially in the eastern end of Long Island Sound. As it was in August, Fishers Island Sound is one of the best areas to look for them, and they may run to the western end of Long Island Sound in some years. This is almost entirely a boater's game, although a few are caught from shore by local sharpies. Schoolie bass fishing is still a bit slow, but as the month goes on, the bass get biting. Most striper action is still on the night tides, although daytime fishing, including dusk and dawn, kicks in by October.

Just as in neighboring Rhode Island, October is prime time for the Nutmeg State. Bass, bluefish, bonito, and false albacore are all feeding hard, and on some special days, they may all be mixed together in one mighty blitz. Striped bass are busy, with both low-light and bright-light action, although if you're looking for a monster bass from shore, you're still better off under the stars. About the third week of the month, stripers that have been sitting far up inside the Connecticut River all summer migrate down to the sound. The lower end of the river should be good for a week or more before these fish spread out along the coast. Fishing in the Norwalk Islands should be excellent, too; there are plenty of big bass and bluefish in this pretty area of the coast.

Bluefish are also around in October, and the fishing for them is good to excellent until the third week of the month. From the last moon of September to the first moon of October, many anglers are totally focused on Atlantic bonito and false albacore. This is the peak of the season for them, and they should be feeding pretty heavily, especially in the Race and Plum Gut, but some action also occurs closer to the mainland. You'll frequently find them in the rips off Black Point in Niantic or along Two Tree Channel and Bartlet's Reef near Waterford. Expect the best bite to be early in the month on the moon tides. By the end of the month most years, this action has faded.

Bonito can hang around into early November, but the false albacore are usually gone by the end of October. In some years, small pods of false albacore will last into November as well, but only when there are a lot of small menhaden near shore. Look for these late-season false albacore to be thickest in the warm-water release at Millstone Nuclear Plant in Waterford.

The longer north winds hold off, the longer fall fishing in Long Island Sound continues. Come November, schoolie action is still likely, but in recent years, the bite has not lasted past the middle of the month. One place to look is around the mouth of the Thames River, where stripers stage before running upriver to winter over. Ocean Beach and Harkness State Park are two access points. Bass in the lower Connecticut River favor the west side in November, especially from Ragged Rock Creek down to the mouth. The South Cove Causeway gives shore anglers a shot at them. The lower Housatonic also has bass at this time of year. Low stages of the tide concentrate the fish and allow anglers to wade out to them. And in these last two rivers, there should be some hickory shad mixed in. The bite in the Thames gradually works its way upstream toward Norwich, and there may be fairly good fishing for small bass well into December.

In the early days of November, the final push of bluefish may occur. This action is spotty at best and is located where big blues are pushing menhaden down the coast. At roughly the same time, a few last-ditch bonito may be caught by diehard anglers willing to work deep. In the 1980s, schoolie action went on until December along much of the state's coastline. Now it wanes by mid-November. The only place you can see some bass action with reasonable certainty is in the upper Thames River.

New York

Saltwater fishing in New York revolves almost entirely around the waters of Long Island. As in Connecticut, New York anglers enjoy the protected waters of Long Island Sound, but they also have the exposed south shore to fish, as well as the tip of Montauk, which is justly famous for its fall action. New York has a few spots where you can catch stripers even in the dead of winter. The best known is found at the LILCO power plant's warm-water release in Northport Bay, on the north shore of Long Island.

More realistically, the season for stripers gets underway in mid- to late March in the Hudson River. The river from Catskill downstream to the Tappen Zee Bridge contains fish. Croton Point and Haverstraw Bay are good areas, but generally, the later you go into May, the peak action lies farther north, from Kingston to Catskill. This Hudson River spring striper fishing lasts about two months, ending in June. The best fishing is focused wherever herring runs exist. Edges of the canal and the tributary mouths are hot spots.

Hudson River bass are going two directions in the spring: Some are headed upstream to spawn, while those too young for procreation are heading downstream to the salt. That means the larger bass are in the river until late May or early June, before they too journey downstream to open water.

By early April, schoolie bass are entering Long Island Sound via the East River. Along the western end of Long Island's north shore, a series of bays continues out to Port Jefferson. After that, the north shore straightens considerably as it runs to Orient Point. For many New York anglers, these western bays and harbors hold the first fly-rod striper action of the season. Little Neck Bay is well known, as is Manhasset Bay and Hempstead Harbor. If the weather is cold, this fishing may not really get rolling until May. But with each warming day, the fishing improves, and the bass work their way eastward toward Orient Point. From late May into early June, a push of larger breeder bass that have dropped down the Hudson move eastward along the same north shore.

Along the north shore, there are several good access points for fly rodders. A few of the best, from west to east, are Caumsett State Park, Crab Meadow Park, Sunken Meadow State Park, Wildwood State Park, and Mattituck Inlet. As with all public-access locations, obey parking and permit regulations.

The striper season on the south shore of Long Island gets going about the same time as on the north shore, or perhaps a week or two later. But the south shore is a different-looking coast. Much of it is open surf, and as with such conditions anywhere, it can be a tough game with a fly rod. Fortunately, there are also numerous inlets to fish, and these inlets lead to large protected backwaters that hold striped bass, bluefish, and weakfish in their seasons. These protected bays are relatively easy to fly-fish, hold large amounts of baitfish, and contain flats for sight fishing, although boat traffic is apt to be high.

On the western end of the south shore is Gateway National Recreational Area, located in the Rockaways. This area offers good shoreline access to anglers, as does the nearby Breezy Point at the head of Rockaway Inlet, which is famous for bass and bluefish. It has open water, jetties, and some tidal mudflats as well. The Park Service also oversees Breezy Point. Jones Beach State Park gives you a chance to fish Jones Inlet, which enters into East Bay. Robert Moses State Park gives anglers access to Fire Island Inlet, which feeds into the huge Great South Bay. Great South Bay runs roughly 30 miles to Moriches Bay, which is fed by Moriches Inlet. The third large bay is Shinnecock Bay, fed through Shinnecock Inlet.

These shallow waters warm fairly quickly. They are protected backwaters that offer good fly-rodding potential. Southern shore striped bass fishing, like its north shore counterpart, begins in April on the western end. Places like Breezy Point and Great South Bay should have schoolie bass by midmonth. As April gives way to May, the fishing steadily picks up along the entire southern coast. Bigger bass start mixing in around the last moon of May. And by June, bass fishing is red hot. Shinnecock Inlet and Moriches Inlet are known for good June bass bites. June fishing around Orient Point, Plum Gut, Plum Island, and Fishers Island is in full swing too.

May finds bluefish slowly invading both the northern and southern shores of Long Island, as well as New York Harbor. In some years, they even run partway up the Hudson. On the ocean side of Long Island, they should be in Jamaica Bay, especially if the menhaden show up on schedule. Expect bluefish in Great South

Bay, too, although they are apt to be smaller. Other known early-season bluefish hangouts are in Peconic and Gardiners Bays by late in May. These May bluefish are not apt to provide hot fishing, but by next month, bluefishing should begin to heat up. By June, bluefish are well spread out along both the north and south shores of Long Island. By July, bluefish action is running at full tilt.

Weakfish arrive shortly after the first bluefish, by late May, although in years when bluefish are numerous, weakfish generally are not. Like the blues and the bass, weaks are found on both north and south shorelines. Look for them in the Rockaways, along Jones Beach, and in the big bays and inlets along the south shore as well. Given their love of shrimp, they are also found in the grassy estuaries and salt marshes. On the north shore of Long Island, Peconic Bay historically has been an early-season hot spot for weaks. Oyster Bay and Hempstead Harbor can be good, too. By July, weakfishing tapers off near shore, until it revives in September.

The eastern bays, such as Shinnecock and Moriches, have bonito and false albacore to cast a fly to. While Spanish mackerel are somewhat of a rare sight in Long Island Sound, they are more common here along the southern shore of Long Island. Look for them well outside the inlets, although at times they come in range of shoreline anglers. August and September are the only two months that hold water warm enough for these southern speedsters. Whereas ebbing tides are best for bass and bluefish action, look to the flood for Spanish mackerel. The flats and heads of the bays fish better on the flood.

In the fall, the inlets along the south shore of Long Island provide some of the best fishing New York has to offer. September and October are prime, as mullet runs form near the inlets and their adjacent ocean beaches. Bluefish are in top form from late September through October, and on into the early half of November. October has bonito and false albacore action from Montauk, and striped bass are here, too, starting in October and lasting well into November.

As in Connecticut, September is a time for blues, which can pop up just about anywhere. Striper fishing improves gradually during the month. Weakfish are on the move back to the south this month, and most of them are gone by the middle of October.

From September on, Montauk becomes a legendary mecca for saltwater anglers. Tremendous numbers of migrating fish make their southerly turn here. The shorelines, especially right under the Light, are not really for fly-rodding.

The north shore along Gin Beach, from Swagwon Reef back to the harbor, is good, however. And on calm days, you might get in on the south side of the Light as well. The bass can be right on the beach.

As September wears on, bonito and false albacore action picks up rapidly. If the wind blows steadily from the north, the bonito and false albacore in southern New England waters drop quickly to Montauk. But it's in October that tuna fishing usually heats up out at Montauk. Striped bass and bluefish are also on a roll in October. Bluefish may last until the first or second week of November if the north winds hold off. Striped bass action is hottest in late October, although there are still bass around in November. Many are staged around the city of New York, waiting to run up the Hudson River.

By early November, a few big blues are still waiting to smash a fly, but don't expect them to stay around much longer than the second week of the month, and even then they are likely to be found only in a few prime locations where large schools of bait still exist. Schoolie bass are pushing through in large schools on their way to their wintering grounds, so action may extend into December if the weather cooperates. And some bass are caught in New York Harbor up until Christmas.

New Jersey
New Jersey is home to some of the most dedicated saltwater anglers on the entire coast, and there is plenty of saltwater fly-rod history here, dating back to the Salt Water Fly Rodders of America. The state is bounded on the north by Raritan Bay and on the south by Delaware Bay. Much of the coast in between is protected by a long barrier beach, behind which lie the extensive shallow waters of Barnegat Bay, and farther south, from Ocean City to Cape May, narrower backwaters laced with islands and bays. The barrier beach is punctuated by several openings, including Manasquan and Barnegat Inlets and Great Bay.

Late March sees the slow start of schoolie action in the rivers. Mullica, Egg Harbor, and Toms Rivers are good bets. Overwintering fish here are apt to be in the deep holes, right on the bottom, so fish low and slow. By mid-April, the action picks up. Also try Little Beach at Great Egg Harbor. The fastest action during mid-April is in the southern portions of the state, but by late in the month, bass are biting north to Sandy Hook.

Weakfish arrive in Barnegat Bay in two batches. The first group arrive at the end of April. These are smaller weaks, mainly 2–4 pounds. In early May, a slug of bigger breeders comes in to spawn, many in the 7- to 10-pound range with the occasional larger fish. The smaller weaks hang out in Barnegat Bay and Great Egg Bay until at least September, but the big tiderunners quickly drop back to deeper water. Most are gone by Memorial Day.

Spring bass action peaks in May. By midmonth, blues are in the southern portion of the state, spreading northward with each passing day. Expect them on the outside beaches and in the protected backwaters too. Barnegat Bay has a good bite. In recent years, these fish have been in the 6- to 9-pound range. Generally this bluefish bite lasts about a month.

By July the striper fishing trails off, even up at Sandy Hook, and what bite there is happens at night. Bluefishing is best from boats, although some beach action still exists. Small weaks provide action in the bays right through the summer months. The majority of the bite is between dusk and dawn. Expect to find these weaks in the deeper holes. Chumming works well, as it does farther north. In the 1980s and early 1990s, July saw Atlantic bonito active offshore over the humps, such as the Klondike and Manasquan Ridge. This fishery has faded in recent years, but as anywhere else in the salt, it may return.

August is slow. Bluefish start to reappear toward the end of the month, but it will be a while before they reach their fall peak. When September rolls around, things are ready to bust wide open. There is an anchovy run in the inlets and neighboring surf, and by the last moon of the month, a mullet run too. Now bluefish are ready to rumble. They'll be in the surf slamming everything, including schools of small weaks, which are leaving the bays for the winter. Striped bass action is slow along much of the Jersey coast, with the exception of the Cape May rips. This is wild water, combining strong currents, shoals, and breaking waves, but an experienced captain can safely find some monster bass and blues.

Around Barnegat Inlet, false albacore pop up during early October. Get them quick; they don't hang around for long. While anglers today affectionately refer to Cape Pogue on Martha's Vineyard as Albie Alley in honor of its excellent false albacore fishing, a spot off Beach Haven carried the same name in the early 1970s for the same reason. The time of year was September and October, and the anglers catching these fish were not fly rodders, but you can bet they were smiling just the same.

Bluefishing falls off after October, but a few blues remain well into November. In November, however, Jersey coast stripers hit their peak. They're migrating down from the north and juvenile menhaden are pouring out of the inlets. The combination promises whirling gulls and swirling bass. Sandy Hook is a great place for late-season striper action. It offers seven miles of oceanfront and a protected bay with coves and islands. There's a good rip up by the Coast Guard Station as well. The bass blitz goes well into December, as long as the north winds don't blow too hard. Until the water temperature drops below 45 degrees, you can catch bass.

Delaware

At this time, there is not a lot of saltwater fly rodding going on in this state, but I expect that to change pretty quickly. The Delaware River, Delaware Bay, and the oceanfront are the main fishing grounds. The river has spawning striped bass that run far upriver. Indian River Inlet, in the southeast corner of the state, also has stripers.

Striper fishing is just getting under way in March. Expect the action to increase as April rolls around. By late April and into May, the spring bass fishing peaks. By mid-April, weakfish put in an appearance in Delaware Bay. The bay is famous for its weakfishing, and one of the best places historically has been Brandywine Shoal. Weakfish are found in the Indian River Inlet as well. From this point southward, the weakfish joins its cousin the spotted seatrout.

Bluefish are going strong in June, and the striper bite tapers off and switches to night tides. In July, the blues are really revved up, but the striped bass are not, and the only bite is apt to be after dark. Weakfishing is slowing down in July.

August is slow except for bluefishing. Blues are feeding heavily during September, and bonito and false albacore are also around offshore. The striper game is only fair at best, although the fall action is coming soon.

Fall action for bluefish hits a peak in October. Bonito and false albacore are there this month as well, but well off the beach. Striped bass fishing is building during the month but may not hit its stride until November.

In November, striped bass fishing picks up again, and lasts well into December. The bluefishing in November is waning rapidly, although an occasional blue is landed out to early December.

Maryland and Virginia

Maryland and Virginia share the famous waters of Chesapeake Bay, a huge estuary with a wealth of important rivers entering on both shores. On the Virginia side the major ones are the Potomac, Rappahannock, York, and James Rivers; on the Maryland side, the Susquehanna, Choptank, and Nanticoke Rivers. The bay also has thousands of points and numerous islands, coves, and channels to explore. All told, it's more water than you could cover in a lifetime. The bay is also home to a great many species of game fish, including bass, blues, Spanish mackerel, hickory shad, American shad, spotted seatrout, and weakfish.

Around the second moon of March, striped bass gather and head for the spawning grounds in the rivers. The spawn begins in April and lasts through May. The Maryland striper fishery is closed during this time with two exceptions. A trophy season outside the rivers usually runs from late April into May. Fishing is also allowed during April on the Susquehanna Flats and in the main stem of the river. Check regulations carefully.

In April and May, the weakfish and spotted seatrout are entering the lower end of the bay to spawn, and their numbers will continue to build into the summer months. Bluefish are entering at this time as well, and in recent years Atlantic croakers have been showing up during May. These drumlike fish are mainly caught with bait, but will take a fly. They stay until August and grow to about 4 pounds.

April also sees the start of hickory shad runs in the upper bay, and in the last five years fish numbers have been rising. Soon after, the American shad start their run. Expect the hickory fishing to last into June. The Susquehanna River below Conowingo Dam sees plenty of shad action, as does Deer Creek, a tributary of the Susquehanna. Octoraro Creek is another good bet. At this writing, fishing for American and hickory shad is strictly catch and release.

By June, striper fishing in the tributaries has opened in Maryland. The lower ends of the rivers generally hold the best opportunities. By now most of the big bass have left for northern waters, but plenty of smaller bass remain. Weakfish, bluefish, and spotted seatrout are spreading out into many areas. The weakfish like eelgrass beds but often prefer to stay 20 to 60 feet down, so reaching them with a fly can be difficult. The bluefish run between 2 and 4 pounds, although 15-pounders have been caught in years past. Weakfish average 14 to 18 inches, with some to 28 inches and the occasional bigger fish. The bay record of 19 pounds was caught twenty years ago near the Chesapeake Bay Bridge Tunnel.

In July, some Spanish mackerel arrive. The bass have gone deep along with the weakfish, and the action in the shallows is largely a night fishing game. By September, however, the fishing picks up, and thousands of gulls may mark the best blitzes. There is fishing for bluefish, bass, weakfish, and Spanish mackerel. While fish are caught throughout the bay, the Eastern Shore often holds good action. Focus on the stretch from Kent Island down to Tangier Sound. Proven spots include Kent Island Narrows, Love Point, Bloody Point Bar, the "Diamonds," Eastern Bay, Poplar Island, Poplar Island Narrows, and the mouth of the Choptank.

In October, bluefish are on a roll, with the best bite coming in November. Weakfish action usually tops out in October, although in some years the bite goes longer. The Spanish mackerel are gone, but bass fishing is slowly gathering steam, and by late October there are bass in the 20- to 35-pound class in the middle bay. Like the weakfish, these fish are deep in the channel and are hard to reach with a fly. Breezy Point is one place to look. Most of the fall striper fever, however, is concentrated in the lower bay and especially around the rips and rock piles of the Chesapeake Bay Bridge Tunnel. Sometimes you'll find the bass boiling on top, but often you have to go down after them with sinking lines. This fishing heats up well into December, often lasting until Christmas.

North Carolina

North Carolina has a tremendous amount of fly-rodding opportunities, both inshore and offshore, and a nearly year-round season. Species include Atlantic bonito, bass, bluefish, cobia, drum, hickory shad, false albacore, Spanish mackerel, spotted seatrout, and weakfish. The state also has a myriad of regulations, so be sure to read them before wetting a line.

The coastline's main feature is the Outer Banks, a 200-mile barrier beach running from Virginia Beach to Cape Lookout. Behind this wall of sand lie several protected sounds, including Pamlico and Albemarle. Connecting the sounds with the sea are the churning waters of Oregon Inlet, Hatteras Inlet, Ocracoke Inlet, and Barden's Inlet. The season and the size of the fish can vary considerably from north to south. Generally speaking, the fishing in the sounds is best from April until September. Anglers walk the marsh banks, wade, or fish from a boat. The Atlantic-facing beaches are best from September through December. Boaters do well, but you certainly can fly-rod these beaches. The surf is formidable at times, but there are plenty of sloughs to work when the waves are down, and there are also great opportunities around the inlets and bridges.

In March the water temperature off the open beaches reaches the upper forties, but the sounds may be a full 10 degrees warmer. That warmth starts some schoolie action in the sounds, but it's slow going and highly weather-dependent. Manns Harbor Bridge over Croatan Sound is one of the early-season hot spots. Also try farther north, in the Kitty Hawk Pier area. Stripers here average 20 to 24 inches, occasionally bigger. Small redfish, known locally as "puppy drum," can be found too. By the second moon of March, stripers are staging off the Roanoke River in preparation for a spawning run. Traveling upward of 100 miles upstream from Albemarle Sound, these fish spawn near the town of Roanoke Rapids. The fishing is done from boats, not by wading. The run peaks in early May and the fishing lasts into June. After the spawn, many of the bass return to the salt.

Several other rivers that feed into Albemarle Sound or Pamlico Sound may have striped bass at this time of year. The most well known is the Chowan River, which enters the back of Albemarle Sound near the town of Edenton. It was near the mouth that the biggest bass on record, a 125-pound giant, was taken in a net in April 1891.

Come April, bluefish and weakfish migrate from the ocean into the sounds. Big drum are moving in too and can be found in Ocracoke Inlet or Cape Point in late April. These beasts are huge, upward of 40 pounds. By May, bluefish, puppy drum, and weakfish are increasing in numbers and becoming more aggressive. The blues can be right on top, but the weakfish rarely are. You have to go down to get them, although some are taken right in the surf. May also sees a few Spanish mackerel arriving. Worm hatches occur in the sounds during April, but better ones happen in May. They produce a daytime bite, and the warmer waters of the ebb tide fire up the action. You can expect the worms to draw bluefish, puppy drum, striped bass, and perhaps weakfish. Also in the ocean in May is a run of Atlantic bonito averaging 6 to 8 pounds.

Early June finds cobia running and exciting sight fishing for this large, powerful fish. The state all-tackle record fish of 103 pounds was taken in 1988. Hatteras and Oregon Inlets are places to try, as are the waters around Pea Island. Spanish mackerel are popping up more regularly now, and there are also plenty of small blues and some schoolie stripers. Spotted seatrout are red hot and will remain so right up to September. Most are less then 4 pounds. By now weakfish are dropping back through the inlets to deeper water. At the end of June, Ocracoke Inlet sees small schools of tarpon, but they're very hard to hit with a fly.

By August, Spanish mackerel are in full force, and king mackerel are feeding in the ocean. Kings are mostly found offshore, although they do come in close at times, especially around the inlets. Offshore, you'll find false albacore are biting over the wrecks if the weather allows you to get there. In September, puppy drum fishing gets going and really kicks in by month's end. The Kitty Hawk area and Oregon Inlet should hold some action. Spanish mackerel and small bluefish are also biting hard this month. There also may be a few black drum around, and cobia fishing may see a second surge.

The legendary run of big blues along the Outer Banks takes place in October and November. After a thirty-year gap, this run again occurred in 1966, with blues averaging 14 pounds. The size of the fish peaked several years later at around an 18-pound average. In 1972, the world all-tackle record bluefish of 31 pounds, 12 ounces was landed here. A northeast wind is what you pray for; it pushes the blues in close, where you have a shot at them from the beach. Southerly winds drive the bait and blues out.

In October the false albacore are moving in. They'll put on a show that lasts to Thanksgiving and even into December if weather permits. The inlets and the Harkers Island area are your best bet. These false albacore are not only numerous but very large. Fifteen-pound fish are commonplace; it takes a 20-pounder to raise any eyebrows. If you come for this bite, plan on staying several days. Stormy weather often keeps you in port for a day or more at a time. This month finds tremendous numbers of spotted seatrout down at Cape Lookout. October also sees striper fishing starting to gather steam. This action builds with each passing week. There are still schoolies, but many of these fall bass are in the 20- to 30-pound range, and sometimes they can be found in schools.

Early November has good fishing for blues and Spanish mackerel, but both species will be pulling up stakes soon. False albacore are still chewing away, and so are the bass. Spotted seatrout are still biting down at Cape Lookout. Some bass are in the sounds, getting ready to winter over in the rivers. But the biggest bass bite is out front in the surf, where they're snacking on peanut bunker. Nags Head is one of the better places to look for them. These are likely big Chesapeake Bay bass that will eventually move offshore for the winter.

These blitzes of big bass on the Outer Banks can go right into January, if the weather cooperates. And you may find some nice drum around Pea Island. If the wind goes northeast, however, you're in trouble; it drives the water temperature down rapidly. When that happens the fishing stops dead. If you get lucky, an eddy off the Gulf Stream will ride into shore and pump the water temperature back up.

MIGRATION PATTERNS

If you look carefully at the above calendar, you will find some migratory patterns. The striped bass migration, for instance, moves northward and eastward in the spring and then reverses in the fall, as those bass return southward and westward. You can literally follow the action from state to state. You can catch the peak fall action in Long Island Sound during October and then head down to New Jersey a month or so later for the peak fishing there.

Many anglers assume that bluefish, bonito, false albacore, and weakfish migrate in much the same manner as striped bass—northward in the spring and southward in the fall. While some north-south movement does occur, it's far from the total picture. These other species also have an inshore-offshore response to the changing seasons: in toward shore during the spring or summer and back to deeper water during the fall.

The net result is this: Unlike striped bass fishing, the action for these other species does not move up and down the coast in a wave. Rather, these fish can arrive and depart from different parts of the coast at roughly the same time. For instance, anglers see peak bluefish action in many places of the seaboard during the same month. Autumn bluefishing peaks in October in both Long Island Sound and New Jersey. This same synchronicity is seen in the spring: Bluefish arrive on Martha's Vineyard in May, which is the same month they arrive in Long Island Sound and New Jersey. Likewise, early season weakfishing gets underway in late May in southern New England as well as in Barnegat Bay.

Weakfish are capable of both a coastal migration and an inshore-offshore migration. This seems to be related to size more than anything else. Smaller weaks, those under 22 inches, generally move along the coast during the spring and fall, while larger, tiderunner weaks move inshore and offshore. The largest weaks migrate the farthest north, moving to places such as Martha's Vineyard.

Atlantic bonito and false albacore likely have a basic north-south agenda built into their annual migration patterns, but equally important, there seems to be an inshore-offshore component. Therefore, these tunas do not run the coastline the way striped bass do; they move toward shore and then back to deep water. Bonito most likely come north in May and June to spawn offshore well to the south of New England. After spawning, they move in to feed in southern New England waters.

Of all the species, the false albacore's migration covers the shortest amount of time and often is the most abrupt, especially on the fall end. False albacore can, at times, disappear overnight. Likely the reason for this is that of all the species, they are the most in need of relatively warm water. For anglers, this means that you have to fish for them inside a short window. As a result, some anglers don't fish for other species until after the false albacore are gone.

In years when the forage is particularly abundant in southern New England, as in 1998, the false albacore may linger a few extra weeks beyond their normal departure time. The reverse is true, too; in lean years, one quick northerly blow, and the false albacore hightail it south.

In the fall, Atlantic bonito and false albacore migrate southward, working their way from southern New England waters over to Montauk. Once those fish round the outermost tip of Long Island, there does not seem to be a progressive bite along the south shore or into the mid-Atlantic beaches. Most likely, these tunas take an offshore route south. In fact, the false albacore bite along the Jersey coast occurs in October, the same time this species is still on the chew in southern New England.

The North Carolina false albacore action comes later than it does in the north. I'm not convinced, however, that these Outer Banks fish are the same ones that fed in New England in September and October. It's possible, but for one thing, these North Carolina fish are, on average, quite a bit larger. More likely, these fish are feeding at this time because this is when the near-shore forage fish are migrating to deeper water for the winter.

Changes in Migration Patterns

Over the years, I've seen changes in the migration patterns of bonito, bass, bluefish, false albacore, and weakfish. These are mostly temporary trends based on the relative abundance of a given species. Changes in the relative abundance of important forage species seems to be a very important factor, and global warming may also be having an effect.

Since the late 1990s, striped bass seemed to enter New England waters earlier than they had previously. Where it was once unusual to catch striped bass in late March and early April, it is now commonplace. The fall migration is different as well. There was a time when the fall fishery extended well into late

November and even into early December, but now the fishery seems to shut down rapidly after mid-November.

Both of these changes may be related. At present, the bass population consists of mainly young fish, which as a rule migrate earlier and return earlier than older fish. And spring water temperatures are frequently warmer than they were years ago, primarily because the winters are milder and hence the water doesn't get as cold.

Perhaps the most disturbing trend here is the disappearance of the late-season big-bass bite. Big bass once moved down the coast late in the fall, well into November. That push of big bass no longer seems to exist. It could be simply that there are not enough large fish left to make this migration noticeable to anglers. It also seems possible that this famous component of the fall fishery was made possible by the existence of schools of very large menhaden. These jumbo forage fish would have been migrating southward at that time and likely were the forage that the late-season big bass were following. Those larger menhaden, age five years and up, are no longer a sizable part of the population. But those menhaden were partly what drove big blues farther north during the 1980s.

In the late 1980s, bluefish began to dramatically disappear from the Atlantic coast. This trend gradually moved northward, finally hitting the remaining epicenter of larger bluefish in southern New England waters around 1991. The controversy as to whether this was a true population crash or simply a relocation of bluefish to offshore waters goes on today. But one thing is sure: Bluefishing has never been the same since.

When the bluefish population is large, with many older members, as it was in the 1980s, the big bluefish migrated farther north than they would have otherwise, reaching into the Gulf of Maine. For many years prior to 1977, anglers in Maine never saw these toothy critters. Then, all of a sudden, big blues were an annual angling event. The other component is forage, in this case menhaden. Those Maine-bound blues were hot on the heels of large menhaden. With the baitfish, too, age makes a difference, as it's only the older menhaden that are capable of making the trip that far north. In those years, come fall, both the big bluefish and the big menhaden cascaded down the coast, much to the delight of anglers from Cape Cod to Montauk.

During those years, the fall migration in New England made for great fishing. Day after day saw wheeling gulls and busting fish. Bass and bluefish blitzes were regular events along the coast.

If you're new to this sport, you've never seen the classic fall migrations of old. But things can change rapidly, particularly if enlightened fisheries management takes hold. The good, old days could come roaring back.

When bluefish disappeared, it left an inshore niche for other predators. One that quickly jumped into the gap was the hickory shad. The wonderful bonito and false albacore fishing in southern New England during the last ten years also may be due to the decline in bluefish. This is partly supported by the fact that the bonito and false albacore that were a regular feature in offshore waters of New Jersey have gone, perhaps having moved north.

CHAPTER EIGHT

Solving Common Problems

Saltwater fly rodding has its share of problems. Some of them are beyond anyone's control—too much wind, not enough fish. Nevertheless, many of the problems we anglers face can be greatly reduced or even eliminated with a little thought and preparation.

TANGLED FLY LINE

For the saltwater fly rodder, one maddening problem is a fly line that tangles during the cast. You make a great backcast, a fine haul, and then wham—the line comes up out of the stripping basket in a wicked snarl and jams in the guides, spoiling the whole deal. If this continues cast after cast, it can ruin your entire day.

Tangling can be greatly minimized by giving your fly lines a little TLC and following a few simple rules. First off, if the interior bottom of your stripping basket is smooth, add one of the devices intended to stop the line from sliding around. They can be home-made or purchased. Some are cone shaped; others are short stubs of heavy mono.

Never keep more line in your stripping basket than you intend to cast. Anything extra is just inviting trouble. When you place fly line in the stripping basket, be certain it goes into the basket in the right order, with the forward end of the line on top of the pile. Don't allow loops of line to hang outside the basket.

And don't walk, run, or wade any distance with a lot of fly line in your stripping basket. The motion tends to shuffle the line into knots; always reel up the line before you move. Having excess water in the bottom of the stripping basket will exacerbate the problem, so frequently empty any water that has accumulated.

Be sure the fly line you use was made for the water temperatures you'll encounter. A line designed for use in the tropics will work poorly in the cold waters of New England. Don't store your fly lines on the reel for prolonged periods of time; they will develop a memory and lie in tight coils. Instead, peel them off the spools and hang them in large, loose loops. While you're at it, inspect the line for cracks. A cracked fly line will also tangle and should be replaced as soon as possible.

When tangling occurs in the field, try reducing the amount of force you employ on the forward part of the cast. Overpowering the cast creates excessive line speed. This sends large amounts of line funneling into the first stripping guide, where they jam together. Sinking fly lines and the latest generation of fly lines boasting superslick coating are particularly a problem in this regard, as both produce higher line speeds right out of the box.

Tangling is often caused by one or more factors related to the condition of your line. The most common source of tangling is line twist. Fly lines often develop twists during heavy use, especially when you're casting large flies, but you can also twist a line by rolling it underfoot on the deck of a boat. When twisted, the line tends to roll around itself as it comes out of the stripping basket.

Dirt is another frequent culprit. When a fly line gets dirty, rarely does it do so uniformly along its entire length. Rather, there are sections of relatively clean line followed by sections of dirty line. When dirty fly line enters the guides, it drags, slowing the rate at which line exits the rod. Meanwhile, the line coming up from the stripping basket is still charging ahead. The result is a collision.

To prevent dirty or twisted lines, you should regularly prep them before heading out. The first step is to stretch the *entire* line. Some manufacturers may scream at that suggestion, but I find it is the only practical way. Stretching not only reduces any twist in the line, it also reduces any memory caused by storing the line on the spool.

Take the reel outdoors, and attach or tie the leader to a suitable object. You need something that's not sharp, and it should be roughly waist-high for ease of operation. I drove a galvanized roofing nail into the side of the back porch for this purpose. To attach the leader, I simply slip a loop knot over the nail head.

Turn the drag off and walk out into the yard, allowing line to peel from the reel. Once you're down to the last couple of turns of fly line, stop. Never go into the backing when stretching a line. Holding the reel firmly, slowly draw the reel backward, stretching the fly taut. Give it about 3 pounds worth of pressure. Hold the pressure for thirty seconds, and then slowly release it, permitting the line to lower to the ground. Repeat the process. Then let the line relax on the lawn for an hour or so.

The final step in the process is to run the line through a soft cloth moistened with fly cleaner. There are several on the market and you can also get away with ArmorAll if need be. Pulling the line through the folded cloth seems to also help eliminate twists, as long as you don't squeeze the line too hard. You can clean a fly line with soap and water if you prefer; just be sure to rinse it well.

To check your line for twists, pull off about 4 feet of fly line, and hold the end of the line about chest-high, slowly lifting the reel off the ground. Does the reel hang motionless or does it want to spin? If it quickly goes into a spin, there is twist in the line.

Sooner or later, you'll have to deal with line twist while you're in the field. There are a couple of ways to do it. The most fun method is to stretch your line on a fish. After the hookup, if possible, allow the fish to take out most of the fly line. Then lean back, slightly applying a bit more pressure on the rod than you might ordinarily do. Ease off a tad, and then slowly reapply the pressure. It works.

If your fishing buddy doesn't mind helping out, you can make a two-person project out of stretching a line. Have your friend hold one end of your fly line while you stretch from the other end. Do it over the water if you can, so the line doesn't drop onto the ground or sand and get dirty. If you're alone, try stretching 3-foot sections of line between your hands. It's slow, but it gets the job done.

Many anglers will tell you that dragging a fly line behind a boat with the fly removed will eliminate twists. It's worth a try, but in my experience, this trick is of limited value.

GETTING LINE OUT FOR THE NEXT CAST

When fishing, most anglers don't retrieve the fly all the way back, instead leaving sufficient line on the water to start another cast. People new to fly casting, however, can't cast that far to begin with, so by the time they retrieve any distance, the fly is so close to the rod tip that starting a fresh cast is difficult. Also, there are times when the fish are feeding within 15 feet of you, especially in the trough. But even when an experienced fly caster retrieves the fly back within 15 feet of the rod tip, it can be a nuisance to get enough line back out to start another cast.

If the fish are very close to you, the easiest thing to do is to simply back up so that you need not retrieve as much line inside the rod. But the real issue here is how to get enough line back out of the rod tip in order to start another cast. You could stop, put down the rod, and pull out line by hand, but that would be a lot of extra work. You could try to make a series of quick false casts, but this would waste time and energy too.

When fishing calm waters, a roll cast is often the answer. Let's say the retrieve ends, and your 9-foot rod is pointed down at the water with only 10 feet of fly line outside the rod tip. Very slowly raise the rod to vertical in preparation for a roll cast, but as you do, permit line to freely slip out through the guides as the rod moves upward. If all goes well, by the time the rod reaches the vertical, you'll have anywhere from 20 to 28 feet of line hanging outside the rod. Now make your roll cast. Immediately as the line lands, start a backcast, using the resistance of the line on the water to help load the rod. This is called a water haul. At this point, the forward cast should be a piece of cake.

HOW TO SET THE DRAG

Every angler knows that the drag's performance is critical to fighting and landing big fish. And therefore many of us are willing to spend considerable money on a quality saltwater reel with a finely engineered drag system. Yet many anglers have no idea how much drag pressure they should use.

As a rule, for bonito, false albacore, or bass or blues, for that matter, set your drag at about 10 percent of the breaking strength of your tippet. So with a 12-pound tippet, tighten the drag to about $1\frac{1}{2}$ pounds of resistance. Don't attempt this with the line strung through the guides, however. Set it straight off the reel, using an accurate spring or digital scale. After you've done it a few times, you'll develop a feel for it and be able to adjust the drag by hand.

An experienced angler does not fight these species with the drag tightened way down. It's a sure ticket to getting busted off, and a sure sign of a novice. In fact, for fish under 50 pounds, the only time you use the drag cranked any further is when fighting a big fish in a place loaded with obstacles, particularly sharp ones. In this case, I'd set the drag at 20 percent of the tippet's breaking strength.

So are you going to fight fish with only a pound and a half of pull? No. After you string up the rod and put a bend in it, that pound and a half of drag rises quickly. And you can add further pressure by squeezing the line to the rod blank, or if you have an exposed rim on your reel, you can palm it. Altogether, this creates a powerful and yet flexible system with which to fight a big fish.

KNOWING HOW TO USE YOUR ROD

When you latch on to a fish of less than 10 pounds, you can make plenty of mistakes and still win the war. But when you lock horns with the fish of a life-time, you'd best know what you're doing. Setting the drag is only half the equation. Knowing how to properly use your rod is equally important.

As with setting the drag, I strongly suggest that you do a little practice at home to get the feel of the equipment, rather than wait until you're on the water. A 9- or 10-weight rod, in good condition, should be capable of producing upward of 5 pounds of pull, if you know how to do it. But too few anglers do.

With the drag set as described above, string up your rod, and double-check that the ferrules are properly assembled. This is important. A ferrule not fully assembled may well break. Next, pull out 60 feet of line. You'll need a friend and an accurate spring scale. Attach the scale to the end of the line, and have your friend hold it to the ground. Walk back and pick up the rod. Pinch the fly line tightly to the rod blank, and then bend the rod gradually. Have your friend tell you when you reach 2 pounds of pull.

You'll find that this is difficult to accomplish if the rod is held fairly vertical. With the rod vertical, you're fighting the fish mainly off the tip of the rod, the weakest portion. Instead, point the rod toward the scale. Then, with the line tight, raise the rod to roughly a 45-degree angle. Now the tip-top guide and the last few snake guides should be in a straight line, with the rod bent mainly through the middle of the blank, where the power lies. Now it's easy to reach 2 pounds of pull.

Study how the rod looks and feels under this load. Gradually increase the load by squeezing the line or palming the reel until you attain 3 pounds. Again note how the rod looks and feels. Finally, bring the load up to 4 pounds. Again study the shape of the rod. With a little practice, you'll be able to quickly tell by looking at the rod how much pressure you are applying to the fish. Do this for all the rods you regularly use. You can't expect rods designed for lighter line weights to reach 4 pounds, but an 8-weight, for example, can generate 3 pounds of pull.

If you fish mainly from a boat, you may want to try this same rod-bending routine from a second-story window. That way, you can see how the rod reacts when lifting a fish up from the depths. This time your friend should be directly below you. And this time your neighbors may be staring, or even laughing, over the fence. But you'll be the one doing the laughing when that big fish tries to sound next to the boat.

ORGANIZING CASTERS IN A BOAT

First, let's set up a hypothetical situation, one to use as a platform for our discussion. The boat in question is a center console of anywhere from 17 to 22 feet in length. There are two right-handed fly casters aboard, and a 15-knot wind is striking the boat abeam on the port (left) side.

It makes the most sense to cast downwind, so both casters should be facing starboard. A right-hander casting from the stern is in good shape. Both the forward cast and the backcast are away from the center of the boat. But for the caster in the bow, it's a different story. That person's cast is going to send the fly directly over the center of the boat. And that's how hooks end up where they don't belong.

Short of befriending a left-hander, here's what you can do. First off, the right-hander in the front of the boat should move as far toward the bow as is safely possible. This increases the distance between the two casters. Next, the bow caster must not cast sidearm. Sidearm casting lowers the rod tip, and therefore the fly line, as it travels back and forth, and a lower fly line increases the chances of the hook striking the boat or one of the occupants.

Instead, the angler in the bow must cast in an overhead manner, with the rod as vertical as possible. Surprisingly, many inexperienced saltwater casters, particularly those who have long used a sidearm approach in fresh water, find it difficult to keep the rod up high. When that is the case, that angler should move to the stern, and the more experienced caster should go forward. Another option is to have the person in the bow cast backhanded. It's awkward, but veteran saltwater fly casters can do it fairly well. Once again, the more experienced caster should be in the bow.

In this example, the wind is on the port side. If, however, the wind was striking the boat on the starboard side, and again there were two right-handed casters, the more experienced caster should be in the stern and the less experienced one in the bow. If you're not sure why, draw yourself a diagram. I think the reasoning will quickly become obvious.

If both anglers cast directly downwind, there is little chance of their back-casts ever becoming entangled. If the boat is drifting fast, however, casting 45 degrees to the centerline of the hull makes fishing easier. The boat does not overtake the fly so quickly. Even with a left-hander in the bow, the backcasts can interfere with one another. The best solution is for the casters to agree to alternate the timing of their backcasts. It takes a little cooperation.

Many of today's boats are designed specifically with fly casters in mind. They have clean decks and an environment free of snags. I still like to have a stripping basket aboard. The caster can either wear it or simply place it on the deck and drop line into it. It can give you an edge when you need to quickly fire off a long cast. If you leave the fly line lying on the deck, take care that it doesn't snag under your shoe. You can avoid this hassle by going barefoot when weather allows.

MISSED STRIKES

Every angler occasionally misses a strike. The long-awaited tug comes, but you can't slip the steel home. Sometimes wet hands are the culprit. Sometimes it's a bad hook. Perhaps the point is broken off, rolled over, or just plain dull. And sometimes it's the fish in front of you that are the source of the trouble. They are either not very aggressive or quite small.

Butterfingers and dull hooks can both be remedied easily. Carry a small hand towel in your jacket, especially in cold weather, and use it frequently to dry your hands. Make a conscious effort to hold the line firmly in your hand during the retrieve. To avoid dull hooks, always carry a hook hone, and use it frequently.

Short-striking fish may require a bit more effort. When fish nip short, the first thing to do is to make a significant change in your retrieve speed. If your retrieve has been fast, slow it way down, or vice versa. Sometimes the answer is to stop the retrieve. When water temperatures are 50 degrees or cooler, small schoolie bass may lightly tap the fly without taking it deep into their mouth. You'll feel the tap, yet often you can't seem to hook up. In this situation, after you feel the tap, stop retrieving. Many times the bass will immediately hit the fly a second time, but much harder, allowing you to drive home the hook.

If that doesn't help, try a different size fly. Often I've had small fish nip at the tail of a long fly. When I switched to a much shorter fly, I got solid hookups. You can't expect to hook bass or blues of less than 4 pounds on a large 2/0 popper. The fly is simply too big for them to latch on to. In such cases, either use a much smaller popper or go subsurface with an appropriate-size streamer.

Missing the occasional fish is one thing, but if you're missing a lot of strikes across the span of the season, you're doing something wrong. Usually the cause is one of two things: too much slack in the line during the retrieve or attempting to set the hook with an improper motion. Of these two, the first is by far the more common. When you're fishing, always keep this in mind: If you can't feel the subtle weight of the fly at the end of the line during the retrieve, you can't expect to feel the strike in time or deliver enough force to drive the hook home. It's that simple.

To remove excess slack in the line, you need to be aware of a few things. First, during the retrieve, the greater the distance between the rod tip and the water, the more slack you have, and the more fish you'll miss. This is especially a problem for anglers working from a boat, since they're standing well above the water, but it affects beach-based anglers, too. The rule here is this: The rod tip must be pointed down at the water during the retrieve. Don't forget it. If you're wading, the rod tip can even be in the water.

Current and waves can also cause slack in the line. When a fly line is cast across a rip, the current produces a belly in the line. That belly is slack between you and the fly, and should the strike come before the fly reaches the end of its swing, it will make setting the hook very difficult. One way to reduce the belly is by following the fly's progress downcurrent with the rod tip. This decreases the curve in the line, and thereby gives you more control of the fly.

Another strategy is to cast slightly downcurrent instead of straight across. This gives the current less of an opportunity to belly the line, although if you're working with a sinking line, the line also has less opportunity to sink. With a floating line or a sinking line with a floating running line, you can make an upcurrent mend just as a freshwater angler does. When properly done, this removes much of the belly in the line.

Waves cause slack for a different reason. As a wave passes under the fly line, it lifts the line momentarily, creating slack. A sinking fly line is one solution, since it gets you under the waves and therefore out of trouble. If you don't have or want to use a sinking line, you can switch to a weighted fly, which produces more resistance in the water and is therefore easier to feel. Or you can pick up your retrieve speed as a wave passes under the fly line. This removes slack and gets you back in contact with the fly. As the wave passes by,

If you miss strikes often, it may be because your rod tip is too high off the water. Keep the tip down.

you can then resume a normal retrieve speed, but be ready to speed up again should another wave approach.

Other things can also account for missed strikes. Fish that strike at the end of the retrieve can be hard to hook, especially for anglers that habitually set the hook by raising the rod. This tends to yank the hook upward and out of the fish's mouth, and it also tends to cushion the force of the hook set. A better way to strike with the rod is to sweep it to one side rather than lift it skyward. Setting the hook by using the line rather than raising the rod is the most positive hook set, however. As the fish takes, simply pull back on the line without changing the rod's position. When you feel the fish's full weight, the steel is home. Then, as the fish turns and runs, allow line to slide out through your hand, maintaining some resistance. Once the fish is on the reel, slowly raise the rod on a tight line.

KNOTS THAT FAIL

Knots should rarely fail. When they do, it's usually because the tier either improperly tied the knot or failed to draw it tight. Learning the correct method is easy, and there are books on the subject to help you. Drawing a knot fully down requires that you wet the line and use sufficient strength to close things up. When you're done, make it a habit to examine the knot. Is it neatly formed? Are all the wraps or turns in the knot in order, or do some jump out of line? If it looks wrong, retie it.

A large jump in diameter between two sections of a leader is apt to cause trouble, too. For instance, knotting 12-pound-test mono directly to 25-pound-test is asking for a problem, even if you tie the knot perfectly. When you must do it, be sure to employ a knot known to be able to join two pieces of mono of greatly dissimilar size. The surgeon's knot is one. Another solution is to use a loop-to-loop connection, such as the surgeon's loop.

Attempting to join two different brands of monofilaments can make things go awry, too. Monofilaments can be so dissimilar in their physical properties that they are very difficult to properly join. Some have harder coatings than others and will quickly cut through other brands when placed under load. Consequently, as a general rule, it's best to use the same brand of monofilament for the entire leader, unless you've tested two brands and found them to knot well together. A simple backyard test with a spring scale is sufficient to determine if this is the case. Construct two leaders of equal length and strength, one using a single brand of mono, the other using the two brands you wish to check. Attach the butt end of the leaders to a stationary object and tie a surgeon's loop in the ends of the tippets. Wet the leaders. Connect an accurate spring scale to the tippet of one leader and slowly apply pressure, noting at what poundage the leader breaks. Do the same for the other leader. If the two-brand leader proves noticeably weaker and consistently fails where the two are joined, you can assume the two monos are incompatible.

NAVIGATING THE BEACH AT NIGHT

There are several problems you're likely to run into when fishing at night. In an effort to lighten the load, anglers frequently put gear down on the beach while they fish, only to have difficulty locating it later in the dark. Another problem occurs when looking for the trail back through the dunes to your car. In the inky darkness, it can be hard to spot.

One way to reduce these types of frustration is to carry lightweight plastic reflectors—the kind that are intended to be mounted on a tree to identify a driveway at night. They can be purchased at most hardware stores and are inexpensive, lightweight, and impervious to salt air.

When you put equipment down on the beach, drop one of these reflectors on top. When you swing your light searching for the stuff later, the reflector will beam back at you. To mark a trail, stick one high in the side of the dune where you come onto the beach. When you want to find your way back later, scan the dunes with your flashlight until the reflector shines back. Be sure to pick them up as you go.

Anglers often wade out to a bar at twilight only to find themselves unsure of the route back as darkness descends. Assuming you used the shallowest route on the way out to the bar, you'll want to use that same route back. Finding it in the dark, however, can be a problem unless there are sufficient landmarks on the horizon. One solution is to plant two cold light sticks, of the type used by bait fishermen and boaters, in the beach when you first head out to the bar. They're inexpensive and can be purchased in tackle and marine accessory shops. Activate them and then set them above the high-tide mark directly in front of where you plan to enter the water. The lights should be 6 feet apart, one behind the other. As you wade out, look back at the lights. They should appear almost as one. Expect them to burn for a couple hours. Later, when you want to return, move along the bar until the lights are again lined up. You're ready to cross back.

THE PERSON NEXT TO YOU IS CATCHING ALL THE FISH

Sooner or later you'll find yourself in a situation where the person next to you is catching fish after fish, but you can't hook a thing. Don't get frustrated; get focused. Take a deep breath, and watch out of the corner of your eye; study what is going on. Begin by matching the other angler's retrieve speed. Often this is the key. At the same time, note where your neighbor is catching the fish. Are they at the end of the cast? Are you casting that far? Or are those fish hitting in close and you're picking up your fly too soon? Adjust as necessary. When the angler unhooks a fish, get an idea of how big the fly is, and compare it with the one you're using. Change flies if needed.

Finally, recognize that sometimes fish are highly concentrated into a small area. Even though you're standing only 50 feet away, you may be casting over empty water while your neighbor is throwing the fly right into a school of fish. It happens. In that case, you may have to move. Try going to the other side of the angler in the hope that this will put you in front of the fish. But never crowd the other angler in the process.

CHAPTER NINE

A Guide to Lobsterville Beach and Dogfish Bar

Every June for the last dozen years, it's been my good fortune to travel to Martha's Vineyard. I do it with one thing in mind: fishing for striped bass on what is likely the most famous fly-fishing stretch of sand on the Atlantic—Lobsterville Beach and Dogfish Bar.

Together they sit on the northwest end of the island, amounting to 4 miles of strand starting from Menemsha Inlet and running westward. This is a fairly protected shoreline, with hyaline water and some mighty scenic views. To my way of thinking, every coastal fly rodder worth his or her salt ought to make at least one journey here. And with that in mind, I'd like to close this book by giving readers a brief overview of how to fish this legendary location.

The ferry from the mainland leaves from Woods Hole and drops you in either Vineyard Haven or Oaks Bluff, both on the island's eastern end. Regardless of which port you arrive in, within a ten-minute ride there are two tackle shops that specifically cater to fly rodders: Coop's Bait and Tackle and Larry's Tackle. These shops have fine, knowledgeable folks behind the counters, who are always willing to give you an update on the present fishing conditions. So by all means, stop into both shops and take advantage of the advice.

Both places offer excellent guide services, too, and a night on the beach with a local expert is worth its weight in gold. While you're in one of the shops, ask for directions to the parking lot at Lobsterville Beach. It's a bit of a ride, and before you get behind the wheel, I suggest that you get some sodas and sandwiches. There are far fewer services where you're headed down at the west end of the island.

Eventually you'll come to Lobsterville Road. Turn right and head down to the water. As soon as the road begins to bend to the right, slow down. The parking lot at Lobsterville Beach is at hand. I use the term lot loosely; in reality, it's a small pull-off area on the left side of the road, with barely room for a dozen cars. Obey the parking signs, and keep your vehicle out of the sand and off the vegetation; it's fragile stuff.

From the lot, you look northward into Vineyard Sound and, more specifically, into a portion of the sound known as Menemsha Bight. It is postcard perfect. Across the way, on the horizon, sit the Elizabeth Islands. There are actually four or more islands in the chain, but from here, they all look as one. To your right down the beach, as far as you can see, is Menemsha Inlet, while to your left, out of view, lie the shores of Dogfish Bar. At the moment, you're standing roughly midway between them.

Over the years, June has shown me many faces. I've fished through sweltering dog days when the mercury hung at 90. And I've braved nights of horizontal rain, whistling winds, and air temperatures down into the forties. Best keep an eye on the weather, particularly the wind. If it's a southwest wind, that's good news, as it keeps the stripers happily slurping. And the stronger it howls, sometimes the better. Anything from the north may ignite a furious bite, but it won't stay lit for long. At best, you'll get a tide's worth of action, and then the fishing dries up, perhaps for days. But as soon as the wind swings to the southwest again, get back to the beach. Things will tear wide open.

The worst wind is undoubtedly a northeaster. Against a rising tide, it'll quickly paint whitecaps across the sound and send waves banging against the beach. Not only does the fishing fall away like a stone, but the water murks up to boot. A southeast wind is more of a mystery; it could be good or bad. Often it brings fog, which sneaks up from behind you. And one thing is for sure: A southeast wind is nearly always a sign that the weather is changing.

For these shores, I suggest anything from an 8- to a 10-weight rod. Take your pick, with one word of warning: The 8 is fun, but some of the bass here are true beasts. If you latch on to one, it'll make that little rod groan into the corks. Whatever rod you elect to use, arm it with both an intermediate and a floating fly line. The intermediate does 90 percent of the task, but on dead calm nights, the floater can work like a charm. From the parking lot to Menemsha Inlet, you won't be walking into the water much, so hip boots are adequate. But down at Dogfish Bar, things are different. There you'll want chest waders.

On a calm, sunny day, you'll see a dark blue drop-off out about a quarter of a mile from the parking lot. If it's a good year for juvenile Atlantic herring, they'll be schooled up along this edge during the middle of the day, and the bass will be blasting them. Flocks of busy gulls let you know if it's going on. While the bite is a long way off the beach, its presence is nevertheless an excellent sign. Expect those herring to move in come late afternoon and the bass to blitz them right on the beach.

Lobsterville Beach is drop-dead gorgeous, but in terms of edges, it's pretty nondescript. Consequently, the bass move in and out of here with the changing light and rarely take up permanent station in any one spot. Nevertheless, once they come in, this stretch cranks out some mighty fine fishing, and some monster bass have touched the sand. Why? There can be some good current here, but the biggest reason is right in front of you: the trough usually holds zillions of sand eels.

The bottom next to shore is made up of small stones, but out 100 feet or more it drops away and turns to sand. As the sun lowers, big bass frequently cruise this edge, so you should watch the water for large swirls in this vicinity. A large streamer or slider is best. If you can't chuck a big fly that far, no problem; as the light lowers further, there will be bass right at your feet.

When bass herd those small herring against the beach in late afternoon, this is one of the locations where the action often erupts. If it happens, you can't miss it. There will be big patches of nervous water being ripped apart with explosion, and you'll see bait spraying up on the sand. The blitz usually occurs in clusters up and down the beach and moves around a bit. Put the fly anyplace close and you'll soon be hooked up.

Given its position inside Menemsha Bight, Lobsterville Beach gets a fair amount of current, particularly on the ebb. That helps fuel things. On the drop, the current is pretty close to the beach, moving from right to left, and that draws fish in tight to feed. At night, the bass are right in the trough, but they can be tough at times. Small sand eel flies or small sliders do most of the work. And the right retrieve is a creep. This holds true along the entire 4 miles.

To your right, the shore wraps around in a gigantic bowl, a long, sweeping curve that runs all the way to Menemsha Inlet, a distance of just under 2 miles.

This stretch of sand does not see much angling pressure, for one simple reason: Most folks don't want to walk that far, especially since there's so much good fishing right by the parking lot. Making the trek in guarantees you'll have some elbow room, however, and some fine fishing, too.

If you elect to make the hoof, look for a culvert sticking out from under the road a short distance down the beach. This culvert is a drain for a small bog situated on the south side of the road. Most Junes, the pipe is bone dry. Yet in a wet spring, a dark, tannic stream gushes forth and over the beach. If it's running, by all means stop and fish here. Where the stream joins the salt, a delta forms, and around this edge, forage and stripers stack up. It's a nice little spot.

After that, except for the trough, the bottom doesn't have a lot of edges, so the action in the bowl tends to move around a lot. Look for the places where the bait is stacked up. Since the water is gin clear, that's not hard to do. As twilight approaches, watch the water closely for swirls. The ones in close are apt to be schoolies; the big boys are more likely out 50 to 100 feet or more.

Study the slope of the beach carefully as you walk in. If you're a good detective, you'll discover a section where the water close to shore is noticeably deeper. The fishing can be super here. In fact, when juvenile Atlantic herring are abundant, they often come and drop anchor here in around 5:00 in the afternoon. I'm not going to tell you exactly where this edge is, but I'll give you a hint: You'll need your canteen.

The last 300 yards of beach leading to the west wall at Menemsha Inlet can be a very fishy location. If you're interested in it, rather than walk down from the Lobsterville parking lot, drive down West Basin Road to the lot at the inlet, and then walk back to the west. As you come over the dune, the pocket of water where the beach greets the jetty wall holds a lot of bait and is an excellent place to begin, although on a windy day, there may also be a lot of floating debris.

Though you can't see the shore of Dogfish from the lot, with a keen eye you can see a portion of the actual bar. It's about a mile away to your left, well out into Vineyard Sound. When the tide is low, there are waves breaking over it, but even when not, you can see the change in color of the water. At the moment, you're looking at just the tip of the eastern end. From there, the bar arcs back toward Gay Head Light and probably covers a couple square miles. All told, Dogfish is an enormous structure.

When anglers say they fished Dogfish Bar, typically they don't mean they were on the bar itself, but rather on the shoreline directly facing it.

This shoreline is home to all kinds of edges and a good, sweeping current, particularly on the ebb. To reach it, walk to the west from Lobsterville Beach. Like heading east into the bowl, this march demands some serious legwork, and you may debate whether to do it given the excellent fish right in front of the parking lot.

Initially the shoreline runs fairly straight, but several hundred yards down, you'll come to a broad cusp in the beach. This bend is nothing radical, but often it's a hot spot just before dark and sometimes very late at night. I know of no clear demarcation where Lobsterville Beach ends, but once you round this first bend, you are entering the realm of Dogfish Bar.

Behind you, the trail home disappears around the bend, and the beach before you straightens again, but this time only briefly. Up ahead, the next bend lies in plain view. It juts out more sharply, and as you walk toward it, you'll notice that the beach around you takes on the feel of a small cove. Good fishing can be had along this "cove," and at low tide you can wade out a fair ways.

When you reach the second bend, stop for a moment and take a breather. Now you're in the final quarter mile of the journey. Ahead to the west are two more bends, each one jogging the beach outward farther. Together, these three jogs are like a set of stairs in the shoreline. These "steps" have a wealth of edges—troughs, sandbars, slough, rips, and holes—all of which you should easily find.

On the ebb, the "steps" are alive with current. The tide comes right along the beach and kisses the tips of all three bends, causing rips to form. The bass feed in these rips. As the hours go by, the current falls farther and farther off the "steps," leaving pockets of stillwater between the bends. There may still be oodles of bass slurping away in close, but they are fussy and apt to be quite small. The bruiser bass are out in the remaining current, if you can reach them.

Bibliography

Saltwater Fly Fishing

Abrames, J. Kenney. *Striper Moon.* Portland, Or.: Amato, 1994.

Brooks, Joe. *Salt Water Fly Fishing.* New York: Putnam's Son, 1950.

Brooks, Joe. *Salt Water Game Fishing.* New York: Harper & Row, 1968.*

Brooks, Joe. *Bermuda Fishing.* Harrisburg, Pa.: Stackpole, 1957.*

Burns, Brad. *The L.L. Bean Fly Fishing for Striped Bass Handbook.* New York: Lyons Press, 1998.

Daignault, Frank. *Striper Surf.* Chester, Ct.: Globe Pequot, 1992.*

Earnhardt, Tom. *Fly Fishing the Tidewaters.* New York: Lyons & Burford, 1995.

Karas, Nicholas. *The Striped Bass,* rev. ed. New York: Karmapco & Lyons, 1993.*

Kreh, Lefty. *Fly Fishing in Salt Waters.* rev. ed. New York: Lyons Books, 1986.

Mitchell, Ed. *Fly Rodding the Coast.* Mechanicsburg, Pa. : Stackpole, 1995.

Moss, Frank. *Successful Striped Bass Fishing.* Camden, Me.: International Marine, 1974.*

Nix, Sam. *Salt Water Fly-Fishing Handbook.* Garden City, N.Y.: Doubleday, 1973.

Post, Robert. *Reading the Water.* Chester, Ct.; Globe Pequot, 1988.*

Rosko, Milt. *Secrets of Striped Bass Fishing.* London: Macmillan, 1966.*

Sands, George. *Salt Water Fly Fishing.* New York: Knopf, 1970.

Sosin, Mark. *Practical Light-Tackle Fishing.* New York: Lyons/Doubleday, 1979.*

Sosin, Mark, and Kreh, Lefty. *Fishing the Flats.* New York: Lyons & Burford, 1983.*

Tabory, Lou. *Inshore Fly Fishing.* New York: Lyons & Burford, 1992.

Tabory, Lou. *Stripers on the Fly.* New York: Lyons Press, 1999.

Woolner, Frank. *Modern Saltwater Sport Fishing.* New York: Crown, 1972.*

Woolner, Frank, and Henry Lyman. *Striped Bass Fishing,* rev. ed. New York: Winchester Lyons, 1983.*

* Includes section on fly fishing.

Saltwater Fly Tying

Abrames, J. Kenney. *A Perfect Fish.* Portland, Or.: Amato, 1999.

Saltwater Fly Tying *continued*
Bates, Joseph. *Streamers and Bucktails.* New York: Knopf, 1979.*
Bates, Joseph, *Streamer Fly Tying and Fishing,* rev. ed. Harrisburg, Pa.: Stackpole, 1966.*
Bay, Kenneth E. *Saltwater Flies.* New York: Knopf, 1972.
Gartside, Jack. *Striper Flies,* 2nd ed. self-published. www.jackgartside.com
Jaworoski, Ed, and Bob Popovics. *Pop Fleyes.* Mechanicsburg, Pa.: Stackpole, 2001.
Kreh, Lefty. *Salt Water Fly Patterns.* Fullerton, Calif.: Maral, Inc., n.d.
Leiser, Eric. *The Book of Fly Patterns.* New York: Knopf, 1987.*
Meyer, Deke *Saltwater Flies: Over 700 of the Best.* Portland, Or.: Amato, 1995.
Steward, Dick, and Farrow Allen. *Flies for Saltwater.* North Conway, N.H.: Mountain Pond, 1992.
Ververka, Bob. *Innovative Saltwater Flies.* Mechanicsburg, Pa.: Stackpole, 2000.
Wentink, Frank. *Saltwater Fly Tying.* New York: Lyons & Burford, 1991.

* Mainly on freshwater patterns but has useful references to saltwater flies.

Saltwater Baitfish
Caolo, Alan. *Fly Fisherman's Guide to Atlantic Baitfish.* Portland, Or.: Amato, 1995.
Roberts, George. *Saltwater Naturals and Their Imitations.* Camden, Me.: Ragged Mountain Press, 1994.
Tabory, Lou. *Lou Tabory's Guide to Saltwater Baits and Their Imitation.* New York: Lyons & Burford, 1995.

Southern Saltwater Fly Fishing
Babson, Stanley. *Bonefishing.* New York: Harpers & Row, 1965.
Beck, Barry and Cathy. *Fly-Fishing the Flats.* Mechanicsburg, Pa.: Stackpole, 1999.
Brown, Dick, *Fly Fishing for Bonefish.* New York: Lyons & Burford, 1993.
Kaufmann, Randall. *Bonefishing with a Fly.* Portland, Or.: Western Fisherman's Press, 1992.

Saltwater Environment
Bulloch, David K. *The Underwater Naturalist.* New York: Lyons & Burford, 1991.
Ross, David. *The Fisherman's Ocean.* Mechanicsburg, Pa.: Stackpole, 2000.

Index

Page numbers in italics refer to photos or illustrations.

A

Albacore. *See* false albacore
Albemarle Sound (North Carolina), 196, 197
Albie Alley, 181, 193
Alewife, 77, 127
American shad, 77, 79, 80, 195
Anchovy. *See* bay anchovy
Annapolis River (Nova Scotia), 173
Annelids. *See* worm hatches
Apogee moon, 40
Aquinnah, cliffs of (Martha's Vineyard), *173*
Atlantic bonito, 1–25
  best time of day for, 19–21
  birds and, 6, *6*, 8, 12
  fighting, 21–25
  flies for 5, 25
  habits, 3–6, 10, 14–16
  locations for, 3, 4, 9, 11, 88, 106, 117, 128
  preparing to fish for, 5, 11, 12
  presenting a fly to, 13, 15
  season for, 3
  releasing, 24
  run of, 22
  spawning, 186
  spotting on top, 5, 6
  tactics from shore, 7–11
  tactics from a boat, 11–21
  water temperature and, 16
Atlantic croakers, 195
Atlantic herring, 35
Atlantic menhaden (bunker), 57, 62, 74, 80, 90, 96, 132, 147–153, 168, 169, 201
  baby menhaden or peanut bunker, 35, 148–150, *149*, 152, 153
  fishing over adult menhaden, 150, 151
Atlantic silversides, 18, 90, 96, 99, 116, 132, 146, 147, *147*
Autumnal equinox, 165

B

Baby menhaden. *See* Atlantic menhaden
Backing, 5, 22
Back-reeling, 22
Backwash, 87
Barden's Inlet (North Carolina), 196
Baitfish. *See* forage
Bars. *See* sandbars
Bass. *See* striped bass
Barnegat Bay and Inlet (New Jersey), 192, 193
Barnstable Harbor (Massachusetts), 179
Barometric pressure, 32, 169, 170
Bartlet's Reef (Connecticut), 188
Bathurst Harbor (New Brunswick), 174
Bay anchovy, 137–141, *140*
Bay of Fundy (Canadian Maritimes), 172, 173
Beaches
  edges on, 82–86
  estuaries and, 127–130
  etiquette on, 42
  fishing rules for, 86
  importance of baitfish on,
  navigating at night, 37, 212, 213
  points, 32, 41, 42, *85*
  rock piles, 122–127
  sandbars, 102–110
  shape and slope of, 84–86
  sloughs, 95–102
  tidal creeks on, 74, 127, *128*, 129, *130*
  trolling from, 94
  troughs, 86–95. *See also* fishing from shore for various game fish species
Berry Brook (New Hampshire), 176
Big flies, 25, 64, 80, 116, 126, 133, 151, 152
Billinsgate Shoal (Massachusetts), 178
Birds, 6
  hooded gulls, 12
  terns, 142, 143

Black Point (Connecticut), 188
Blitzes, 12, 13, 35, 45, 57, 60, 62–64, 130, 133, 150
Block Island (Rhode Island), 183, 184
Bloody Point Bar (Chesapeake Bay), 196
Bluefish,
  biting schoolie bass, 66
  blitzing on top, 57, 62
  chumming for, 66
  daisy chaining, 65
  dawn fishing for, 58, 59
  diet of, 57
  fighting and landing, 67, 68
  flies for, 57, 63
  jumping, 68
  locations for, 56, 57, 88, 96, 106, 111, 115, 117, 128
  night fishing for, 60, 61
  poppers and, 62, 63, 67
  retrieve speed, 62, 67, 68
  shock tippets for, 67, 68
  tactics from shore, 57–63
  tactics from a boat, 63–66
  teeth of, 56, 69
  water temperature, 56, 61
Bob's Banger (Bob Popovics), 152
Bonito. See Atlantic bonito
Bourne Pond (Massachusetts), 177
Brandywine Shoal (Delaware), 194
Breezy Point (Chesapeake Bay), 196
Brewster Flats (Massachusetts), 178
Bunker. See Atlantic menhaden
Buzzards Bay (Massachusetts), 178

C
Calves Island (Connecticut), 185
Camp Ellis (Maine), 175
Canadian Maritime fishing, 77, 172–174
Cape Cod (Massachusetts), 40, 97, 141, 145, 177, 178, 180, 181
Cape Cod Bay (Massachusetts), 178, 180
Cape Cod Canal (Massachusetts), 177
Cape Hatteras (North Carolina), 149
Cape Lookout (North Carolina), 196, 198
Cape May (New Jersey), 192, 193

Cape Pogue (Martha's Vineyard), 4, 178, 181
Cape Point (North Carolina), 197
Casting, 92, 93
  getting line out for, 205, 206
  fan-casting 13, 34, 34, 99, 105
  night, 38
  tactics in the trough, 88, 89
Caumsett Park (New York), 190
Chaleur Bay (New Brunswick), 174
Channels, fishing in, 32, 75, 117–122
  bends, 118, 119
  end of, 119
  tides for, 120, 121
Charlestown Breachway (Rhode Island), 184
Charley Cinto, 179
Chatham (Massachusetts), 177, 178, 181
Chesapeake Bay (Maryland), 172, 185, 194
Chesapeake Bay Bridge Tunnel (Maryland), 195
Choptank River (Maryland), 195
Chowan River (North Carolina), 197
Cinder Worm (Eric Petersen), 161
Clamworms. See worm hatches
Cleats, 9, 124
Clouser Deep Minnow, 80, 114, 145
Cold fronts. See fronts and weather
Compo Beach (Connecticut), 187
Connecticut fishing, 184–189
Connecticut River, 79, 162, 168, 171, 185, 186, 188
Conowingo Dam (Maryland), 195
Conimicut Point (Rhode Island), 182
Cotuit Bay (Massachusetts), 178, 179
Coop's Bait & Tackle (Martha's Vineyard), 214
Corsair Sand Eel (Jack Gartside), 133
Crabs, 18, 116, 154–156, 155
Crab flies, 113, 114
Crab Meadow Park (New York), 190
Crazy Charlie, 80
Crease Fly (Joe Blados), 153
Creeks. See tidal creeks
Croton Point (New York), 189

Current, 95–101
    channels and, 118–120
    estuaries and, 127, 128, *128*, 130
    longshore currents, 95, 104
    rock piles and, 122–126
    sandbars and, 104, 106, *107*, 108, *109*, 110
    sloughs and, 96–101, *97*
    troughs and, 94,95
    See also rips and tides
Cuts. *See* sandbars
Cuttyhunk (Massachusetts), 179, 181

D
Dawn fishing, 95
    bluefish and, 58, 59
    sand eels and, 143, 144
    striped bass and, 36, 37, 41, 50
    seasonal aspects of, 41
    hickory shad and, 79
    weakfish and, 74
Deceiver. *See* Lefty's Deceiver
Deep Candy (Bob Popovics), 140
Deep Sparkling Sand Eel (Chris Windram), 145
Deer Creek (Maryland), 195
Delaware fishing, 194
Delaware Bay and River, 172, 192, 194
Devils Bridge (Massachusetts), 26, 181
Dogfish Bar (Martha's Vineyard), 214–218
Drag, 206, 207
Drop-offs, 47, *84*, 87, 106, 118, *118*, 120, 129
Dropper flies, 134–137
Dusk fishing,
    bluefish at, 59
    hickory shad, 79
    striped bass, 36, 37, 41, 50
    weakfish, 74
    sand eels and, 143
    seasonal aspects of, 41

E
East Beach (Rhode Island), 184
East River (New York), 189
Eastern equine encephalitis, 117

Edgartown Great Pond (Martha's Vineyard), 177
Edgartown Harbor, (Martha's Vineyard), 4
Eelgrass, 74, 122
Eldridge Tide and Pilot Book, 40
Elizabeth Island Chain (Massachusetts), 179, 181
Enfield Dam (Connecticut), 185
Estuaries, fishing in, 41, 42, 127–130, *128*, *129*, *130*

F
Falmouth (Massachusetts), 4, 177, 178
False albacore, 1–25
    best time of day for, 19–21
    birds and, 5, 6, *6*, 8, 12
    fighting and landing, 21–25
    flies for, 5, 25
    locations for, 3, 7, 9, 11, 88, 106, 117, 128
    preparing for, 5, 11, 12
    presentation of fly to, 13, 15
    reviving, 24
    runs of, 22
    tactics from shore, 7–11
    tactics from a boat, 11–21
    seasons for, 3
    spotting on top, 5, 6
Fan-casting 34, *34*, 99, 105
Ferry Landing State Park (Connecticut), 185
Fighting fish. *See* various species
Finger bar. *See* sandbars
Fishers Island Sound (Connecticut), 184, 186, 187
Flashlights, 37, 38, 95
Flies, *(see also color plates)*
    baitfish imitations, 132
    bay anchovy flies, 139, 140
    big flies, 25, 64, 80, 126, 133
    Bob's Banger (Bob Popovics), 152
    Clouser Deep Minnow, 80, 145
    Cinder Worm, (Eric Petersen), 161
    Corsair Sand Eel (Jack Gartside), 133
    Crease Fly (Joe Blados), 153

Deep Candy (Bob Popovics), 140
Deep Sparkling Sand Eel (Chris Windram), 145
dropper flies, 134–137
epoxy flies, 139
fouled fly, 39
Gurgler (Jack Gartside), 133
Inner-Flash Baby Bunker (Bob Popovics), 153
Jiggy (Bob Popovics), 80, 133, 145
Lazer Bay Anchovy (Bob Veverka), 139
Lefty's Deceiver, 100, 135, 140, 144, 146
Mark's EZ Body Squid (Mark Lewchik), 157
poppers, 61–64, 76, 91, 100, 106, 124, 135, 150, 152, 156
Pop Lip (Bob Popovics), 133
Presto Felt Worm Fly (Phil Farnsworth), 161
Razzle Dazzle (Kenney Abrames), 135, 152
sand eel flies, 27, 135, 99, 114, 142
shrimp flies, 75, 76, 135
Siliclone (Bob Popovics), 154
sliders, 38, 80, 91, 100, 114, 145, 146
squid flies, 144, 157
3-D Shimmering Squid (Bob Veverka), 157
worm flies, 161
Fly lines, 203–205
intermediate, 10, 45, 90, 91, 99, 113
floating, 91, 92, 113, 121, 145
sinking, 9, 10, 11, 44, 45, 64, 74, 91, 99, 100, 108, 120
stretching, 204, 205
tangles in, 203, 204
twists in, 204
Fly rods, 44, 45, 68, 73, 80, 91, 99, 100, 101, 114, 121, 136
applying pressure with, 207, 208
keeping tip down, 38, 90, 126
pumping, 23, 54
under the arm, 10, 51, 54, 90
Fog, 32, 59
Forage, 56, 82, 87, 90, 96, 101, 127, 131, 200
See also individual species
Fronts, 32, 50, 59, 75. See also weather

G
Gardiner's Bay (New York), 191
Gateway National Recreational Area (New York), 190
General Sullivan Bridge (New Hampshire), 176
Gin Beach (New York), 192
Goldsmith's Inlet (New York), 4
Great Egg Bay (New Jersey), 193
Great Island (Connecticut), 185
Great Pond (Massachusetts), 177
Great South Bay (New York), 190, 191
Greenwich Bay or Cove (Rhode Island), 182
Griswold Point (Connecticut), 185
Gulf of St. Lawrence (Canada), 172, 174
Gurgler (Jack Gartside), 133

H
Hammonasett State Park (Connecticut), 187
Hampton River (New Hampshire), 176
Hampton Beach State Park (New Hampshire), 176
Harkers Island (North Carolina), 198
Harkness State Park (Connecticut), 187, 188
Hatteras Inlet (North Carolina), 196
Haverstraw Bay (New York), 189
Head of the Meadow Beach (Massachusetts), 181
Hedge Fence (Martha's Vineyard), 180
Hempstead Harbor (New York), 189, 191
Herring Cove (Massachusetts), 181
Housatonic River (Connecticut), 185, 186, 188
Hickory shad, 70, 77–81, 78, 88, 128, 202
diet of, 80
fighting and landing, 81
flies for, 80
locations for, 79, 88, 128
population cycle of, 78
soft mouth of, 81
High dawn, 36
Highland Light (Massachusetts), 180
Hudson River (New York), 172, 189, 192

I

Indian River Inlet (Delaware), 194
Inlets, 3, 4, 9, 10, 19, 41, 42, 75, 96, 129, 130, 142
Inner-Flash Baby Bunker (Bob Popovics), 153
Isle of Shoals (New Hampshire), 176

J

Jamaica Bay (New York), 190
James River (Virginia), 195
Jetties, 9, 10, 75
Jiggy (Bob Popovics), 80, 133, 145

K

Kennebec River (Maine), 172, 175
Kent Island Narrows (Maryland), 196
Kitty Hawk Pier (North Carolina), 197, 198
Knots, 136, 211, 212
   surgeon's loop, 136
   with different brands of mono, 212
Kouchibouguac River (New Brunswick), 174
Kukonen, Paul, 75, 76

L

Lake Tashmoo (Martha's Vineyard), 178
Landmarks, using at night, 37
Larry's Tackle (Martha's Vineyard), 214
Leaders, 35, 38, 90, 91, 114, 127
   checking, 64
   for droppers, 136
Lee River (Massachusetts), 178
Lefty's Deceiver, 100, 135, 140, 144, 146
Light level,
   Atlantic bonito and, 19–21
   bluefish and, 58, 59
   false albacore and, 19–21
   sand eels and, 143, 144
   striped bass and, 29, 30
   tides and, 20, 36, 42, 44, 50, 59
   weakfish and, 74
Light penetration, 30, 41, 43, 45, 120
LILCO power plant, 189
Lines. *See* fly lines
Little Narragansett Bay, 4
Little Neck Bay (New York), 189

Little tunny. *See* false albacore
Lobsterville Beach (Martha's Vineyard), 143, 179, 214–218
Long Island Sound, 66, 78, 142, 148, 153, 154, 167–170, 184, 185, 187, 188
Longshore bar. *See* sandbars
Longshore current, 95, 104
Love Point (Maryland), 196
Lyme disease, 117

M

Magaguadavic River (New Brunswick), 173
Maine fishing, 40, 174, 175
Manasquan Inlet (New Jersey), 192
Manhasset Bay (New York), 189
Manns Harbor Bridge (North Carolina), 197
Mark's Baby Bunker fly, 153
Mark's E-Z Body Squid, 157,
Marsh banks, 116, 119, 120, 129
Martha's Vineyard, 80, 177, 178, 180, 181
Maryland and Virginia fishing, 194–196
Massachusetts fishing, 177–181
Mattituck Inlet (New York), 4, 190
Menemsha Bight (Martha's Vineyard), 1, 169, 216
Menemsha Inlet (Martha's Vineyard), 4, 190
Menemsha Pond (Martha's Vineyard), 178
Menhaden. *See* Atlantic menhaden
Merrimack River (Massachusetts), 174
Merry Meeting Bay (Maine), 174
Mickey Finn, 75
Migration, 163–171, 199–201
   Atlantic bonito, 165, 166
   baitfish, 163
   bluefish, 164, 166, 167
   currents and, 167, 168
   day length and, 165, 166
   forage and, 168, 169, 200
   moon and, 167, 168
   striped bass, 164, 165–167
   water temperature and, 166, 168, 169, 170
   weakfish, 164
   weather and, 166, 169

Millstone Nuclear Plant (Connecticut), 20, 187, 188
Missing strikes, 38, 209–211
Miramichi River (New Brunswick), 174
Monomoy (Massachusetts), 180
Moons, 116
  apogee, 40
  current and
  full moons, 37, 41
  migration moons
  new or dark moon, 37, 41
  perigee, 110
Montauk (New York), 3, 171, 190, 191
Moriches Bay & Inlet (New York), 190, 191
Mousam River (Maine), 174
Mudflats, 115–117
Mullet, 92, 96, 153, *154*
Mummichogs, 80, 116
Mung weed, 180
Mussel bars, 104

N
Nags Head (North Carolina), 198
Nanticoke River (Maryland), 195
Nantucket, 177, 178, 180, 181
Nantucket Shoal, 171
Napatree Point (Rhode Island), 182
Narragansett Bay, 4, 182, 183
Narragansett Town Beach, 183
Narrow River (Rhode Island), 183
Nauset, 178, 181
Nayatt Point (Rhode Island), 182
Nereis. *See* worm hatches
New Brunswick (Canada), 172, 173, 174
New Hampshire fishing, 175, 176
New Jersey fishing, 192–194
New York fishing, 189–192
New York Harbor, 192
Newburyport (Massachusetts), 178, 181
Niantic River (Connecticut), 185
Night fishing, 3, 6, 60, 61
Night vision, 38
Nobska Point (Massachusetts), 180
North Carolina fishing, 160, 196–198

Northumberland Strait (Canada), 174
Norwich Harbor (Connecticut),

O
Ocean Beach (Connecticut), 188
Ocracoke Inlet (North Carolina), 196, 197
Octoraro Creek (Maryland), 195
Odiorne Point State Park (New Hampshire), 176
Old Orchard Beach (Maine), 175
Oregon Inlet (north Carolina), 196–198
Orient Point (New York), 189, 190
Oyster Bay (New York), 191
Outer Banks (North Carolina), 196, 198
Overcast conditions, 59

P
Pamlico Sound (North Carolina), 196, 197
Parsons Beach (Maine), 174
Pawcatuck River (Rhode Island), 182
Pea Island (North Carolina), 197
Peanut bunker. *See* baby menhaden
Peconic Bay (New York), 191
Penfield Reef (Connecticut), 187
Perigee, 110
Petersen, Eric, 135
Pettaquamsett River (Rhode Island), 183
PFD, 92, 109
Plankton, 32, 135, 142, 151
Piscataqua River (New Hampshire), 176
Plum Island (Massachusetts), 179, 181, 188
Plum Gut (New York), 3, 170, 171, 185, 190
Pogy, *See* Atlantic menhaden
Points of land, 32, 41, 42, 85, *85*
Point Judith (Rhode Island), 4, 182, 183, 184
Polarized sunglasses, 87, 96, 98, 111
Poplar Island Narrows (Maryland), 196
Popham Beach (Maine), 175
Pop Lip (Bob Popovics), 133
Poppers, 55, 61–64, 76, 91, 100, 106, 116, 124, 135, 150, 152, 156
Popovics, Bob, 74, 139
Popponnesset Bay (Massachusetts), 177
Port Jefferson (New York), 189

Potomac River, 195

Presenting a fly, 13, 64, 132–134, 145, 160
  bay anchovy flies, 140, 141
  dead drift, 94, 145, 161
  deep in a rip, 44, 45, *45*
  in channels, 120, 121
  on flats, 114
  sand eel flies, 145, 146
  to fussy fish, 64, 132, 133
  worm flies, 160, 161

Pressuring the fish, 207, 208

Presto Felt Worm Fly, (Phil Farnsworth), 161

Presumpscot River (Maine), 175

Prime edges, 83, *84*, 94, 101, 108

Prince Edward Island, 174

Protective eyewear, 43

Providence River (Rhode Island), 183

Pugnose bass, 52

Pumping the rod, 23, 53, *53*, 54

Q

Quick's Hole (Massachusetts), 179

Quonochontaug Breachway (Rhode Island), 184

R

Race Point (Massachusetts), 180

Race Point Beach (Massachusetts), 181

Race, the (Connecticut), 3, 171, 185, 186–188

Ragged Rock Creek (Connecticut), 188

Rain, 59, 114

Rappahannock River (Virginia), 195

Raritan Bay, 192

Razzle Dazzle fly, 135, 152

Reversing Falls (New Brunswick), 172

Rhode Island fishing, 160, 181–184

Richibucto River (New Brunswick), 174

Rips, 3, 15, 32, 39, *45*, 63, 64, *85*, *107*, 108, *109*, 118, *119*, 120, *123*, *126*, *128*, 142, 171, 174

Roanoke River (North Carolina), 197

Robert Moses State Park (New York), 190

Roberts, George, 157

Robinson's Hole (Massachusetts), 179

Rockaway Inlet (New York), 190

Rocky Neck State Park (Connecticut), 187

Rock piles, 32, 122–127, *123*, *125*, *126*

Rods. *See* fly rods

Rye Harbor State Park (New Hampshire), 176

S

Saco River (Maine), 175

Safety, 37, 41–43, 47, 92, 93, 109, 110, 117, 121
  dropper flies and, 137

Sandbars, 32, 83, 84, 96
  cuts, *101*, 104, 106, 107
  finger bars, 103, 104, 107, *107*, *109*
  longshore bar, *101*, 103–105, *105*, 109
  tides, 106–109, *107*, *109*

Salt ponds, 3, 117, 119, 142, 158, 159, 161

Sand eels, 80, 90, 92, 99, 96, 141–146
  at dawn or dusk, 143, 144
  at night, 143
  fishing over, 143, 144
  flies, 27, 99, 114, 135, 142, 145, 146
  retrieve speed of flies, 145, 146
  young-of-the-year, 142, 145
  wounded as prey, 144, 145

Sand flats, 110–115, *118*

Sand lance. *See* sand eel

Sandy Hook (New Jersey), 40, 192, 193

Scarborough River (Maine), 175

Sea breeze, 38

Sea herring. *See* Atlantic herring

Seekonk River (Rhode Island), 182

Setting the hook, 8, 10, 21, 90

Shad. *See* American and hickory shad

Shad dart, 80

Shape and slope of the shoreline, 84–86,

Sherwood Island State Park (Connecticut), 187

Shinnecock Bay & Inlet (New York), 4, 190, 191

Shock tippet, 67, 68, 76

Short Beach Park (Connecticut), 185

Shrimp, 18, 116

Shrimp flies, 75, 76, 135

Shubenacadie River, (Nova Scotia), 173
Sight fishing, 35, 48, 110–114
Silicone, (Bob Popovics), 154
Silversides. *See* Atlantic silversides
Sinking fly lines, 9, 10, 11, 44, 45, 64, 74, 91,
    99, 100, 108, 120
Slack in the line. 51, 90, 126, 210
Slicks, 65
Sliders, 38, 80, 91, 100, 114, 145, 146
Sloughs, 95–103
    forage in, 96
South Cove Causeway (Connecticut), 188
Sow and Pigs Reef (Massachusetts), 181
Spanish mackerel, 180, 187, 191, 195–197
Spotted seatrout, 71, 198,
Squeteague, 71. *See also* weakfish
Squid, 99, 144, 156, *156*, 157
Squid Fly, 144, 157
Stetzgo, Tony, 134
Stewiacke River (Nova Scotia), 173
Stretching a fly line, 204, 205
Striped bass,
    best times of day for, 29, 30, 33, 36, 37,
        41, 43, 50
    big bass,39–42, 99, 101, 102, 104, 115,
        124, 167
    birds, 46, 47, *43*
    diet, 140
    fighting, 51–54, *53*
    habits of, 27–29
    landing 49, 50, 54, *53*, *93*
    locations for, 87, 88, 89, 96, 99, 101, 102,
        106, 111, 112, 115, 117, 122, 124, 128,
        129, 167
    pugnose, 52
    season for, 39–41
    sight fishing for, 35, 48
    tactics from a boat, 43–54
    tactics from shore, 29–43
    under blues, 64
    water temperature and, 34, 52
St. Croix River (New Brunswick), 173
Summer solstice, 165
Sunken Meadow Park (New York), 190
Surgeon's loop, 136

Susquehanna River (Maryland), 195
Swagwon Reef (New York), 192

T
Tabusintac River (New Brunswick),
Tangling fly lines, 11, 63, 203, 204. *See also*
    stretching a fly line
Terns, 88, 142, 143
Thames River (Connecticut), 185, 188
3-D Shimmering Squid (Bob Veverka),
    157
Thunderstorms, 32, 41, 59
Ticks, 117
Tidal creeks, 74, 127, *128*, *129*, *130*
Tidal flats. *See* mudflats and sand flats
Tides, 74, 92, 106–110, 115, 116, 120, 121,
    128
    apogee, 40
    channels and, 120, 121
    current and, 19, 120, 130
    effect on migration, 167, 168
    estuaries and, 128, *129*, 130
    flats and, 115, 116
    importance to fishing, 18, 19, 30, 31
    light level and, 20, 36, 42, 44, 50, 59
    perigee, 110
    sand bars and, 106–109, *107*, *109*
    sloughs and, 100–102
    troughs and, 94, 95
Tippets, 23, 50, 90, 91, 114, 127, 136
Toms River (New Jersey), 192
Troughs, 86–95

U
Under-the-arm retrieve, 10, 51, 54, 90

V
Vernal equinox, 165
Vineyard Sound, 179, 180
Virginia fishing. *See* Maryland and Vir-
    ginia fishing

W
Wader belt, 92, 109
Wading staff, 9, 124

Wareham River (Massachusetts), 178

Water color, 86, 76, 96, 98, 103, 117
  discolored, 34, 116

Water temperature, 166, 168 *See also* Atlantic bonito, bluefish, hickory shad, striped bass

Waquoit Bay (Massachusetts), 177

Wasque Point (Martha's Vineyard), 178

Watch Hill (Rhode Island), 3, 157, 182, 183, 84

Waves,
  dangers of, 91, 92
  landing fish in, 93
  sandbars and, 101
  slack line caused by, 210

Weakfish, 70–77, 164, 199
  best time of day for, 71, 72
  diet of, 75
  habits of, 72–74
  fighting, 76
  flies for, 75
  following bluefish, 72
  locations for, 88, 96, 104–106, 111, 115, 117, 128
  releasing, 76, 77
  season, 74
  soft mouth of, 76, 77
  teeth, 72
  tiderunners, 71, 74, 75, 104, 106
  weather and, 75

Weather, effects on fishing, 31, 75, 166, 169
  colder than normal, 41
  fog, 32, 59
  overcast, 59
  See also barometric pressure, migration, wind

Weekapaug Inlet (Rhode Island), 184

West Haven sandbar (Connecticut), 186

Westport River (Massachusetts), 178

West Nile Virus, 117

Weweantic River (Massachusetts), 178

Woods Hole (Massachusetts), 157, 177, 178, 180

Worm hatch, 157–162, *158*, 178, 182, 197
  flies for, 161
  salt pond, 159
  tactics for, 160–162
  tidal creek, 158, 159

White, Capt. Jim, 75

White perch, 177, 182

Wildwood State Park (New York), 190

Wind, 31, 32, 41, 59, 74, 95, 170
  plankton and, 32
  water temperature and, 169
  See also migration

Windram's Squid Fly, 157

Winter Solstice, 165

Y

York River (Virginia), 195